Moving from Teacher
Isolation to Collaboration

**Other Books Edited by
Sharon Conley and Bruce S. Cooper**

*Finding, Preparing, and Supporting School Leaders: Critical Issues, Useful
Solutions*

*Keeping and Improving Today's School Leaders: Retaining and Sustaining
the Best*

Moving from Teacher Isolation to Collaboration

Enhancing Professionalism and School Quality

Edited by Sharon Conley and
Bruce S. Cooper

ROWMAN & LITTLEFIELD EDUCATION

A division of
ROWMAN & LITTLEFIELD
Lanham • New York • Toronto • Plymouth, UK

Published by Rowman & Littlefield Education
A division of Rowman & Littlefield Publishers, Inc.
A wholly owned subsidiary of The Rowman & Littlefield Publishing Group, Inc.
4501 Forbes Boulevard, Suite 200, Lanham, Maryland 20706
www.rowman.com

10 Thornbury Road, Plymouth PL6 7PP, United Kingdom

British Library Cataloguing in Publication Information Available

Library of Congress Cataloging-in-Publication Data
Conley, Sharon C.
Moving from teacher isolation to collaboration : enhancing professionalism and
school quality / Sharon Conley and Bruce S. Cooper.
pages cm.
978-1-4758-0269-6 (cloth : alk. paper) — 978-1-4758-0270-2 (pbk. : alk.
paper) — 978-1-4758-0272-6 (electronic)
1. Teachers—In-service training—United States. 2. Effective teaching—
United States. 3. Teachers—Professional relationships—United States. 4.
Professional learning communities—United States. I. Conley, Sharon. II.
Cooper, Bruce S.
LB1731 .C632 2013
371.120973—dc23   2013014458

∞™ The paper used in this publication meets the minimum requirements of
American National Standard for Information Sciences—Permanence of
Paper for Printed Library Materials, ANSI/NISO Z39.48-1992.

Printed in the United States of America

Contents

Preface

Bruce S. Cooper and Sharon Conley

Teachers perform a critical role in society, preparing children for a productive and happy life. Yet all too often teachers are treated as less than equal, as they lack the status and power of other occupational groups such as doctors and lawyers. In addition, teachers work semi-isolated—in their classrooms, insulated mostly from other colleagues and supporters. The bell rings, they close their doors, and for the majority of their working day, they work alone. They are separated from other teachers by the "tyranny of the classroom walls" (Wise, 2012) that keeps them from working alongside other teachers as a team of professionals.

Dan Lortie, in his classic book, *Schoolteacher: A Sociological Study* (1975), called this loneliness, this physical separation, a root cause of their "semiprofessional" status; for teachers have been robbed of close working relationships with colleagues who can directly help them and work at their sides. While doctors, lawyers, and other professionals are largely in charge of themselves—and take responsibility for their other colleagues' behaviors—teachers may have the worst of both worlds: being denied the opportunity to become team players and, therefore, according to some, real professionals.

"Team teaching"—with two or three teachers working together in the same space—also didn't work, as it was deemed too expensive and too complicated. Thus, teachers find themselves in the worst of both worlds: neither functioning as real independent craftspeople nor having a team effort in their classes. As one new teacher explained, "I am on two teams, which can be problematic; I share sixty kids with another teacher in the same classroom for two periods, and I'm also part of a ninth grade family, where kids have the same teachers and we have a common prep but don't share a classroom."

Or as another observer (Cushman, 1998) of teachers lamented:

> Again and again, these teachers speak of emerging from the isolation of their classrooms into partnerships, teams, and networks marked by collaboration among peers. Such initiatives have their tensions and costs, they acknowledge; and at every stage of their careers teachers require explicit supports to carry them out. But they also yield intellectual and personal rewards, which often renew their energy and commitment to continuing in a profession under siege. (p. 1)

Thus, team teaching started up in the 1970s and died out. It was deemed too costly, too stressful, and too ineffective in improving work quality or productivity. But short of working in teams in the classroom, teachers can and do consult with one another, share techniques and ideas, and collaborate in their subject and grade-level work. In the 1980s, the notion of teachers working collaboratively was already being defined by Judith Warren Little (1982) in her classic work, *Norms of Collegiality and Experimentation: Workplace Conditions of School Success*. Little's work recognized the value of furthering existing collaboration among teachers and extending it.

This edited book explains and demonstrates just how collaboration and renewed teamwork can help to enhance the professionalism and productivity of teachers, both new and experienced, by overcoming teachers' isolation in the classroom, in the school, and in their work.

THE CHAPTERS

In chapter 1, "Teaching as a Profession—and More: Why? And How?," Bruce S. Cooper and Carolyn A. Brown begin by defining and explaining ways to enhance teachers' professionalism as worthy efforts and critical goals within schools and districts. The authors point out that teachers face many demands. The teachers' role does not only include the classroom: it also includes working with colleagues, with the principal, and with parents. As there are currently more and more demands from teaching, this chapter shows what an extraordinarily complex job teaching is. Thus, a sharing approach points the way to improving accountability and increasing classroom effectiveness—and student learning.

In chapter 2, "Restricted Professionalism of Teachers: Implications for Collaboration," Mary Antony Bair points out that collaboration has often been used as an umbrella term to incorporate many different concepts. The chapter's historical overview indicates why collaboration is crucial for a vibrant and sustainable teacher professionalism. She maintains that preservice education should reinforce teacher responsibility not only to students in the classroom but also to other teachers. In addition, sustained collegial professional development is required throughout the career of teaching. Further, collaboration with researchers might provide "content and pedagogical knowledge" that can help ensure continual teacher growth for success.

In chapter 3, "Rejuvenating Teacher Teams: Back to Basics," Terrence E. Deal and Donna Redman take a historical and contemporary look at teaming and collaboration in schools. They point out that the current accountability movement paved the way for schools to create professional learning communities (PLCs). However, a bureaucratic approach to PLCs results in "compliance," resistance, and anxiety. They identify principles of successful collaboration from looking at teams in both schools and other sectors. The chapter examines both the promise and pitfalls of teaming.

In chapter 4, "Organizational Design in Support of Professional Learning Communities in One District," Scott C. Bauer, S. David Brazer, Michelle Van Lare, and Robert G. Smith refer to groups of teachers who work within a larger professional PLC as collaborative teams (CTs). Situated in a suburban district in the mid-Atlantic region of the United States, the research reported uses a theory of decision making to view collaborative teams as a *web of stakeholders* interested in a particular set of problems, each contributing knowledge and experience, and each having influence within the web. The authors describe the district design of the structure of and support for collaborative teams, as well as the role school leaders played in this design process. Interviews with ten principals shed light on the design and support of CTs, including considerations of structure, process, and support.

In chapter 5, "Influences on Teacher Sharing and Collaboration," Tanya F. Cook and Vivienne Collinson draw on a qualitative study within a multischool computer technology innovation project (Collinson

& Cook, 2004a; Collinson & Cook, 2004b) to provide some recent conceptual work on organizational learning. This chapter creates a dynamic picture of the opposing influences that teachers find either motivate or restrain their ability to collaborate (including interpersonal relationships, work locations, teacher attitudes/dispositions, student interest, and time constraints). Special attention is given to teachers' interpretations of their uses of time and the ways time affects collaboration. The chapter also explores the relative merits of increasing motivation versus removing barriers and discusses ideas about increasing and supporting teacher sharing.

In chapter 6, "Teaming to Break the Walls of Isolation: Collaboration in Elementary Grade Level Teams," J. John Dewey and Sharon Conley draw on Hackman and Oldham's (1980) conceptual framework and Crow and Pounder's (2000) qualitative investigation of middle school teacher interdisciplinary teams to investigate teachers' experiences with teaming at two California elementary schools. The practices of teaming suggest a natural inclination toward collaborative activity and the maintenance of collegiality and support, with variation in the degree of self-direction that teachers are afforded in their teams.

In chapter 7, "Collaboration in Middle School Departments: A Work Group Effectiveness Perspective," Sharon Conley and Frank C. Guerrero report on a survey study of 120 middle school teachers in five California schools. The authors analyze teachers' perceptions of collegial work features (e.g., motivating task characteristics, coordination of efforts) within their departments. Several of these features predicted teachers' perceptions, such as: (a) department strategies that were effective in promoting student learning and teaching; (b) teachers who were committed to the team; and (c) department work that had met school-wide standards.

In chapter 8, "Professional Learning Communities Using Evidence: Examining Teacher Learning and Organizational Learning," Michelle D. Van Lare, S. David Brazer, Scott C. Bauer, and Robert G. Smith suggest that PLCs exist in part as a result of larger organizational forces and influences from outside the formal organization of schools and districts. Using interviews and observations with administrators, teachers, and instructional coaches in a large suburban school district, the researchers consider how PLC members analyzed and utilized evidence of student learning. They also examine the possibility of gaps between espoused theories and theories in use that may be addressed through organizational learning.

In chapter 9, "Teacher-Principal Collaboration: Partnerships or Power Plays?" Vivienne Collinson explores what teachers appreciate and dislike most about school administrators in the teachers' efforts to work creatively with their supervisors/leaders. Teachers may prefer to work as partners with leaders who keep their focus on learning and support classroom resources and improvement. Based on interviews with exemplary teachers, the chapter identifies ways in which teachers deal with principals: among them (1) working as partners, (2) modeling or piloting desired changes, (3) finding alternative solutions, or (3) even doing it themselves or working around administrators. A call is provided for examining the different ways teachers and administrators might think and behave as twenty-first-century technology-driven schools demand collaboration along with new skills, attitudes, ideas, and discussions of what is desirable.

REFERENCES

Collinson, V., & Cook, T. F. (2004a). Collaborating to learn computer technology: A challenge for teachers and leaders. *Leadership and Policy in Schools*, *3*(2), 111–33.

Collinson, V., & Cook, T. F. (2004b). Learning to share, sharing to learn: Fostering organizational learning through teachers' dissemination of knowledge. *Journal of Educational Administration*, *42*(3), 312–32.

Crow, G. M., & Pounder, D. G. (2000). Interdisciplinary teacher teams: Context, design, and process. *Educational Administration Quarterly*, *36*(2), 216–54.

Cushman, K. (1998). *Teacher renewal: Essential in a time of change*. Coalition of Essential Schools. Retrieved from: http://www.essentialschools.org/resources/51

Hackman, J. R., & Oldham, G. R. (1980). *Work redesign*. Reading, MA: Addison-Wesley.

Little, J. W. (1982). Norms of collegiality and experimentation: Workplace conditions of school success. *American Educational Research Journal*, *19*(3), 325–40.

Lortie, D. C. (1975). *Schoolteacher: A sociological study*. Chicago: University of Chicago Press.

Wise, A. E. (2012). End the tyranny of the self-contained classroom. *Education Week, Commentary*. January 25, 2012, *31*(18), p. 24.

Chapter One

Teaching as a Profession—and More

Why? And How?

Bruce S. Cooper and Carolyn A. Brown

Is teaching a real "profession," and thus are teachers "professionals"? These related questions have concerned, if not plagued, the field of education for a long time, as teachers have yearned and struggled to gain higher role status, better pay, and a stronger voice with their colleagues as they work with the nation's 55 million children in both public and private school K–12 classrooms. Furthermore, narrowing teachers and teaching down to being called "professional" or "semiprofessionals" is an oversimplification, for life in the classroom is more complex and interesting than that.

Teachers are other things, too, besides being deemed professionals: they are important adult figures for children; and they are performers—if not artists—as they seek to hold the attention of students for hours daily, getting students to laugh, have fun, and feel the meaning and importance of what they're learning and experiencing with their teachers.

They are also key authority figures, earning and holding the attention and respect of their students over a nine-month period and beyond. And they are "experts" in their respective fields, such as mathematics, science, foreign languages, language arts, English, social sciences, and history. Some of these teacher qualities are associated with being "professionals," and some are just good human and interpersonal skills and practices. But whatever the categories we apply, teaching is far more interesting and complex than the traditional view of them simply as "professionals" at best and "semiprofessionals" at the least (see Etzioni, 1969; Lortie, 1975).

This chapter, as the start of our analysis in this book, both widens the perspective of seeing teaching in its real setting and looks also at its actual behaviors. We hope to explain fully in the coming chapters how we can understand the role and job of teachers, and how their positions can be taught in teacher preparation programs, evaluated and analyzed on a regular basis in schools, and the work improved as teachers pursue their careers. Somehow, we argue, teaching must become more cooperative, collegial, and shared as teachers work to become a community of scholars and practitioners.

TEACHERS AS PROFESSIONALS AND TEACHING AS A PROFESSION

Prominent occupational sociologists such as Dan C. Lortie (1975) in *Schoolteacher: A Sociological Study*—and more recently in a follow-up study by Eugene F. Provenzo Jr. and Gary N. McCloskey (1996), authors of *Schoolteacher and Schooling: Ethoses in Conflict*—have conceptualized and analyzed school teaching from many perspectives. For if teachers are to end the classroom isolation of their work and lives, currently labeled the "tyranny of the self-contained classroom walls" (Wise, 2012, p. 24), and become esteemed professionals, then teaching will have to change its prerequisites for membership, work, and visibility in public life.

In the *British Journal of Education*, Jonathan Smilansky (1984) reported a study of teachers, comparing what they felt "inside" their classrooms, working with their students, versus what effects their external work environment had on them. He also related the world of teachers to their sense of overall job satisfaction.

Smilansky (1984) found, not unexpectedly, that feeling good about teaching and effective in their work was mostly related to their *classroom work*, while personal job stress was triggered by "external factors" like working with the principals and being reviewed and rated by ever-critical school systems. As Smilansky (1984) explains:

> Teachers' general satisfaction and stress at work were found to relate mostly to their reported feelings about what happened within the class rather than to administrative or policy questions. Satisfaction as a teacher was related to internal factors (e.g., satisfaction in life in general and feelings of self efficacy) while reported stress was related to external factors (e.g., principal and pupil ratings). The "better" teachers, according to external ratings, were willing to report more stress in their work situation. (p. 88)

The following sections outline Lortie's (1975) contribution to understanding teacher professionalism, the history of the semiprofession, working in isolation, and the arrival of unionization.

Lortie's Contribution

Dan Lortie (1975) began his research when working on his master's degree, studying the careers and work of a group of then lower-status anesthesiologists as doctors (1950); and his doctorate was on the status of lawyers (see *Laymen to Lawmen*, 1963). Then, when interviewing schoolteachers, Lortie determined, based on his research on teachers in Dade County (Miami), Florida, that teachers were viewed as "semiprofessionals." For teachers lacked the social status, collective career control, and the prestige of true professionals (e.g., lawyers, doctors, accountants, dentists).

Also in line with Lortie's research, Amitai Etzioni (1969) edited the book, *The Semi-Professions and Their Organization*, which included chapters on social workers, nurses, and teachers (written by Lortie), as examples. In the foreword to his book, Etzioni summarized some of the limits of the three semiprofessional jobs: teaching, nursing, and social work. Etzioni (1969) states: "Their training is shorter, their status is less legitimate, their right to privileged communications is less established, there is less of a specialized body of knowledge, and they have less autonomy from supervision or social control than 'the' professions" (p. v).

Goode (1969), also a contributor to the Etzioni book, saw two key differences between "real" professions and teaching: that teachers (1) do not have an arcane, "specialized body of knowledge" such as in law, medicine, and engineering, and (2) nor do they enjoy "the ideal of service." However, Hall (1985) found that among the eleven professions he studied that "it was teachers in the sample who felt most strongly that they were of real service" to the public and humanity (pp. 229, 232).

As one student of sociology recollected from his coursework in becoming a teacher:

> Dan Lortie was one of the many authors that I read for Sociology, and his work was one of my highlights of the course. Lortie researched teachers' work lives and his argument is basically that teachers are conservative [i.e., not inclined to advocate major alterations in classrooms or schools]. The fact

that teaching is a flat career where salaries plateau quickly tends to attract [these] conservative entrants in the first place. (Cameron Paterson posted this note on December 17, 2010)

Lortie (1975), likewise, noted that prior to taking up their first posts, teachers had already been living and growing for sixteen years in the classroom and nonacademic activities, learning traditional patterns of thought and practice as participants in K–12 education as students them-selves. In fact, most students actually "grow up" in their schools over thirteen years.

The extent and degree of socialization are potent forces, and students' later introduction as teachers—often being the only adult in charge in the classroom—can lead them to fall back on this lengthy "apprenticeship of observation" that they undertook when they were students in schools themselves. Teaching in some funny ways is like "starting school over."

The "conservatism" of the job is emphasized as part of the initial training experiences, as fellow teachers often encourage novices to view teaching as an individualistic rather than a collegial enterprise. And many teachers long remember their first weeks as the only adult in their class-room, trying to get children's attention and ensure their safe, polite, and attentive behavior. Students likewise know that they will "test" their new teachers, to see what these new pedagogues are "made of," what they as pupils in the classroom can "get away with," and just how focused and strong their new teachers can and will really be.

Teachers and their supervisors report that children can drive the inexpe-rienced teacher from the classroom in tears during those first weeks, as a result of trying to manage student misbehavior and inattention—while the neophyte struggles to take control of the environment, help students get their behavior on track, and form supportive relationships with colleagues and supervisors.

Isolated as the adults in their cellular classrooms, teachers often find that the individualistic, lonely nature of teaching continues throughout their career. Lortie (1975) is worth a read as his work explains why school reform is so difficult. All three semiprofessions treated in the Etzioni (1969) book—teaching, social work, and nursing—besides being fields traditionally dominated by women, shared five characteristics that often prevented them from being considered and treated as professionals:

1. *Lack of an arcane knowledge base and work skills*: Compared to law-yers pleading a case before the Supreme Court, or doctors performing surgery, teaching appears much simpler and less life-threatening on the surface.

2. *Ease of entry*: Becoming a teacher now can take as little time as a sum-mer and a term in an alternative certification program, while preparing for medicine or law can take three to nine years of advanced training, internships, and residencies.

3. *Relatively limited control by teachers of their own preparation and practices*: While teachers and their associations and unions (e.g., the American Federation of Teachers [AFT] and National Education As-sociation [NEA]) have a primary concern with teacher training (AFT, 2012), it can be argued that doctors through the American Medical Association (AMA) and lawyers through the national and state bar associations have historically had higher participation in credentialing agencies for their professions.

4. *On average, much shorter careers for teachers*: High rates of teachers moving from or leaving their jobs are generating significant concern nationally (Ingersoll, 2001); doctors, lawyers, and engineers tend to persist in (often lifetime) careers after their training and credentialing.

5. *Work isolation for teachers in the classroom*: Teachers mainly work alone in their classrooms with often few other adults present. In con-trast, doctors and lawyers might practice their professional activities in teams, such as surgeons collaborating with anesthesiologists, other surgeons, and nurses; and lawyers often practice their work in teams, handling major clients and cases.

In education, open concept classrooms—"forces [that encourage] teach-ers to collaborate" (Cohen, Deal, Meyer, & Scott, 1979, p. 30)—hardly lasted a decade (in the 1970s) although the chapters in this book discuss various forms of collaboration for "breaking down the walls of separation" and building "professional learning communities (PLCs)," collaborative programs, teamwork, and shared common interests.

As mentioned in his first study of professionalism (or really semiprofes-sionals) for his thesis, Lortie (1950) found that anesthesiologists lacked the status of other medical doctors, as he reported in a paper presented to the In-ternational Anesthesia Society. Lortie (1950) wrote in their medical journal:

This ambiguity results from the fact that there is no clear-cut "definition of the job" in regard to anesthesia. In many places in America, the work is defined as "nurse's work." Patients, hospital personnel, and physicians expect this function to be executed by a nurse, not an MD. (p. 181)

History of the Semiprofession

Stories abound throughout history of how education grew up, and the less than desirable working conditions of teachers. Rural teachers, scattered across the country, worked virtually alone, as they were often the only educated adults in their rural, semiliterate communities—and thus had few to no colleagues.

For example, Kate Rousmaniere (2005) detailed the historical development of the U.S. "common school," and the difficulty that women teachers, in particular, faced in trying to keep schools going in scattered rural, pioneering areas in the south and west. She reported the story of one such teacher:

Ellen Lee, who was so successful as a teacher in Indiana, still suffered the isolation of her placement: "In my school I am content, and happy for I am doing good, but I am entirely deprived of sympathy, and good society. I have no human beings here, in whom I can confide, or who possess kindred feelings with mine." (p. 11)

Urban teachers often faced a different problem, but one equally distressing. Historically, they worked in overcrowded schools and classrooms with anywhere from fifty to a hundred multiaged students together in a kind of "school-as-factory" model. These "factories" often used a "monitorial instruction system," where students sat by age and were drilled en masse. Based on models of "efficiency" and "economy," students were taught to memorize a standard set of skills, and individual and group recitations were used to keep students in line and learning together. Finklestein (1989) reported on what one observer noted in 1868 in a New York City monitorial classroom:

To manage successfully a hundred students, or even half that number, the teacher must reduce them as near as possible to a unit. Nothing must be done that all cannot do at the same time. Everything must be sacrificed to regularity, everything like spontaneity repressed. The children must be like so many pins—so much alike that all undergo the same process in exactly the same way. (p. 319)

Working in Isolation

As schools became more "progressive" and "child centered" in the twentieth century, the classroom was made into a more human setting for children and teachers, as Dewey, Montessori, and other reformers sought to move from an industrial instructional model, where children's education was "mass produced," to a more human, familial environment—where the teacher sought to know and help each child individually. Yet, still, teachers were often adult "loners" in the cellular structure of schools. And the standards for teaching changed very little, although more and more teachers attended a four-year college (instead of a two-year teachers training program, called a "normal school," a name based on the desire to establish "norms" for the teaching field). And later, many if not most teachers went on to receive a master's degree in education.

Unionization Arrives

Perhaps the most significant development for teaching in the schools of many states in the United States was the move for teachers to organize into unions, giving them a greater collective voice in setting their salaries and benefits, and influencing their working conditions. The collective bargaining movement came relatively late in U.S. history (between the 1960s and 1980s), on a state-by-state basis, as legislatures passed laws allowing public employees, including public school teachers, to organize, to bargain for their pay and benefits (e.g., health, retirement), and to protect their rights in a formal contract.

Also, nationally and regionally, teacher unions became major representatives for teachers and for support of public education in the nation, as other public employees such as police officers, firefighters, and other civil servants were unionizing in all but six of the states. As public education expanded—with more than 5 million public school teachers as members of the NEA and AFT, which is affiliated with the American Federation of Labor and Congress of Industrial Organizations (AFL-CIO)—the question became, what are the ways teacher unionism and collective bargaining can further professionalization of the teaching profession (Shedd, 1988)?

And what can teacher representatives and districts do to encourage teachers to work more closely together on improving pedagogy and enhancing student learning? It appears that unions have historically fought for the big picture—better salaries, benefits, and working conditions—and are increasingly defining their professional concerns in terms of collegial participation and mutual support.

For example, one local teachers' union worked with the school district to change "to an interest-based bargaining model rather than the traditional adversarial model" (Richardson, 2007, p. 6). The collaborative model focused on high-quality professional development, specifically creating time for teachers to work together and for teachers and administrators to attend a monthly meeting around professional learning. The union president noted initial challenges and resistance but emphasized that "we have to model that it really is for the benefit of everyone to work in a collaborative way" (p. 7).

As Joseph B. Shedd (1988) maintained in his analysis of the teacher professionalization movement and collective bargaining, in the future:

> Bargainers will focus more on *building closer relationships among teachers*. The growing tendency to define "professionalism" in terms of collective participation in decision making, collegial assistance, and mutual responsibility for the quality of education—rather than in terms of the individual teacher's autonomy—can be expected to keep issues such as team teaching, peer review and coaching, and teacher responsibility for staff development at the forefront of attention. (p. 412)

This volume will look at the role of teachers, and what can be done to enhance their work, their professional status, and the dynamics of collaboration, in a way that helps break down the isolation of the self-contained classroom.

ADDED ELEMENTS OF TEACHING

Treating teachers as professionals—or not—is really only part of the job, for teachers—as they live and work—are also artists who engage and even entertain their students, of all ages. They are counselors and "parent figures" who help children to grow and learn together. They are performers, attention holders of groups of children, who can find classes to be fun, caring, and happy places. And they are managers making the process move ahead on time, running their classrooms, working around requirements and timelines, and responding to federal, state, and local requirements, expectations, tests, and standards.

Treating teachers as professionals is critical but a great oversimplification of a very complex job. This chapter presents three key dimensions of their in-the-classroom work as examples, each of which is a different but essential role of teachers as:

1. Field-discipline-academic pedagogical specialists who work to keep up with developments in their areas;
2. Artists who need to engage and hold students' interests over the 183 days of classes each year; and
3. Counselor-parenting figures who care about and tend to the developmental and behavioral needs of children, ages five to eighteen.

Field-Discipline-Academic Pedagogical Specialists

Teachers are experts, specialists, in their respective fields and disciplines, working to keep up with developments in their areas, such as science, math, language arts, English, and social studies concepts and issues (Cuban, 1993). And as teachers, they must know and practice the skills of meeting all of their students' needs to enable them to meet high standards by working with individual students, groups of students, and fellow teachers. For as Gajda and Koliba (2008) explain:

> According to the National Board of Professional Teaching Standards (NBPTS, 2004) and the National Commission on Teaching and America's Future (NCTAF, 2003), instructional quality and school effectiveness depend on the degree to which teachers work in a professional partnership with colleagues. Furthermore, the American Federation of Teachers (AFT, 2004) considers the process of collective teacher inquiry focused on the improvement of practices as the means for attaining essential school outcomes. (p. 133)

It seems clear that as specialists in their field and work, teachers need opportunities and support in their classrooms, from other teachers, specialists, and school leaders. Levine and Marcus (2007) explain that,

> Prescriptive reforms that reduce teachers to technicians are not likely to facilitate teachers' understanding of their work or their ability to adapt it to new circumstances or specific students. Such approaches seem less likely to help teachers internalize new values or new practices that they might later use on their own. (p. 120)

Artists: An Attention-Holding Dimension

Spend an hour in a classroom with a good teacher and one becomes aware of the fun, excitement, and attention grabbing. As one teacher explains:

> We must vary what we do, must constantly stimulate and indeed should consider giving them kinesthetic learning that involves touch, smell, sound and (should health and safety considerations permit) taste. Of course, this is all very difficult. For a start, television with its carefully scripted presentations, skilled presenters and large-scale special effects has set an impossible standard. For another, this is not a carefully controlled stage situation: we grapple with dodgy digital projectors, students arriving late, less than totally satisfactory rooms, and so on. (chriswalley.blogspot.com/2009/02/on-teaching-and-entertainment.html, 2/13/09)

But even a professional entertainer, a man like sitcom star Tony Danza, when taking on the role and job of teacher, found the going rough, since teaching is more than entertainment. What happened when Danza moved into Room 230 at a large urban public high school?

> Danza underwent weeks of [preparation] and new-teacher orientation before starting at Northeast, a diverse 3,400-student public high school in a blue-collar neighborhood. . . . Initially, it's rough going for the boss of Room 230. Danza talks too much and gets corrected by a student in front of the class. He deals with cheating and violence, meets with parents of obstinate students, and tries to balance discipline with empathy—all while teaching *Of Mice and Men* and other books to teens with varying academic abilities. It's overwhelming. Danza cries several times in the first few episodes.

As Monica Prendergast (2008) explains, "Teaching quite easily lends itself to performative *metaphors*: the 'captive audience' of students in a classroom, the teacher onstage at the front of the room, charged with the tasks of engagement and enlightenment, even (in Egan's [1986] model) storytelling" (p. 2).

Therefore, teaching is not merely entertainment; it must be engaging but more than just a sitcom show. And making children feel safe, secure, and happy in the classroom and in their schools is important as teachers are proud, happy, and creative adults who can make their classrooms in "performing arts," places of collaboration and imagination, as Robyn Ewing (2010) explains:

> For example, the work of Damasio (1994) and Williams and Gordon (2007) demonstrate that the human brain must feel comfortable or safe before it can engage in explorative, creative or problem-solving processes. Damasio (1994) explicitly talks about the interrelationship between emotion, cognition and performance, and how embodiment through the performing [arts] can enable engagement in learning and enhance the development of the imagination and metaphor. Collaborative strategies common in creative dance, music, visual arts and drama activities have been shown to achieve an increase in brain synchrony and associated bonding. The ability to empathize or "walk in someone else's shoes" is also important in understanding diversity and the need to be inclusive. (p. 34)

And in the modern hi-tech era, teachers can use a host of tools to help attract and entice their students:

> Most educators hope that their teaching touches students in exciting ways so that the information conveyed makes an impact. One sure way to engage students is to make their educational experience fun. New teachers just starting out as well as experienced teachers who could use a breath of fresh air in their curriculum will love all the great tools available on the Internet to help make their teaching more entertaining. Some of the following tools will have teachers and students exploring wikis, open courseware, Twitter, blogging, comics, videos, and incorporating plenty of other tools that will help make learning fun. (See Study Hall, 100 Free Tools. www.onlineschools.org/study-hall)

In fact, all of life could be considered a performance; as experienced teachers know, why should this activity stop in the classroom, so that students are bored and turned off? For Prendergast (2008) reminds us that,

> Sociologist Erving Goffman (1959) argues that we perform our everyday lives, and his work has had great effect on the development of performance theory. So, the broadest metaphor we can apply to performance is *as life*. This, of course, is mimesis. But this is also a very broad metaphor indeed, and one that needs some fine-tuning, some focusing, in order to become clearly useful in the context of this essay. (p. 111)

Thus, when a classroom is a cold, lifeless place, with hours of sitting and looking at the floor, students get bored and learning often stops (see Vogel-Walcutt et al., 2011). Sara W. Sparks (2012) portrays what happens when schools are dull, uninteresting places:

> One glance, and any teacher knows the score: That student, halfway down the row, staring blankly at his tapping pen, fidgeting, sneaking glances at the wall clock roughly every 30 seconds, is practically screaming, "I'm bored!" While boredom is a perennial student complaint, emerging research shows it is more than students' not feeling entertained, but rather a "flavor of stress" that can interfere with their ability to learn and even their health.
>
> "I think teachers should always try to be relevant and interesting, but beyond that, there are other places to look" (Eastwood, 2011, p. 22). By definition, to be in the state of boredom is to say the world sucks out there in some way. But often that's not the case; often it's an interior problem, and [students] are looking in the wrong place to solve the problem." Boredom is one of the most consistent experiences of school and one that can be frustrating and disheartening for teachers. (p. 16)

Teachers know that schools and classrooms must be happy and lively places, providing an engaging approach to teaching and learning, or the students simply "zone" out. How to prepare and support such teaching is not well defined; we know it when we see and feel it, and so do the students at every level of education.

Counselor-Parenting Roles

Finally, besides their roles as experts, artist-entertainers, and authority figures, teachers and their classrooms are children's "home away from home" and teachers often fulfill a parental role as guardian, counselor, and adult advisor to children whom they teach. Thus, teachers are expected to know and understand the capacities and skills appropriate for each age and stage of human growth. Many teachers in their preparation take "developmental psychology" courses, to understand the needs and abilities of children as they mature.

As Teachers College, Columbia University, in New York City, explains,

> Developmental psychology focuses on the development of individuals across their lifespan within the context of family, peer groups, child-care and after-school programs, schools, neighborhoods, and larger communities and society. It considers the well-being of children, youth, and adults, vis-à-vis the cognitive, emotional, social, academic, and health domains . . . with a concern about disparities among groups (e.g., gender, resources such as parental income and education, ethnicity, and immigrant status) as well as the ways in which equity among groups may be promoted.

For just as parents often treat their children differently and uniquely based on their age, development, personality, interests, and maturity, so too do teachers work to tailor their teaching and interactions with children to youngsters' needs. Thus, teaching is more than a "profession" or "semiprofession," as it resembles living and working in a classroom "family." For purposes of training teachers in their work, as Knight and Lee (2008) explain in their *Guide to Teaching Developmental Psychology*:

- Provides a unique wealth of concrete suggestions and a clear roadmap for successfully teaching developmental psychology;
- Links chapters to major areas of a lifespan development course, including research methods, teaching infant development, and teaching adolescent development;
- Offers practical, hands-on tips for novice teachers and experienced instructors alike; and
- Includes sample syllabi and lecture outlines, reading quizzes, critical thinking; assignments, and references for helpful videotapes and websites.

Thus, we can see in the psychological domain just how complicated teaching can be, as teachers work as professionals, authority and parental figures, and experts in pedagogy and psychology.

PROLOGUE

Teaching embodies many roles—not only in the classroom and in teacher-student interactions, teaching extends beyond the classroom and well beyond interactions with children. Therefore, it is important that teachers are not isolated in their attempts to fulfill these roles. The chapters in this book are concerned with helping to strengthen these roles and fill gaps that can occur as teachers continually try to change hats to meet changing expectations. This book considers the complexity of the role, and the need to end the isolation and build a working community in the classroom and school. Teachers need each other, to break the "tyranny of the classroom walls" (Wise, 2012) and to work together as skilled professionals for the benefit of children and the teaching profession.

This sharing and collaboration will not be easy after historic patterns of isolation. But this book explores the "teacher work group," "PLC" (see Astuto et al., 1993) and its similar concepts, as a way of helping teachers and improving education in all schools and communities, including these five attributes covered in this book (see SEDL, Olivier & Hipp, 2010):

1. supportive and shared leadership
2. collective creativity
3. shared values and vision
4. supportive conditions
5. shared personal practice

This book examines these issues and attributes, and presents solutions and suggestions for making teaching better, more personally rewarding and collectively effective for both teachers and students alike.

REFERENCES

Astuto, T. A., Clark, D. L., Read, A-M., McGree, K., & Fernandez, L. de K. P. (1993). *Challenges to dominant assumptions controlling educational reform.* Andover, MA: Regional Laboratory for the Educational Improvement of the Northeast and Islands.

AFT (2012). *AFT task force takes new look at teacher preparation.* Washington, DC: American Federation of Teachers. Retrieved from: http://www.aft.org/newspubs/news/2012/013112teacherprep.cfm

Cohen, E. G., Deal, T. E., Meyer, J. W., & Scott, W. R. (1979). Technology and teaming in the elementary school. *Sociology of Education, 52*(1), 20–33.

Cuban, L. (1993). *How teachers taught: Constancy and change in American classrooms, 1890–1990* (2nd ed.). New York: Teachers College Press.

Damasio, A. (2006/1994). *Descartes' error: Emotion, reason and the human brain.* London: Vintage.

Danza, T. (2012). *I'd like to apologize to every teacher I ever had: My year as a rookie teacher at Northeast High School.* New York: Random House.

Developmental Psychology Programs, Teachers College, Columbia University. (2013). Retrieved from http://www.tc.columbia.edu/hud/devpsych/.

Egan, K. (1986). *Teaching as storytelling: An alternative approach to teaching and curriculum in the elementary school.* Chicago: University of Chicago Press.

Etzioni, A. (Ed.) (1969). *The semi-professions and their organization: Teachers, nurses, social workers.* New York: The Free Press.

Ewing, R. A. (2010). *The arts and Australian education: Realising potential.* Camberwell, Victoria, Australia: Australian Council for Educational Research.

Finkelstein, B. F. (1989). *Governing the young: Teacher behavior in popular primary schools in the nineteenth century United States.* New York: Falmer Press.

Gajda, R., & Koliba, C. J. (2008). Evaluating and improving the quality of teacher collaboration: A field-tested framework for secondary school leaders. *NASSP Bulletin, 92*(2), 133–53.

Goffman, E. (1959). *The presentation of self in everyday life.* Garden City, NY: Doubleday.

Goode, W. J. (1969). The theoretical limits of professionalization: In A. Etzioni (Ed.), *The semi-professions and their organization: Teachers, nurses, social workers* (pp. 266–313). New York: The Free Press.

Hall, R. H. (1985). Professional/management relations: Imagery vs. action. *Human Resource Management, 24*(2), 227–36.

Ingersoll, R. (2001). Teacher turnover and teacher shortages: An organizational analysis. *American Educational Research Journal, 38*(3), 499–534.

Knight, E. B., & Lee, E. L. (2008). *A guide to teaching developmental psychology.* New York: Wiley-Blackwell.

Levine, T. H., & Marcus, A. S. (2007). Closing the achievement gap through teacher collaboration: Facilitating multiple trajectories of teacher learning. *Journal of Advanced Academics. 19,* 116–38.

Lortie, D. C. (1975). *Schoolteacher: A sociological study.* Chicago: University of Chicago Press.

Lortie, D. C. (1950). The sociologist looks to the profession of anesthesiology. *Current Researches in Anesthesiology and Analgesia.* July–August, *29*(4), 181–89.

National Board of Professional Teaching Standards (NBPTS, 2004). *What teachers need to know and be able to do.* Retrieved 12/2/05, from http://www.nbpts. org/about/core-props.cfm#prop5

National Commission on Teaching and America's Future (NCTAF, 2003). *Summary report.* Washington, DC: Author.

Olivier, D. F., & Hipp, K. K. (2010). Professional learning communities: What are they and why are they important? *Issues . . . about Change, 6*(1), 1–14.

Paterson, C. (2010, December 17). Sociology and Dan Lortie. Retrieved 2010/12, from http://learningshore.edublogs.org

Prendergast, M. (2008). Teacher as performer: Unpacking a metaphor in performance theory and critical performative pedagogy. *International Journal of Education & the Arts, 9*(2), 1–19.

Provenzo, Jr., E. F., & McCloskey, G. N. (1996). *Schoolteacher and schooling: Ethoses in conflict.* Greenwich, CT: Greenwood Press.

Richardson, J. (2007). Bargaining time: Union contract spells out how and when professional learning will happen. *The Learning System, 2*(6), 47–48.

Rousmaniere, K. (2005). In search of a profession: A history of American teachers. In D. M. Moss et al., *Portrait of a profession: Teaching and teachers in the 21st century.* (pp. 2–26). Westport, CT: Praeger.

Shedd, J. B. (1988). Collective bargaining, school reform, and the management of school systems. *Educational Administration Quarterly, 24*(4), 405–15.

Smilansky, J. (1984). External and internal correlates of teacher satisfaction and a willingness to report stress. *British Journal of Education Psychology, 54*(1), 84–92.

Sparks, S. W. (2012, October 12). Studies link students' boredom to stress. *Education Week, 32*(7), 1, 16.

Study Hall, 100 free tools. (n/d). Tweetbuzz. Retrieved from http://tweetbuzz.us/entry/130255811/www.onlineschools.org/study-hall/100-free-tools-to-make-your-teaching-more-entertaining/

Taylor, H. W. (1919). *Shop management.* New York: Harper & Brothers.

Walley, C. (2009, February 13). On teaching and entertainment. Retrieved 2/13/09 from chriswalley.blogspot.com/2009/02/on-teaching-and-entertainment.html

Williams, L., & Gordon, E. (2007). Dynamic organization of the emotional brain responsivity, stability and instability. *The Neuroscientist*, 13, 349–370.

Wise, A. E. (2012). End the tyranny of the self-contained classroom. *Education Week,* Commentary, January 25, 2012, *31*(18), 24.

Vogel-Walcutt, J. J., Fiorella, L., Carper, T., & Schatz, S. (2011, October 13). The definition, assessment, and mitigation of state boredom within educational settings: A comprehensive review. *Educational Psychology Review*. Published online, Springer.

Chapter Two

Restricted Professionalism of Teachers
Implications for Collaboration
Mary Antony Bair

Collaboration is often used as an umbrella term to incorporate many different concepts, such as team teaching, teacher mentoring, and teacher collective decision making. This chapter provides a historical synopsis to indicate how teacher autonomy and professionalism came to be included under the umbrella of collaboration.

Throughout much of the nineteenth century and into the first half of the twentieth century, teaching was perceived to be a *craft* that lacked a knowledgebase and therefore required little preparation. Teachers worked individually in classrooms isolated from one another and learned to teach through trial and error. During this time, teacher professionalism largely consisted of the ability to manage students. Attempts to professionalize teaching in the 1960s and 1970s were made through demands for autonomy, and individualism continued to be the hallmark of teacher professionalism. Teachers worked in isolation from one another, albeit now in an isolation of their own choosing.

While the 1980s and 1990s saw an increase in collegial collaborations through site-based management and professional learning communities (PLCs), teachers were arguably still isolated from colleagues both within and between communities. They were also isolated from much of the research being conducted in universities. Of greatest importance, they were isolated from meaningful decision making. During this period, although the notion of collegiality gained significance, professionalism continued to be defined by local norms.

In the twenty-first century, attempts by teacher educators and professional organizations to inculcate an extended sense of professionalism are being thwarted by the regulation of teachers by educators and noneducators.

The accountability movement appears to be furthering the inspection and regulation of teaching by local boards, state departments of education, and federal policymakers. Collaboration is one way to counter these efforts to undermine teacher professionalism.

In this chapter, Hargreaves's (2000) conceptual framework about the historical phases of professionalism is used to explain why a restricted notion of professionalism seems to dominate teaching. Notions of professions and professionalism are discussed, followed by an examination of the isolation that has characterized the professional life of teachers. In conclusion, collaboration is recommended as one way to counter forces that threaten to undermine teacher professionalism.

THE TEACHING PROFESSION AND
TEACHER PROFESSIONALISM

Professions

Professions have been traced as far back as sixteenth-century England, where the term referred primarily to the fields of divinity, law, and medicine (Abbott, 1988). By the nineteenth century, a system was established that distinguished professions from businesses, trades, and crafts. Several scholars have tried to identify the distinguishing characteristics or traits that an occupation needed to possess to be deemed worthy of the status of a profession.

According to Flexner (1915), the hallmark of the professions was that the activities engaged in were "essentially intellectual in character" (p. 154). Hence, the original professions were referred to as the *learned* professions. Professions were socially closed occupational groupings; those seeking entry into a profession needed to first complete an extended and elaborate process of professional training (Abbott, 1988). This training culminated in the acquisition of formal credentials, which were evidence of the individual's mastery of the arcane knowledge that characterized the profession. These credentials were awarded by a regulatory body made up of members of the profession. Since the regulatory body controlled both the training and the entry into the profession, professions were said to have autonomy in licensing.

Professions were also self-regulating (Sockett, 1993). This was based on the belief that those within the profession possessed the discernment to best regulate the profession. The regulatory body was also charged with the responsibility of ensuring that members of the profession were competent and executed their duties in an ethical manner (i.e., individual members were held to a code of professional ethics and standards).

Finally, professions were thought to be inherently altruistic. That is, they were guided by service, "only incidentally (albeit deservedly) reaping pecuniary and other rewards" (Goodlad, Soder, & Sirotnik, 1990, p. 39). These characteristics have been summarized by Sexton (2007) as the knowledge, autonomy, and service attributes.

There has been much debate about the professional status of teaching. Pratte and Rury (1991) asserted that while other professions require mastery of a body of conceptual or formal knowledge, teaching only requires embodied knowledge that is learned through experience. According to Etzioni (1969), when compared with professions like clergy or law, teaching is a semiprofession because the "training is shorter . . . there is less of a specialized body of knowledge" (p. v) (e.g., see Cooper & Brown, chapter 1, this volume). Also, teachers do not have control of standards for entry to their profession (Labaree, 2008). Unlike doctors and lawyers, teachers do not belong to a single umbrella organization that establishes, maintains, and enforces the ethical standards the profession has set for itself. Further, at the local level, as Lortie (1975) pointed out, "teachers work in settings where formal authority is vested in board members who do not belong to their occupation and are therefore beyond the reach of its internal controls" (p. 6).

Professionalism

Professionalism, a closely related term, is often described in terms of the ideals of practice to which individuals within the occupational groups aspire (Pratte & Rury, 1991). The essence of professionalism, according to Hargreaves and Fullan (2012), "is the ability to make discretionary judgments" (p. 92) drawing upon the collective wisdom and experience of the profession.

It is important to note that professionalism is not simply the quality of individual practice; rather, it is "conduct within an occupation" (Sockett, 1993, p. 226). Professions exist because they are well-organized. What distinguishes a profession is not "autonomy of individual conduct, but the collective establishment of widely recognized rules of good service and standards for admission to practice" (Kerchner & Caufman, 1995, p. 108). This organization allows for a profession-wide system for doing work. Thus, professionalism connotes a common set of norms and skills that are used by a community of practitioners (Glazer, 2008). It includes legal and ethical guidelines or standards; a code of professional conduct; and the expectation of professional responsibility toward oneself, toward one's clients, and toward the profession.

In applying the notion of professionalism to teachers, Hoyle (1980) distinguishes between *extended* and *restricted professionalism.* Extended professionalism, according to Hoyle, entails a wide vision of what education involves, valuing the theory behind the pedagogy and the adoption of a rational, not just practical, approach to the job. Extended professionalism is more than content knowledge and it is more than the application of universal principles and techniques of teaching. Teachers work in complex contexts of schools and classrooms. They deal with unique problems on a case-by-case basis, using their judgment to make decisions that maximize the learning of all students, keeping in mind that what happens in the classroom is affected by matters outside the classroom. It is these qualities of professional decision making in context that exemplify extended professionalism.

However, when asked about their understandings regarding professionalism, teachers tend to associate the term with individual behaviors observable in the classroom or school setting (Raymond, 2006). Hoyle (1980) uses the term *restricted professional* to refer to this focus on the immediate day-to-day practical reality of the classroom—that is, classroom management and instruction. Many equate teacher professionalism with behaviors such as politeness, punctuality, appearance, use of proper language, and respectful communication with students, parents, and colleagues (Helterbran, 2008). However, this characterization has been described as the "trivialization of teacher professionalism" (Raymond, 2006, p. 31). To understand why this restricted notion of professionalism is so prevalent, and what has prevented teachers from becoming full professionals, it is important to examine the notions regarding the teaching profession and teacher professionalism that have prevailed throughout American history.

HISTORICAL ISOLATION OF TEACHERS

Physical Isolation

During the nineteenth century, no formal preparation was required for teachers. Instead, teachers were hired by local religious leaders based on their moral character and general knowledge of reading, writing, and arithmetic (Angus, 2001). Often, local individuals were hired who needed a job and could maintain order in the classroom (Labaree, 2008). Most teachers received their certification to teach from local officials based on their performance on an exam. While initial exams were oral, later these exams developed into longer written assessments.

During this "pre-professional age" (Hargreaves, 2000, p. 153), while it was acknowledged that teaching was a demanding job, it was considered to be a technically simple task. The assumption was that one learned to teach by watching others, through apprenticeship (Lortie, 1975). During this time, teachers' work was limited to their individual classroom. Experienced teachers taught in isolated classrooms, having little interaction with their colleagues and receiving no feedback about their practice (Lortie, 1975).

Improvements in teaching were made through trial and error; there was little ongoing professional education. Throughout the nineteenth century, the citizen, not the professional educator, was in control of the professional preparation and certification of teachers (Angus, 2001). Thus, teacher isolation limited shared practical knowledge and opportunities for professional growth (Flinders, 1988). Since the identity of the teacher was determined by the setting (Labaree, 2008), this isolation restricted opportunities for the development of a common professional identity.

Isolation from the Theoretical Knowledgebase

As mentioned previously, the historic professions were considered the learned professions. One main criticism leveled against teaching is the lack of an arcane body of knowledge that forms the base of professional expertise (Lortie, 1975).

Shulman (1987) has argued that teaching is, indeed, a learned profession. He articulated the "qualities and understandings, skills and abilities and what traits and sensibilities render someone a competent teacher" (p. 4). He pointed out that the knowledgebase of teaching includes content knowledge, pedagogical knowledge (i.e., broad principles of classroom management), pedagogical content knowledge, curriculum knowledge, knowledge of learners, knowledge of educational contexts, and knowledge of the historical and philosophical foundations of educational purposes and values. According to Shulman (1987), what distinguished a teacher from a content expert was the ability to transform the content knowledge from personal comprehension into "forms that are powerful and yet adaptive to the variations in ability and background presented by the students" (p. 15).

Historically, such knowledge was not made available to teachers; the expectation was that the teacher knew a little more subject matter than the students they instructed. It was only in 1867 that "professional knowledge, the theory and practice of teaching" was first required (Angus, 2001, p. 9). During the second half of the nineteenth century, the rapid growth of the common school and a corresponding demand for teachers created a need for standardized teacher preparation. This led to the emergence of *normal schools*—teacher training institutions that provided basic college education to prospective teachers. They were "expected to set the standard—the norm—for good teaching" (Labaree, 2008, p. 292).

Since normal schools were expected to produce large numbers of teachers to staff the rapidly expanding public school system, they did so by "making teacher education easy to enter, short in duration, modest in academic rigor, and inexpensive to maintain" (Labaree, 2008, p. 297). In fact, it was these very traits of teacher preparation that allowed for the successful growth of common schools and the establishment of an American public school system.

These normal schools gradually developed into state teacher colleges, which grew first into state colleges and then into regional state universities. According to Labaree (2008), since teacher education ended up at the university more or less involuntarily, this has led to a tension between the academic and the professional role of teacher preparation. Teacher education programs that evolved from the normal schools tended to be "professionally strong but academically weak" (p. 302). Likewise, Shulman (1987) points out that, historically, much of the focus on teacher preparation has been on the management of students rather than the management of ideas. On the other hand, teacher education programs that evolved within the university tended to focus on research, minimizing the professional preparation of teachers (Labaree, 2008, p. 302).

Isolation from Research Developments

Teacher candidates arrive at the university with preformed values and attitudes about the profession due largely to what is considered an apprenticeship of experience (Lortie, 1975). Such prior experiences have been found to have a stronger influence on the socialization of teachers than the knowledge gained through teacher preparation programs. Teachers prefer information that is experiential (Landrum, Cook, Tankersley, & Fitzgerald, 2007), seeking advice from their peers rather than the pages of a scholarly journal.

In the twenty-first century, the problem is not the lack of a knowledge-base; the problem is that this knowledge is generally not accessible to practitioners (Goodlad et al., 1990). Much of the research is published in journals located in academic libraries and databases to which teachers typically do not have access. Furthermore, these research articles are frequently written in a manner that is inaccessible to practitioners (Berliner, 2008), who might not know how to apply the research findings to their own practice. Finally, when compared to professionals like doctors and nurses, teachers have not historically had a culture where it is expected they will share professional information or new techniques in professional journals or conferences (Lortie, 1975).

Isolation from Shared Norms

Professionalism involves decision making. Professionals draw upon a body of expert knowledge to make judgments and decisions when carrying out their responsibilities (Wills & Sandholtz, 2009). The isolation of teachers from the existing body of expert knowledge means that teacher professionalism is being constrained by local traditions and norms rather than being constructed by a professional organization. Professions have professional associations that are entrusted with the responsibility to encode and enforce the guidelines for professionalism (Sockett, 1993). This requires a well-organized professional body, which establishes, maintains, and enforces ethical standards. The vast majority of teachers belong to strong national, state, and local teacher organizations (e.g., the National Education Association [NEA] or the American Federation of Teachers [AFT]). However, it can be argued that this membership has not resulted in the same professional stature as the professions of law and medicine.

Started in 1857, the National Teacher's Association was the professional organization for teachers. By 1870, this teacher organization developed into the NEA, a coalition of administrators, university professors, and lay citizens that spoke in one voice for the education profession (Goodlad et al., 1990). The NEA was governed by superintendents and college professors; teachers were essentially second-rate citizens within the organization (Kerchner & Caufman, 1995). Over time, various groups that were originally departments within the NEA developed independent organizations. These included the American Educational Research Association (AERA), the Association for Supervision and Curriculum Development (ASCD), the National Association of Elementary School Principals (NAESP), and the National Association of Secondary School Principals (NASSP).

Education professors moved out of the NEA to join the AERA and ASCD, and school administrators left to join the NAESP and NASSP. During the 1960s, the focus of the NEA switched to collective bargaining for the working conditions of teachers, prompted by the strong union activity of the AFT. Currently, and in the teacher professionalization movement of the 1980s and 1990s, attention has been directed to blending union activity with advocacy for improvements to the teaching profession. For example, in Ohio, the Educator Standards Board was signed into law following lobbying activity by the Ohio Education Association and the Ohio Federation of Teachers (Allen, 2004). Practicing PK–12 classroom teachers make up the majority of the board, which develops recommendations for statewide standards for educators.

Self-Imposed Isolation

During the 1960s, teacher professionalism was characterized by individualism and autonomy. Although teachers were isolated from one another because of the egg-crate organization of schools (Lortie, 1975), some of this isolation was self-imposed, even preferred, by those who saw themselves as autonomous decision makers (Flinders, 1988). Thus, this was an age of *professional autonomy*, when teachers felt they had the right to select materials and methods they deemed best for their students (Cooper & Brown, chapter 1, this volume; Hargreaves, 2000). This autonomy was further justified by the growth of teacher participation in preservice and in-service education—education that provided them with the knowledgebase and expertise to practice as autonomous professionals. Consequently, this focus on individual rights further isolated teachers in the classroom, an isolation that eroded the spirit of service associated with teaching (Louis & Kruse, 1995) and the previously held public perception of teachers focusing on the needs of students.

Just as in the preprofessional age, during the age of professional autonomy teachers had few opportunities to collaborate with colleagues in resolving school-wide problems (Holmes Group, 1986). They tended to view their work "in terms of tasks that do not involve collaboration with other teachers" (Flinders, 1988, p. 22). Consequently, teachers' responses to problems were individualistic and *ad hoc*; there were few innovations that were institutionalized throughout the education system (Hargreaves, 2000). Collegiality was not considered a valuable aspect of professionalism.

It was only in the late 1980s that teachers began to feel the need to build collaborations to cope with and respond to the challenges they faced: an expansion of knowledge about teaching styles, the inclusion of students with special needs, and rapidly growing ethnic diversity in the student population. Teacher autonomy was no longer sustainable as a professional goal (Hargreaves, 2000). This led to the development of a professionalism that was *collegial and collective* rather than individual or autonomous. During this period, there was a growth in site-based professional development and PLCs.

CURRENT THREATS TO TEACHER PROFESSIONALISM

Although universities prepare teachers, they do not set the standards for teacher preparation nor do they provide teaching licenses. Public schools are government agencies. "[L]icensing of teachers is a state function, that is, it is the state rather than the members of the profession itself that determines who is allowed to teach in public school" (Raymond, 2006, p. 25). In the early nineteenth century, a license to teach was provided by ecclesiastical authorities. Over the course of the century, this licensing role was passed on to civil authorities.

By the second half of the nineteenth century, most teachers received their certificate to teach from local and then state officials. Even today, as Lortie (1975) pointed out more than a generation ago, "[t]eachers work in settings where formal authority is vested in board members who do not belong to their occupation and are therefore beyond the reach of its internal controls" (p. 6). The hiring of temporary teachers with emergency certification, the rise of charter schools, the rise of Teach for America, and in fact, "any attempt to staff schools with non-certified and non-professionally trained teachers can be seen as a threat to education's jurisdictional control" (Glazer, 2008, p. 173).

Furthermore, in the last decade, the state has expanded its role from licensing teachers to regulating their professional roles. There is a trend toward limiting spaces and opportunities where teachers can develop and exercise their capacity to think for themselves, replaced with the government's prescription of curriculum, pedagogy, and assessment. Now that forty-five states have adopted the Common Core Standards (Common Core State Standards Initiative, 2011), teachers have little control over the generation or selection of knowledge. Their job, according to many districts, is merely to transmit or deliver the curriculum. Likewise, student assessment, which was historically a local matter completed by teachers, is gradually being replaced with assessments developed in distant locales.

For example, thirty-one states are poised to adopt the national formative and summative assessments developed by the SMARTER Balanced Assessment Consortium, one of two consortia awarded funding by the U.S. Department of Education to develop an assessment system aligned to the common core state standards. The primary responsibility of teachers has become raising student achievement scores as measured by standardized assessments. Professionalism has come to mean compliance. This represents a shift from a licensed autonomy to what Apple (1998) describes as a *regulated autonomy*.

Not only is teacher work becoming standardized, it is also being monitored by the state. For example, there is an increase in state surveillance through the use of student achievement in teacher evaluations. By 2015,

student achievement and growth will constitute 50 percent of teacher evaluations in some states (Michigan Legislative Council, 2012). Ball (2003)
calls this the "technology of performativity" (p. 217), where complex processes are translated into simple figures or categories of judgment. What
this implies is that, when compared to other professionals, teachers cannot
be trusted to work in the best interest of their clients.

We are now in what Hargreaves (2000) called an age of *postmodern
professionalism*. This period is marked by an assault on the profession
that threatens to return teaching to a preprofessional stage. The most
significant challenge is a trend toward the marketization of education,
where schools and institutions of higher education are run like for-profit
organizations.

Furthermore, teachers are being subjected to increasing regulations
that are the very antithesis of professionalism: the adoption of prescribed,
centralized curricula; changes in tenure rules; reductions in the period and
level of initial certification of teachers; the proliferation of alternate routes
to certification, including online teacher preparation programs; raising
the caps on charter schools; and reductions in post-certification education
requirements for teachers.

In addition to these attacks on K–12 education, the federal government
questions the importance of teacher preparation, claiming there is no con-
vincing research that teacher preparation makes a difference in student
achievement (U.S. Department of Education, 2004, as cited in Stairs,
2010, p. 47). Legislative actions, such as limiting the nature and number
of courses required for teacher certification, are indicative of attempts by
noneducators to regulate teacher education (Beaudry, 1990). Teaching is
returning to an "amateur, de-professionalized, almost pre-modern craft"
(Hargreaves, 2000, p. 168).

RENEWED PROFESSIONALISM
THROUGH COLLABORATION

The challenges of modern times necessitate a return to the notions of *collegial professionalism* (Hargreaves, 2000). Excessive individualism among
teachers has resulted in exclusion, isolation, and a sense of meaningless-
ness and ambiguity about their work (Ball, 2003; Louis & Kruse, 1995).

It is also destroying the opportunities for teachers to develop a common professional identity and a sense of solidarity with other teachers.

Hargreaves and Fullan (2012) report that teachers who "work in professional cultures of collaboration tend to perform better than teachers who work alone" (p. 112). Furthermore, Louis and Kruse (1995) point out that teachers' work outside their classrooms may be critical to their success within the classroom. Therefore, what is sorely needed is a concept of professionalism that extends beyond the classroom, involves collaboration with colleagues across the profession, and democratically involves groups outside teaching.

However, teachers cannot be expected to develop professionalism by themselves. Rather, educators need to collaborate to improve teaching and learning in schools. This begins with preservice preparation, and continues with in-service professional development and ongoing collaboration with colleagues within and outside the school. As Coleman, Gallagher, and Job (2012) state: "We believe that without a commitment to renewed professionalism, we risk becoming isolated, fragmented, and irrelevant. Through professionalism, we can forge and strengthen linkages with other stakeholders who are committed to excellence in education for all learners" (p. 35).

Preservice Teacher Education

In a climate where teachers are being deprofessionalized, it is urgent for teacher educators to examine how preservice and in-service teachers are socialized into the profession. "Socialization is the process by which the ideologies, technical competencies, and expected behaviors deemed necessary to perform an occupational role are transmitted to novices" (Evans, 2010, p. 185). But socialization is not a passive process. Individuals interpret and construct their professional identities. Furthermore, the influence of a shared social milieu leads to a collective understanding. Thus, professional identity development is a collaborative and contextualized process.

Preservice education offers numerous opportunities for this socialization into the profession. It is important that teacher educators attend not only to principles of practice, but also to heuristics that determine if and when principles are to be applied (e.g., contextual knowledge). Often teacher education programs do not stress the responsibility a teacher has toward the profession. Therefore, teacher educators also need to pay attention to the role of the teacher beyond the confines of the school (Sexton, 2007). This implies a collegial professionalism where the focus is "not just on classroom conduct, but on collegial relations and relations with the parents and the community" (Sockett, 1993, p. 226).

Novice teachers must be provided with analytical tools to critically reflect about school and society, and with the interpretive and normative skills required to understand the broader social context of teaching (Council of Learned Societies in Education, 1996). This notion of professionalism implies a reflective and enquiring teacher who is responsible not only to the students in the classroom but also to other teachers, to the profession, and to the moral, political, social, and philosophical context of schooling (Sexton, 2007).

Professional Development

Darling-Hammond, Wei, Andree, Richardson, and Orphanos (2009) conducted a comprehensive review of professional development in the United States and abroad. They found that teachers in the United States were isolated from one another and had few opportunities for sustained, collegial professional development. They also found that,

> [w]hen schools are strategic in creating time and productive working relationships within academic departments or grade levels, across them, or among teachers school wide, the benefits can include greater consistency in instruction, more willingness to share practices and try new ways of teaching, and more success in solving problems of practice. (p. 11)

PLCs can provide a caring and supportive space for exploring the best ways to enhance student learning. In fact, teacher-to-teacher coaching and mentoring have been found to be more likely to lead to higher-order learning experiences for students than traditional professional development activities (Quick, Holtzman, & Chaney, 2009). However, it is important to note that within PLCs, teachers need to be able to define their own needs, not simply figure out how best to implement the agenda developed by others. The latter will only lead to a *contrived collegiality*, not a true collaborative community (Hargreaves & Fullan, 2012).

Research Collaborations

Collegial professionalism is characterized by collaboration with researchers to increase content and pedagogical knowledge (Cwikla, 2004). Of
even greater importance, collaboration with researchers can help teachers
understand the theoretical rationale behind some practices. If we continue
to neglect the theoretical knowledgebase, "teaching becomes merely a
task for technicians" (Goodson, as cited in Sexton, 2007, p. 94). As Coleman et al. (2012) remind us: "[w]hat defines teaching as a profession, and
thus calls for standards of professionalism, is the idea that it is a praxis
(e.g., a set of practices used in complex ways) that requires reflection and
continual growth for success" (p. 27).

While research (Hatch et al., 2005) has shown that teachers who collaborate with researchers are more reflective about their practice, many
teachers find research inaccessible and even intimidating. Better ways
to communicate research to teachers are sorely needed. In addition to
being consumers of knowledge, collaborative professionals also need to
contribute to that knowledge (Hegarty, 2000). Duke and Martin (2011)
report that "some of the most compelling research arises from collaborations between researchers and teachers" (p. 11). They give the example of
concept-oriented reading instruction, which was a result of collaboration
between teachers and researchers in Maryland.

It is important to point out that authentic collaboration takes mutual
trust and a genuine sense of caring. Research in the fields of nursing and
health services cautions that "bureaucratic organizational structures can
reinforce a form of professionalism that frames caring and collaborative
relationships as unprofessional" (Douglass & Gittell, 2012, p. 267). The
focus on accountability suggests that we are not expected to care about
each other; instead, we are expected to care about results (Ball, 2003).
However, teaching, like other service-based occupations and nonprofit
work, is relationship-based work and the notion of caring undergirds the
profession (Collinson, Killeavy, & Stephenson, 1999). To neglect this
would be to neglect the soul of the profession.

CONCLUSION

Teacher professionalism in the United States is at a crossroads; in the face of
numerous "assaults on professionalism" (Hargreaves, 2000, p. 168), teacher

individualism is no longer sustainable as a professional goal. Collaboration is one way to counter these efforts to undermine teacher professionalism. "Problems can only be resolved by the generation of shared knowledge constructed through dialogue between all parties in a particular context rather than through the 'top-down' application of a universal, 'objective' professional expertise" (Quicke, 2000, p. 304). This requires collaboration among and between educators to articulate the shared knowledge and value base that will provide "a framework for shared, collective, ethical decision making" (Louis & Kruse, 1995, p. 15).

Teachers must reconceptualize a professionalism that is *collegial and collective* rather than individual or autonomous. Teacher educators need to pay attention to the contextual responsibilities of teachers outside the class-room (Sexton, 2007). This might allow American educators to revitalize and sustain their professional character in the eyes of community members and legislators alike, and claim responsibility for their professional behavior rather than be held accountable by others to external standards of practice.

REFERENCES

Abbott, A. (1988). *The system of professions.* Chicago: University of Chicago Press.

Allen, G. (2004, May). Standards for educators: Ohio teamwork gives teachers a voice on professionalism. *NEA Today, 22*(8), 31.

Angus, D. (2001). *Professionalism and the public good. A brief history of teacher certification.* Retrieved from http://www.edexcellencemedia.net/publications/2001/200101_professionalismandpublicgood/angus.pdf

Apple, M. (1998). Under the new hegemonic alliance: Conservatism and educational policy in the United States. In K. Sullivan (Ed.), *Education and change in the Pacific Rim: Meeting the challenges* (pp. 79–99). Wallingford, Oxfordshire: Triangle Books.

Ball, S. J. (2003). The teacher's soul and the terrors of performativity. *Journal of Education Policy, 18*(2), 215–28.

Beaudry, M. (1990). Post-Carnegie developments affecting teacher education: The struggle for professionalism. *Journal of Teacher Education, 41*, 63–70.

Berliner, D. C. (2008). Research, policy and practice: The great disconnect. In S. D. Lapan & M. L. Quartaroli (Eds.), *Research essentials* (pp. 295–326). New York: Wiley.

Coleman, M., Gallagher, J., & Job, J. (2012). Developing and sustaining professionalism within gifted education, *Gifted Child Today, 35*(1), 27–36.

Collinson, V., Killeavy, M., & Stephenson, H. J. (1999). Exemplary teachers: Practicing an ethic of care in England, Ireland, and the U.S.A. *Journal for a Just and Caring Education, 5*(4), 349–66.

Common Core State Standards Initiative (2011). *In the states.* Retrieved from http://www.corestandards.org/in-the-states

Council of Learned Societies in Education (1996). *Standards for academic and professional instruction in foundations of education, educational studies, and educational policy studies* (2nd ed.). The Council of Learned Societies in Education. Retrieved from http://www.unm.edu/~jka/csfe/standards96.pdf

Cwikla, J. (2004). Show me the evidence: Mathematics professional development for teachers. *Teaching Children Mathematics, 10*(6), 321–26.

Darling-Hammond, L., Wei, R., Andree, A., Richardson, N., & Orphanos, S. (2009). *Professional learning in the learning profession: A status report on teacher development in the United States and abroad.* Stanford, CA: Stanford University, National Staff Development Council.

Douglass, A., & Gittell, J. (2012). Transforming professionalism. *Journal of Early Childhood Research, 10*(3), 267–81.

Duke, N., & Martin, N. (2011). 10 things every literacy educator needs to know about research. *The Reading Teacher, 65*(1), 9–22.

Etzioni, A. (1969). *The semi professions and their organization.* New York: Free Press.

Evans, L. (2010). Professionals or technicians? Teacher preparation programs and occupational understandings. *Teachers and Teaching: Theory and Practice, 16*(2), 183–205.

Flexner, A. (1915). *Is social work a profession?* Proceedings of the National Conference of Charities and Corrections, 42nd Annual Session held in Baltimore, MD.

Flinders, D. (1988). Teacher isolation and the new reform. *Journal of Curriculum and Supervision, 4*(1), 17–29.

Glazer, J. (2008). Educational professionalism. An inside-out view. *American Journal of Education, 114*, 169–89.

Goodlad, J., Soder, R., & Sirotnik, K. (1990). *The moral dimension of teaching.* San Francisco: Jossey-Bass.

Hargreaves, A. (2000). Four ages of professionalism and professional learning. *Teachers and Teaching: History and Practice, 6*(2), 151–82.

Hargreaves, A., & Fullan, D. (2012). *Professional capital. Transforming teaching in every school.* New York: Teachers College Press.

Hatch, T., Ahmed, D., Lieberman, A., Faigenbaum, D., White, M. E., & Mace, D. (2005). *Going public with our teaching: An anthology of practice.* New York: Teachers College Press.

Hegarty, S. (2000). Teaching as a knowledge-based activity. *Oxford Review of Education, 26*, 451–65.

Helterbran, V. (2008). Professionalism: Teachers taking the reins. *The Clearinghouse, 81*(3), 123–27.

Holmes Group. (1986). *Tomorrow's teachers: A report of the Holmes Group.* East Lansing, MI: Holmes Corporation.

Hoyle, E. (1980). Professionalization and deprofessionalization in education. In E. Hoyle & J. Megarry (Eds.), *World Yearbook of Education 1980* (pp. 42–57), London: Kogan Page.

Kerchner, C., & Caufman, K. (1995). Lurching towards professionalism. The saga of teacher unionism. *The Elementary School Journal, 96*(1), 107–22.

Labaree, D. (2008). An uneasy relationship: The history of teacher education in the university. In M. Cochran-Smith, S. Feiman-Nemser, & J. McIntyre (Eds.), *Handbook of research on teacher education: Enduring issues in changing contexts* (3rd Ed.). Washington, DC: Association of Teacher Educators.

Landrum, T., Cook, B., Tankersley, M., & Fitzgerald, S. (2007). Teacher perceptions of the usability of intervention information from personal versus data-based sources. *Education & Treatment of Children, 30*(4), 27–42.

Lortie, D. (1975). S*choolteacher: A sociological study*. Chicago: University of Chicago Press.

Louis, K. S., & Kruse, S. (1995). *Professionalism and community: Perspectives on reforming urban schools*. Long Oaks, CA: Corwin.

Michigan Legislative Council (2012). *The revised school code (excerpt) Act 451 of 1976*. Retrieved from http://www.legislature.mi.gov/%28S%282mr uqpiy3thexpvqnn1dbi55%29%29/mileg.aspx?page=GetObject&objectname= mcl-380-1249

Pratte, R., & Rury, J. (1991). Teachers, professionalism and craft. *Teachers College Record, 93*(1), 59–72.

Quick, H., Holtzman, D., & Chaney, K. (2009). Professional development and instructional practice: Conceptions and evidence of effectiveness. *Journal of Education for Students Placed at Risk (JESPAR), 14*(1), 45–71.

Quicke, J. (2000). A new professionalism for a collaborative culture of organizational learning in contemporary society. *Educational Management Administration and Leadership, 28*, 299–315.

Raymond, S. (2006). *Professionalism and identity in teacher education. Implications for teacher reform.* (Unpublished doctoral dissertation). Northern Arizona University, Flagstaff, Arizona.

Sexton, M. (2007). Evaluating teaching as a profession. Implications of a research study for the work of the teaching council. *Irish Educational Studies, 26*(1), 79–105.

Shulman, L. (1987). Knowledge and teaching: Foundation of the new reform. *Harvard Educational Review, 57*(1), 61–77.

Sockett, H. (1993). *The moral base for teacher professionalism.* New York: Teachers College Press.

Stairs, A. (2010). Becoming a professional educator in an urban school-university partnership: A case study analysis of preservice teacher learning. *Teacher Education Quarterly, 37*(3), 45–62.

Wills, J., & Sandholtz, J. (2009). Constrained professionalism: Dilemmas of teaching in the face of test-based accountability. *Teachers College Record, 111*(4), 1065–1114.

Chapter Three

Rejuvenating Teacher Teams

Back to Basics

Terrence E. Deal and Donna Redman

June Davisson is a veteran teacher. She loves teaching and, along with her teammate, is recognized as an outstanding classroom teacher. She explains:

> I have been teaching in a Title I elementary school for twenty-three years. Believe me; I've been through many new things that come and go, usually imposed from the top by a principal or someone in the district office who has read a recent journal article or gone to a workshop somewhere. The one thing that has stuck with us over time because it works is team teaching. Teaming makes it possible for us to group students, plan together, give each other helpful suggestions, and provide mutual support. It also gives us more influence over school-wide decisions normally made by the principal.
>
> Somewhere along the way, they started calling it teacher collaboration. We didn't care. To us it was still team teaching. We just kept on doing what had always made sense to us. This year was different. In the first faculty meeting before school started, a group of young teachers had volunteered to work with the principal on something called professional learning communities or PLCs as they came to be known. These hyped-up teachers pitched the new wrinkle, something about getting together and sharing ideas. To illustrate the concept of PLCs, they spent time playing parlor games, role-playing various scenarios, and reading together from a giant folder of documents. To add to the frustration, the activity kept us all away from doing what we needed to do, working together to get our classrooms ready for the start of the school year. We already know it takes teamwork to get things done. We still team teach just as we did before they rechristened it PLC. (Personal interview with author.)

If this scenario was an exception, we might brush it off as the peculiarities of disgruntled teachers or an unusual school. Unfortunately, it's very typical. Team teaching began as a natural structural response to changes in instructional practices. Teachers in individual, isolated classrooms had difficulty managing these new challenges alone so they formed working relations with others. The new arrangements had an impact on both classrooms and the school. For June Davisson, and many others, team teaching worked. And it still does. Studies have confirmed it. But since the 1970s it has dropped from the radar of promising changes that can help teachers become more effective.

The scarcity of teacher teams today reveals a fundamental flaw in American education. We seem unable to take something new, give it a chance, try to improve it, and stick with it if it seems to have some potential. Rather, we take a potentially good thing, impose it on teachers, give it a quick fling, and quickly move onto something roughly similar with a new name. That is, we believe, what happened to team teaching.

In this chapter, we hope to bring into question the prospects of PLCs and resurrect and reinforce the promises of teacher teams. We will show how work teams have succeeded in other sectors, and offer some suggestions for how teachers working in teams might strengthen their ability to meet the demanding tasks of outcome-based instruction. In conclusion, we raise serious questions about current reform efforts.

PLCS AS ANOTHER PASSING FAD?

The Federal No Child Left Behind Act (Department of Education, 2002) mandated reforms for all schools in the United States. This time around, however, legislation had some teeth. Deadlines and financial penalties awaited districts and states unable to show sufficient student progress on standardized tests. The emphasis on accountability and student achievement paved the way for programs to create professional learning communities (PLCs). These local groups emerged as an infrastructure to address issues of teacher isolation, absence of productive collaboration, and lack of student proficiency (Morrisey, 2000). Although efforts to create PLCs were well intended, they often failed to reach full potential. School administrators, to promote such collaborative communities, often mandated their formation. Teachers, as a result, felt forced into the arrangements and were often asked to do what they already had been doing in their homegrown teacher teams.

If PLCs intend to help teachers work together more productively, then it makes sense that they embody characteristics of successful collaboration. Friend and Cook (1992) have identified these characteristics: (1) being voluntary; (2) requiring parity among participants; (3) based on mutual goals; (4) depending on shared responsibility for participation and decision making; (5) consisting of individuals who share their resources; and (6) consisting of individuals who share accountability for outcomes.

The first of these characteristics, *being voluntary*, is missing from June Davisson's example and from many other efforts to form PLCs. For the idea to work, group efforts have to be voluntary. Mandating PLCs removes the willingness for teachers to work together and creates resistance.

The other characteristics are part of group structure and process that, more often than not, are absent from a group's preparation and training. As a result, groups bog down in procedural details, become hampered by conflict and are unable to deal with typical political and cultural challenges.

A recent study of the Stanford Center for Research on the Context of Teaching expands on this point: a bureaucratic approach to PLCs results in three patterns among teachers: compliance, resistance, and anxiety (Talbert, 2010). The act of requiring teachers to "comply" with a directive to form communities once again deviates from choice as an essential attribute of successful collaboration. Resistance to form local communities stems from the validity that teachers see lacking in the PLCs. Teachers feel it is a waste of time and resources to attend PLC workshops and often resist by dragging their feet or not showing up. Finally, new teachers become anxious because they do not feel fully vested in the culture of the school or don't yet belong to their own informal group. They see resistance from veteran teachers and become anxious themselves. As newcomers, they feel particularly vulnerable.

PLCs might potentially be a good way to encourage a collaborative approach to the challenges of No Child Left Behind and other outcome-based reforms. But the top-down approach, and other deficiencies launching and maintaining the concept, does not auger well for their future. In addition, PLCs seem part of education's endless carousel of reform, giving teacher teams a new name and becoming a poor substitute for an innovation that appeared to work. Teachers still know how to work in teams, and as the June Davisson example suggests, some have been teaming for years. But to Davisson, her colleague, and many other seasoned teachers, PLCs make little sense and have no meaning. They are a blip on the passing parade of innovations that come and go. Pressure for their establishment may even reinforce the sanctity of the self-contained, isolated classroom.

PLCS IN CONTEXT

Coercion to adopt PLCs are easiest to understand in the milieu of educational reform as a constant mantra for improving schools. Reforms come in wave after wave; Larry Cuban (1990) puts it nicely: "Reforming again, again, and again." Waves upon waves of so-called improvements pound against local public school districts and schools. In their wake, they leave many discarded programs and legions of disillusioned teachers much less willing to hitch on to whatever comes next. Currently, the big push is on accountability and test scores, measured on standardized tests. These numerical results have become very close to the exclusive criterion on which we judge our nation's schools.

How did we arrive here? Let's look back to the 1960s and 1970s, a time of rapid change in society and in education. Innovation flourished in schools, often funded by state and federal governments. Teachers witnessed the advent of decentralization of authority, individualized instruction, open space architecture, team teaching, alternative schools, and many other novel ideas. Most aimed at opening up bureaucratized school systems and giving more authority to schools and teachers. Many were grassroots initiatives. Some of these interesting ideas succeeded; others failed. Even more serious, many of these innovations altered the symbolic face of public schools, raising questions about what they were accomplishing (Meyer & Rowan, 1978).

Alongside these developments, movements were afoot to bring rationality and measurement to business and education. McNamara's push to fight the Vietnam War by the numbers. The Polaris Missile System's phenomenal success, credited to the project's reliance on "modern management techniques." No matter both efforts were discredited or reinterpreted later. McNamara admitted: "We were wrong, terribly wrong." Sapolsky (1972) documented how the modern techniques gave Polaris the allure of tight management and control. This belief kept Congress from close, bothersome oversight while the managers of Polaris went about their business in their customary ways. Still, these and other such efforts, with success more imagined than real, became a panacea to rescue the nation's public schools. Program Evaluation and Review Technique (PERT), Planning, Programming, and Budgeting System (PPBS), behavioral objectives, objective tests, the entire panoply of rational programs conjured to make sure schools were performing up to snuff.

A school district in the Midwest was one of the first school districts to become victim to this rising faith in rational approaches. It was selected to experiment with PPBS, a rational system that included setting behavioral objectives for each lesson. A behavioral objective specifies a certain behavior observable at the end of a particular teaching strategy: at the end of X period, a student should be able to demonstrate Y. This shift was hard for most teachers, used to judging how well students were learning by professional intuition or "feel." But behavioral objectives were mandated and applied to nearly every subject. Of course, teachers rebelled and the district was embroiled in turmoil. Harry Wolcott, an anthropologist, spent that year observing and wrote a book describing the incident. In the book's preface he writes, "All the while I was doing the fieldwork and writing this [book], I was bolstered by one sustaining thought: This must never happen again" (Wolcott, 2003). But it has, as specificity, rationality, and modern management have continued to haunt our public schools—even though many businesses and other organizations are moving away from calculating yearly performance solely on bottom-line results.

From the many educational innovations of the 1960s and 1970s that flew by like words or images on a tachistoscope, at least one innovation seemed to make a significant difference: team teaching.

Stanford Study of Team Teaching

In 1973–1975, thirty-four school districts in California's San Francisco Bay area participated in an ambitious three-year study conducted by sociologists in the Stanford Center for Research and Development in Teaching. The districts ranged in size—from one to over one hundred elementary schools, in wealth—from very wealthy to very poor; and in location—urban, suburban, and rural.

Within the thirty-four districts, 101 elementary schools selected randomly participated in the study. The schools varied in size from those with teaching staffs of four to those with staffs of thirty. Both superintendents and principals were interviewed (and completed short questionnaires) twice—once in 1973 and again in 1975. In eighteen of the elementary schools, teachers completed questionnaires in both 1973 and 1975.

Administrators and teachers described instructional and organization patterns from their respective viewpoints. Superintendents described district organization—including policies, roles and relationships, general instructional issues, the local community, and relationships between the community and the district. Principals characterized the school organization, described typical instructional patterns, and portrayed both the local community and school/community relationships. Teachers described their classroom organization and their instructional approaches and techniques.

Comparing perceptions of administrators and teachers from 1973 with those of 1975, it was possible to determine how district and school roles, policies, and administrative practices—affected classroom organization and instruction over time (or vice versa). The study focused on two aspects of classrooms: individualized instruction and team teaching. The guiding theory assumed that the two would be related, that both would be affected by organizational or administrative patterns at either the district or the school level, and that both individualized instruction and team teaching would be affected by characteristics of the community environment: types of students (socioeconomic level), educational values, or special funding.

The results for teacher teaming are intriguing. Although teaming does not affect instructional patterns, individualized instruction leads to teaming. Teachers seem to work together more closely in response to demands created by complex instructional approaches.

In fact, results revealed that "differentiated instruction encourages collaboration among teachers" (Cohen, Meyer, Scott, & Deal, p. 29) and that the newer methods of teaching "tend to move teachers into collaborative arrangements and away from isolated classrooms" (Cohen et al. 1979, p. 29).

These team arrangements are also fragile. Teams form, dissolve, and re-form—but with new members. Teacher organizations have an effect on teaming—but the impact is negative. In districts where teacher organizations were rated as highly influential, close working relationships among teachers actually declined between 1973 and 1975. Subsequent analyses in the smaller teacher samples showed teachers in teams to be more satisfied, feel more autonomous, and to perceive they have more influence over school-wide decisions (Johnson, 1975). Shedd (1988) noted that a strong emphasis of collective bargaining in the 1980s onward would be to support the development of closer relationships among teachers.

Factors influencing the organization of classrooms are similar to those affecting instruction. Open space had an important positive impact. But other features of the classroom, school, district, or community do not affect collaborative relationships among teachers. Teaming is unaffected by district policies, supportive community climates, or—as a surprise to many administrators—even by school-wide policies that formally encourage teachers to work closely together in teams. These findings spawned a new image of schools and classrooms as "loosely coupled" entities and led to the development of institutional theory (Deal, Meyer, & Scott, 1975).

Other studies within the environment for teaching group looked at the impact of teaming on teachers in schools with open space architecture. Open space encouraged teachers to join teams as a way of coordinating activities. They compared responses of teachers in individual classrooms (N=120) with those involved in teams (N=110). They discovered that teachers in open space schools, involved in teams, were significantly more highly interactive with other teachers about instruction, more influential in school-wide decisions, more satisfied with their jobs, and, surprisingly, felt more autonomous. Teachers felt satisfaction in their work because they had "a forum of colleagues for discussion of their work, which results in their feeling of success in accomplishing their tasks" (Brunetti, Cohen, Meyer, & Molnar, 1972, p. 95) There was also an increased feeling of joint authority and joint responsibility as teachers work together in a common area, rather than in their isolated classrooms. Thus the isolated position of authority was shifted to that of collaborative and joint responsibility (p. 98).

While this early evidence clearly establishes a promising role for teaming in schools, both it, and open space architecture are today apparently consigned to the ghost parade of innovations wending their way in and out of education.

In business and other sectors, however, teams are flourishing.

TEAMS IN OTHER SECTORS

In recent decades, teams have penetrated nearly every sector of business, healthcare, military and other organizations. In 80 percent of Fortune 500 companies, half the employees work in teams. Management teams are enjoying success in companies such as Apple, General Electric, and Oracle. The notion of teaming is spreading in a variety of organizations because it works. Teams create a shared sense of mission and bond participants together in a tight almost cult-like community. Two recent examples illustrate the point.

On May 2, 2011, Stealth Hawk helicopters carrying two operational units of Seal Team Six's Red Squadron attacked Osama bin Laden's lair in Abbottabad, Pakistan. The outcome of their mission, "to interdict a high value target in a non-permissive environment," now takes its place in military history, although there remain several conflicting accounts of the actual combat itself. The fog of war invites many different interpretations.

Most after-the-fact commentators agree on one feature of Operation Neptune Spear. The real secret of Red Squadron's success is not the unsurpassed courage and pluck of its highly trained operators or its awesome weaponry. They agree on the astonishing teamwork built into a Seal's experience from the beginning. The Seal team's success has engaged the attention of the American public. Seals have recently published three books. An Academy Award Nominee for Best Picture of the Year, *Zero Dark Thirty* (2013), played in movie theaters across the country. The film portrays the close teamwork among federal agencies leading up to Neptune Spear as well as the joint effort among the Seals during the operation.

The second example is Saturn Motors. In 1983, General Motors announced the launch of a revolutionary experiment: the Saturn project, which would produce automobiles in a new way. The Saturn experiment showed what could happen when you place people in teams. After launch by its parent, Saturn quickly achieved levels of quality, consumer satisfaction, and customer loyalty that surpassed those of much of the U.S. automotive industry. What was the secret of the company's success? Saturn's distinctive team structure (Bolman & Deal, 2008).

Company-wide, Saturn employees had authority to make team decisions, within a few flexible guidelines. Restrictive rules and ironclad, top-down work procedures were left behind as the company moved away from what employees called the "old world" of General Motors.

Teams did the actual assembly of the Saturn automobile. More than 150 production teams of eight to fifteen cross-trained, interdependent workers assembled the cars on a half-mile-long assembly line. The traditional system of sequential, repetitive efforts by isolated individuals became obsolete. Saturn created "a work environment where people provide leadership for themselves and others. It is cooperation and self and team management that make Saturn tick. Problems are solved by people working together—they are not kicked upstairs for others to solve" (Deal & Jenkins, 1994, p. 230).

Saturn was eventually absorbed into General Motors and many of its lessons about teamwork applied throughout General Motors. Nevertheless, Saturn lingers on as a symbol of what people can do when given a chance. The idea of self-governing teams paved the way for many companies that are now adopting similar practices.

Some will argue that education has very little, if anything, to learn from teams fighting battles or manufacturing automobiles. Educators, in particular, believe that educational organizations are unique and lessons learned elsewhere do not apply to schools. Another view suggests that at the heart of it, organizations are organizations, teams are teams, and people are people in any enterprise. The basic core is the same. Differences lie in the nature of what they do. Educational organizations have the sacred responsibility of preparing the next generation. Military organizations are oath and honor bound to protect our country. Saturn was devoted to building a high quality car that people would be proud to drive. To achieve these noble ends, a shared spirit, cultivated through teamwork is essential.

Former Visa CEO Dee Hock captures the heart of the issue:

> In the field of group endeavor, you will see incredible events in which the group performs far beyond the sum of its individual talents. It happens in the symphony, in the ballet, in the theater, in sports, and equally in business. It is easy to recognize and impossible to define. It is a mystique. It cannot be achieved without immense effort, training, and cooperation, but effort, training, and cooperation alone rarely create it. (Schlesinger, Eccles, & Gabarro, 1983, p. 173)

The Environment for Teaching study demonstrated that teams once made a difference in the professional lives of teachers. The study showed that "newer methods of teaching tend to move teachers into collaborative arrangements and away from isolated classrooms" (Cohen et al., 1979,

p. 29). The study also showed that open space architecture encouraged teachers to form teams. Now, with both innovations somewhat defunct, how are schools going to reap the benefits of teaming showing up in other sectors?

The path toward that end is not an easy one for several reasons: (1) There is a mythical cultural force supporting the sanctity of the "one room classroom"; (2) Most schools being constructed now reflect traditional "egg-crate" designs; (3) Dominant external forces require schools to become more standardized and rational; (4) The prevalence of test scores used now to evaluate schools and individual teachers makes it difficult to evaluate team performance; (5) Teacher preparation programs often do not prepare prospective teachers for teamwork; (6) Teachers, already weary of innovation after innovation, are sick of reform; and (7) The "catch-22" is that teams could provide needed rejuvenation but will be resisted as another passing reform effort.

In both the Environment for Teaching study and the literature on teaming in other sectors, there is evidence that teams have trouble with group dynamics and often fail because of the lack of training. In the case of Seal Team Six, team training begins early in the first of a tortuous path to one of the squadrons. Saturn employees went through one of the most rigorous team training programs of its time. This leads to another important point. If teacher teams are once again considered as assets in the quest to improve American education, this time we need to go about it in the right way: training teachers to master the dynamics of working together as a cohesive team, and training administrators in the fine art of shaping "team friendly" schools.

TEAMS WORK: BUT WHAT MAKES TEAMS WORK?

Teams too often are formed or thrown together with little regard for what makes a team work. Team members are left on their own to figure out the dynamics they will encounter in moving from a group of individuals to a highly functioning team. Their hit or miss efforts produce results not unlike those in the classic, *Lord of the Flies*. Stranded on an island, the group of students first relied on democracy to elect a leader and then tried to evolve a structure of roles and relationships. Their hard slog was quickly undercut by a power struggle that split the group into factions. The two emerging subcultures then developed their own ways, eventually leading to conflict and warfare. This progression is similar to what happens in forming teams anywhere.

Bolman and Deal (2008) offer a framework for understanding team dynamics. They look at teams through four different lenses or frames: human resource, structural, political, and symbolic. Each frame helps team members identify troublesome areas and suggests ways predicaments can be confronted and resolved before interfering with the team's performance.

Team structure focuses on goals, roles, and work relationships among team members. One key ingredient of a top-notch team is an appropriate blueprint of roles and relationships set in motion to attain common goals or missions. Even highly skilled people zealously pursuing a shared mission will falter and fail if group structure constantly generates inequity, confusion, and frustration. Solving issues of authority, responsibilities, and coordination are one of the first problems teams have to deal with. Teachers do not always receive adequate grounding in the sociology of education, a branch of which would enable them to read the structures of their classrooms or school more effectively.

Interpersonal issues also interfere with how well a team functions. People have needs and dispositions that they bring to the group experience. These must be recognized and resolved as they crop up. Too often team members hold back their true feelings and opinions until they surface in interpersonal conflict. Training in interpersonal dynamics is necessary to help create a healthy group climate. Interpersonal training in preparing teachers often does not emphasize working in teams.

Power and conflict haunt any human group. Coalitions form around different opinions and interests. People vie for power. Conflict is a natural consequence. Effective teams master the skills of good politics: bargaining, negotiating, and facing conflict head on. Most teachers, used to a self-contained classroom, are not versed in the art and strategies of politics. Therefore, they typically shy away from the natural forces of power and conflict in teams. This needs to become part of their training beforehand.

Finally, every team evolves a culture of values and beliefs, heroes, rituals, ceremonies, stories and a network of informal players—priestesses, gossips, and so on. This will happen on its own, but can be shaped positively by team members who understand the role of symbols in human and other groups. Shaping an effective culture also needs to become part of a team's training.

Teachers will profit from this comprehensive perspective and training. As will their teams.

REFORM OR REVITALIZATION?

Studies of open space and team teaching in 1973 forecast a less than optimistic future for the promising innovations:

> After a time, the innovation loses its bloom of "innovativeness" and is turned into routine practice. The problems are no longer outweighed by the gratifications. People begin to talk about the innovation as a "failure." And the search is on for a new—and temporary—panacea. (Brunetti et al., 1972, p. 100)

Unfortunately, their prognosis was prediction: team teaching fell out of favor along with other innovations of the 1970s and 1980s. But the pace of change in education continued. It is now mandated from the top down rather than stimulated from the school and classroom levels. The main emphasis has shifted to the State and Federal level through directed programs such as No Child Left Behind or Race to the Top.

The aim of these reforms attempts to make schools more rational and accountable. The primary measure of effectiveness became standardized test scores, now education's near exclusive bottom line. Policymakers seem to believe that schools would do better if run more like businesses.

The problem is that the top-performing businesses of America don't have profits as their number one concern. They take pride in their rich history of involving employees in satisfying customers. The bottom line follows. Ritz Carlton employees take great pride in their hotel's unique way of pampering guests. Nordstrom Department Stores will do almost anything to satisfy shoppers. BMW workers are proud of building the most reliable automobiles in the world. All these companies flourish because everyone is devoted to making a difference. Starbucks encourages its employees to pour their hearts into every cup of coffee they serve. Saturn, in its heyday, was proud of its designation, "The Car Company with a Soul."

Heart. Soul. Spirit. In business, the stuff of success. The rapture of making a difference. In schools, the very meaning that has been weakened, if not sacrificed to testing and other measures to make them more accountable. Take the language of education for example. It is now far more technical than natural. In many cases, it misuses and abuses terms. Take the word rubric, for example, now used as a rational measure for ordering and judging assignments. The true meaning is the color red, used in the color of letters to mark sections in medieval manuscripts. Nonetheless, educators stole and misused it. It became part of "Educanese," a language few outside the field of education understand.

Today's students are not just test scores. They are young people whose lives are entrusted to teachers. It's not so much what teachers teach, it's who they are and how they make students feel. That's something that can't be measured. And if it could, it might take years for the effect to show up. Schools, as organizations, exist to provide teachers with spirit, heart, and soul—all the good things that gives them, every day, confidence, faith, and hope that what they do will make a difference. In many instances, this will require changing back to recapture the values that once inspired the teaching profession. There is reason to suspect that team teaching may help in this quest. If so, we need to give it a second chance to see if it will help rejuvenate our schools. To get back to the basics of restoring faith, spirit, soul, and joy to a noble profession.

REFERENCES

Bolman, L., & Deal, T. E. (2008). *Reframing organizations: Artistry, choice and leadership.* San Francisco: Jossey-Bass.

Brunetti, F. A., Cohen, E. G., Meyer, J. W., & Molnar, S. R. F. (1972). Studies of team teaching in the open-space school. *Interchange, 3,* 85–101.

Cohen, E. G., Meyer, J. W., Scott, W. R., & Deal, T. E. (1979). Technology and teaming in the elementary school. *Sociology of Education, 52,* 20–33.

Cuban, L. (1990). Reforming again, again, and again. *Educational Researcher, 19*(1), 3–13.

Deal, T. E., & Jenkins, W. A. (1994). *Managing the hidden organization: Strategies for empowering your behind-the-scenes employee.* New York: Warner Books.

Deal, T. E., Meyer, J., & Scott, R. (1975). Organizational influences on educational innovation. In J. V. Baldridge & T. E. Deal (Eds.), *Managing change in educational organizations.* (pp. 109–32). Berkeley, CA: McCutchan.

Department of Education. (2002). *No Child Left Behind.* Washington, DC: Author.

Friend, M., & Cook, L. (1992) *Interactions: Collaboration skills for school professionals.* White Plains, NY: Longman Publishing Group.

Johnson, R. (1975). *Teaching collaboration, principal influence, and decision-making in elementary schools.* Technical Report No. 48. Stanford, CA: Stanford University, Stanford Center for Research and Development in Teaching.

Meyer, J. W., & Rowan, B. (1978). The structure of educational organizations. In M. W. Meyer & Associates (Eds.), *Environments and organizations.* (pp. 78–109). San Francisco: Jossey-Bass.

Morrisey, M. S. (2000). *Professional learning communities: An ongoing exploration.* Austin, TX: Southwest Educational Development Laboratory.

Sapolsky, H. (1972). *The Polaris system development.* Cambridge, MA: Harvard University Press.

Schlesinger, L., Eccles, R., & Gabarro, J. (1983). *Managerial behavior in organizations.* New York: McGraw-Hill.

Shedd, J. B. (1988). Collective bargaining, school reform, and the management of school systems. *Educational Administration Quarterly, 24*(4), 405–15.

Talbert, J. E. (2010). Professional learning communities at the crossroads: How systems hinder or engender change. (pp. 555–71). A. Hargreaves, A. Lieberman, M. Fullan, & D. Hopkins (Eds.) In *Second international handbook of educational change.* Dordrecht, The Netherlands: Springer.

Wolcott, H. F. (2003). *Teachers versus technocrats.* Walnut Creek, CA: Altamira Press.

Chapter Four

Organizational Design in Support of Professional Learning Communities in One District

Scott C. Bauer, S. David Brazer,
Michelle Van Lare, and Robert G. Smith

Professional learning communities (PLCs) have emerged as one of the most prevalent mechanisms for school reform in the United States. They provide means for teachers to work together to solve difficult problems of practice based on locally available evidence related to teaching and student achievement. A few scholars have written about PLCs' structure and purpose (Talbert & McLaughlin, 1994; Wood, 2007) and their relationship to teacher behaviors and student achievement (Gersten, Dimino, Madhavi, Kim, & Santoro, 2010; Saunders, Goldenberg, & Gallimore, 2009; Vescio, Ross, & Adams, 2008). A number of popular texts provide guidance related to how PLC work should be conducted (e.g., DuFour, DuFour, & Eaker, 2008; DuFour, DuFour, Eaker, & Many, 2010; DuFour, Eaker, & Dufour, 2005), but much less is known about what PLCs actually do in schools and how they are designed as reform initiatives. This chapter is part of a larger study of the microprocesses of PLCs and the contexts in which they exist.

Our research team has decided to refer to groups of teachers who work within the larger PLC as *collaborative teams*, both because that is the term used in our research site and because PLC often refers to collections of teams that create a larger collaborative community. In this chapter, we focus on the question of how collaborative teams are designed and supported across schools in the single, large suburban district studied. The qualitative data analyzed in this portion of the study expose in detail how these collaborative teams work and the role principals play in exercising instructional leadership by designing the organization to focus on improvements in teaching and learning.

INVESTIGATING THE DESIGN OF
COLLABORATIVE TEAMS

This chapter presents one portion of the findings emerging from a district-wide study of collaborative teams (CTs) that asks the general questions: What do CTs actually do? How are they designed and supported? The main interest of this chapter is the latter question, that is, the design and support of CTs.

Purpose

This chapter has two main purposes: (1) to demonstrate what has been learned through field-based research regarding how schools and school districts are designed to support collaborative teams; and (2) to explain the apparent influence of design choices made at the district level on school designs and their potential effects on these teams. These purposes are addressed through the following questions:

- How has one large suburban school district designed the structure of and support for CTs?
- To what extent does organizational design to accommodate CTs differ from school to school?
  - To what extent do schools exercise discretion in how they organize to support CT work?
  - What role do school leaders play in organizing these groups?
- Are there discernible differences in CT practices that can be linked to differences in organizational design?

Rationale and Significance

Much of the more recent PLC literature is advocacy for a particular model (e.g., DuFour et al., 2005; DuFour et al., 2010) and tends not to acknowledge theoretical roots of procedures that are promoted as "best practices" for improving teaching and learning. The academic literature focused on CTs is more helpful for understanding what happens when teachers collaborate, but it tends to be characterized by a lack of connections between current concepts of CTs and the theoretical literature on teacher learning and organizational learning (Servage, 2008). It also appears disconnected from the considerable literature on school-based management and shared decision making (e.g., Bauer, 1998; David, 1989; Lindquist & Mauriel, 1989; Little, 2003; Malen & Ogawa, 1992; Malen, Ogawa, & Kranz, 1990; Murphy & Beck, 1995) that preceded the current interest in CTs. The result is the practice literature is divorced from theory; the research literature is somewhat atheoretical; and both fail to consider the organizational context in which CTs operate.

Like the research on school-based management, work on CTs tends to treat design and implementation like a "black box" (Sharpe, 1996), ignoring nuances related to the processes actually used in schools to implement the reform. Thus, what we know about CTs may be characterized as normative or descriptive of microprocesses and largely disconnected from the organizations (school and district) in which they are embedded.

By focusing on the context of CTs through the lens of organizational design, this chapter opens up the study of these teams to the application of organizational theory. Doing so is important because CTs do not operate in an organizational vacuum, as they have largely been described up to this point. Organizational influences and resources provide opportunities and limitations on teamwork that must be considered if we are to understand the contributions CTs make to student achievement and school improvement. The theoretical foundations discussed next, coupled with close examination of CT work, create new insight into the role and function of these teams within schools displaying common organizational characteristics. The theoretical grounding that we employ in this research—and our investigation into both the micro-level processes of collaborative decision making and the context in which they occur—address previous authors' calls for situating CTs in theoretical traditions so that they can be more clearly understood and not be isolating teamwork from the important district and school contexts in which it occurs (Little, 2012; Servage, 2008).

Practical significance of this chapter stems from the widespread implementation of CTs. As an example, the region in which we have collected data has a handful of large school districts educating well over 400,000 students. All of these districts espouse to have adopted a PLC-type model that intends to drive improved student achievement through the use of CTs. For some, this effort is a continuation of past efforts at shared decision making (Weiss, 1993, 1995) and/or site-based management (Ogawa

& White, 1994), while for others it is a relatively new venture into teacher collaboration. The region in which this study takes place is in the densely populated suburbs of a major city and is typical of similarly situated school districts around the country.

By explaining how CTs are designed and supported, and the role principals play in the design process, this chapter serves to inform school and district administrators and teachers about how these teams work and how the decisions about enactment of the reform can shape the teams' potential and real achievements. Those who wish to use CTs to enhance their practice have the opportunity to learn from the experiences of others represented in the findings of this chapter.

CONCEPTUAL FRAMEWORK

This paper is situated in the broader theoretical framework of our investigation into how CTs make decisions. The decision-making model employed builds on previous conceptual and empirical work that identifies influence webs as a central factor in decision making involving multiple stakeholders (Brazer & Keller, 2006; Brazer, Rich, & Ross, 2010; Winn & Keller, 2001). These stakeholders collaborate in schools and elsewhere in an effort to address limited or bounded rationality (March, 1994; March & Simon, 1993; Simon, 1993). A CT can be thought of as a *web of stakeholders* interested in a particular set of problems, each member contributing experience and knowledge to the group, and each having varying levels of influence within the web. CTs are formed in part to share analysis of student learning and ideas about how to improve it in the belief that having multiple people working together on a set of problems will generate better ideas, thus expanding the limits of any one individual's problem-solving capacity (rationality, in March and Simon's terms). Furthermore, group commitment is thought to be generated when members agree on a particular path toward improvement.

CTs do not operate in isolation and are subject to the objectives of relevant stakeholder groups that are an additional part of the influence web in which the team is located. Examples of such stakeholders include principals, central office support staff, superintendents, and local, state, and national governments. These stakeholders situated outside of the CT can help to form the context in which CTs operate and thus exercise some degree of influence over the team decision making. The school district context and stakeholder web for collaborative teams are depicted in Figure 4.1.

As shown in Figure 4.1, organizational factors shape CT contexts and exercise influence over decision making. The creation of collaborative teams themselves is motivated, at least in part, by pressure that superintendents and their boards perceive to improve student achievement—pressure emanating from federal and state policy and local interests of parents and the community. Expectations about how CTs are intended to act and what they are intended to accomplish generate a "logic of appropriateness" (March, 1994) that is embodied in routinized behavior that may not necessarily be rational in terms of value maximizing. Applying March's conception of appropriateness, teachers and others working within CTs likely take into account their identities as educational professionals, their roles within the CT, and the rules of CT conduct as determined by team

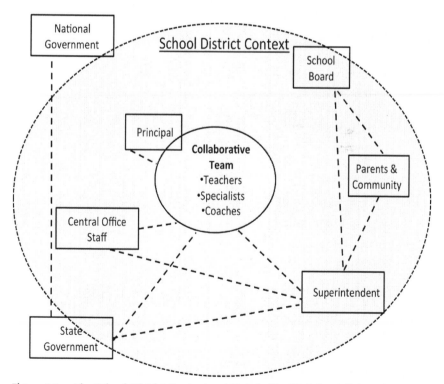

Figure 4.1.   The School District Context and Stakeholder Web for Collaborative Teams

members themselves, principals, or central office administrators and staff. In current educational parlance, appropriate behaviors are articulated as "best practices" that may relate to the internal work of the CT, or to the organizational design and processes employed by the team.

Institutional isomorphism (DiMaggio & Powell, 1983) is related to the logic of appropriateness as an additional determinant of appropriate behavior and design. Institutional isomorphism suggests that making design decisions similar to other groups helps to enhance CTs' legitimacy. Instead of "re-inventing the wheel," they are adopting procedures "known" to work. Thus, the design and operation of CTs may be derived from the institutionalization of the CT concept (Deal & Redman, chapter 3, this volume; Meyer & Rowan, 1977). Districts, schools, and CTs gain legitimacy by looking like other districts, schools, and CTs that are implementing some form of the model. Isomorphism at the district level may become influential at the school or CT level as superintendents and principals invest greater power in CT structures and processes as a means to improve student and school performance.

The end result of one or more logics of appropriateness and institutional isomorphism is a specific organizational design in which CTs are embedded. We adopt a framework to describe organizational design first suggested to explain the design of collaborative decision-making systems by Shedd (1987) and Shedd and Bacharach (1991), and later elaborated and tested by Bauer (1998). These studies identified three broad dimensions that could be used to describe the internal workings of decision-making groups like CTs:

1. **Scope**, referring to the range of issues participants discuss;
2. **Formal structure**, including composition and representativeness of decision-making teams; and
3. **Decision-making process**, dealing with how teams make decisions.

Later, Bauer (2001) added a fourth dimension, **support**, dealing with the *resources provided* to decision-making teams, which is associated with the institutional context of CTs (while **scope**, **structure**, and **process** deal directly with the *communication and decision-making practices* engaged in by teams). Bauer also asserted that the *focus* or *purpose* of collaborative teams, while related to scope, deserved to be treated as an independent dimension of design. Thus, from a design perspective, form follows function; hence how leaders enact various components of team structures and processes is heavily influenced by focus, making it critical to first establish what that focus is espoused to be. Previous studies employing this conceptualization of design showed that all four constructs are important to team success (Bauer & Bogotch, 2001, 2006). As we have indicated previously, the purpose of CTs is to improve student achievement.

METHODOLOGY[1]

The findings in this chapter are focused on interviews conducted with ten principals at the elementary, middle school, and high school levels. We employ a case study design because so little is known about the design and support of CTs (Little, 2012; Merriam, 1991; Yin, 2009).

Setting

Our research took place in a large suburban school district located in the mid-Atlantic region of the United States. The research team gained entry into ten schools (three elementary, three middle, and four high schools) in four of the eight administrative areas of the school district. The schools are diverse in terms of size and student populations served (see Table 4.1), and represent a fair cross-section of the district. Schools were recommended to the research team by the area assistant superintendents who supervise the principals.

Participants

Interview participants for this study included central office administrators, principals, and teachers participating in PLCs. At least two PLCs within each school were represented through interviews and were directly observed by members of the research team. PLC documents were collected during and after observations. Data for this chapter rely on interviews conducted with principals of the ten schools, since we are primarily interested in decisions related to design and the leadership exercised at the

Table 4.1. **Characteristics of Research Sites**

	Size (Rounded to Nearest 100)	% White, Black, Hispanic, Asian (Rounded to the Nearest 5)	% Eligible for Free or Reduced Price Lunch (Rounded to the Nearest 5)
Elementary 1	400	10, 10, 70, 15	85
Elementary 2	700	15, 30, 40, 15	70
Elementary 3	700	50, 10, 20, 20	20
Middle 1	1100	20, 10, 45, 25	60
Middle 2	1000	25, 30, 40, 5	55
Middle 2	1000	60, 10, 20, 15	15
High 1	1600	55, 10, 20, 20	20
High 2	2400	25, 15, 30, 25	50
High 3	2300	40, 20, 25, 20	40
High 4	2700	60, 5, 15, 20	15

Note: School characteristics are rounded to preserve anonymity

school site to shape design decisions. Of the ten principals, six were male and four female; seven were Caucasian and three African American. Four have been principals for one to three years; two have been principals for six to ten years; and the remaining four have been principals for more than ten years, with a high of twenty-four years. On average, the principals have just over ten years' experience in their current role.

Data Collection

Interviews lasting from forty-five to sixty minutes were scheduled with the principals at their convenience at their schools. An interview proto-col created by the research team was used to guide discussion, but the principals were permitted to dwell on topics of interest to them and they were asked to add any information the interviewer may have neglected to address through questions.

Data Analysis

The research team created a central coding list based on a general con-ceptual framework for the larger investigation. The authors used some of those codes but created an additional coding list more focused on design-related issues, derived from the framework presented in this chap-ter. Codes that emerged from reading transcripts were also added. Each code was given a working definition so that all members of the research team would have consistent interpretations and code data in similar ways. Coding discrepancies were discussed and resolved, usually through being inclusive and working out interpretations later.

We employed a constant comparative method (Glaser & Strauss, 1967) to understand what was happening across schools. We used our codes to identify uniqueness among participants and common themes across participants (Maxwell, 2005). We also employed information from the general context, particularly what we learned about district and area level expectations from interviews with central office administrators, to help explain how the principals perceived what is intended for CTs and their implementation of them.

Limitations

The most obvious limitation of this research is that the team was steered to schools that were deemed by administrators to be working well. Finding sites and participants began at the central office with two administrators who were in charge of PLC implementation in various ways, the Director of Professional Practice and the Assistant Superintendent for Professional Learning and Accountability. They recommended which four of the eight area assistant superintendents we should approach, who in turn recommended schools.

The advantage for the research team is that we found willing participants, for the most part. A disadvantage is that we were not able to interview and observe in schools that were deemed to be struggling with the development of their PLC. For purposes of this research on the design and support of CTs, this positive approach seems to be an appropriate criterion for selection; that is, it would be very difficult to assess the design used in enacting CTs in sites where the process was floundering or had not begun to operate. Nevertheless, results should be interpreted with this limit in mind.

FINDINGS: THE DESIGN AND SUPPORT OF CTs

In this section, we illustrate the various elements of design of CTs described earlier, starting with purpose, and continuing with scope, structure, process and support. In addition to our summaries, illustrative quotes are used to share the voices of respondents.

Purpose

All principals were asked directly what they believed regarding the purpose of CTs, yielding consensus about core ideas, with some variability in the details. Perhaps the best representation of the core came from one elementary principal, who said: "A PLC is a group of educators, all with a common goal of making sure all of our students perform to their highest potential." A high school principal elaborated a bit:

> What is a professional learning community? Our [PLC] at this school is based on the work of Rick and Becky DuFour. So, where a school has clearly identified what you want students to know and be able to do [the work involves] assessing that learning, examining the data, and then providing additional support to students who aren't learning. That is the 35,000 foot sort of summary definition of a PLC.

A middle school principal provided a somewhat lengthy, but largely consistent notion of what the CTs are all about:

> Well, for [our district], the [CT] is to get a group of professionals together that service the same content and we work together with English for Speakers of Other Languages (ESOL) teachers, . . . our special ed. teachers, and our core teachers so that we can develop a pre-assessment, unpack standards, and design instruction so that the post assessment shows student results. If you work collaboratively together, then we feel you get a better product because you all are, number one, making sure every child in the school who needs to be taught that specific content is actually receiving the quality of product that you need. If you are all together talking and unpacking what that would look like in a classroom then everybody gets a better understanding of what is expected to be taught and what students should learn. So with us having such a diverse community in [our district], it just gives more of a fair playing field for all students.

One high school principal commented on an important shift in organizational expectations related to purpose: "We've kind of summarized that, basically, the days of the individual teacher hero are gone. Now we've become the team hero as we identify and address the needs of a lot of different kids in our schools." This principal further elaborated:

> It certainly is undergirded by a movement from "we teach in a way and see who it works for" to trying to more systematically make sure that all students

achieve at least a minimum outcome—a minimum positive outcome. Teams are a way to measure that and get to that, and that's why it's the unit used.

The same principal went on to say:

> I think from my perspective, an effective CT claims all of the students of that particular discipline. So, instead of it just being my 150 kids in an English 9, or 10, it's all the kids in English 9. It's also playing to all the strengths of the teachers and also incorporating flexibility—not only in the teachers not only having specific times and places where they teach, but a willingness to change with the needs of the kids.

This was not the only principal who connected CTs to school culture, to "a way of doing things around here" rather than a program, but only a few explicitly made this observation. In terms of why the district adopted CTs, one high school principal seemed to capture the consensus when she said:

> I think the reason that [our district] adopted that model was because I think that we realized that if we could organize teams to work together, we could probably accomplish a lot more. If we can use data more frequently to make decisions, then we'd be able to address challenged areas with our students a little bit better. We are able to re-teach the areas and . . . develop lessons to address those areas and to develop enriching lessons for kids who progress faster than others. We both know we need to differentiate across the whole spectrum of student abilities and [CTs] would make it a lot easier for teachers to do.

The same principal connected the work of the CTs to the improvement of the whole school, something that about one-third of the respondents did in reference to purpose.

> The outcomes that I expect is . . . the discussion centers around student achievement, ways of discovering how we can improve student outcomes not only as a discipline but as a school, and to create systems that are going to help the different subgroups of students we have in the schools then look at it as, they come up with an action plan for the school in general, the entire school.

In summary, two themes seem very clear among these respondents in relation to the purpose of collaborative teams. First, in the schools we visited, the principals espouse that the work of CTs is grounded firmly in what goes on in classrooms. Second, they tend to recognize that this focus represents a fundamental cultural shift in the way the school approaches improving instruction; the change involves making teaching more public and focusing on teachers learning from each other. As one principal explained:

> So it comes through, I think, a more focused, collaborative instructional program. So, you and I, if we were both teaching U.S. history, we're not just behind our doors, doing our own thing. And you know, what we teach is no longer really a question. It's very well defined for us by the state, the [school district]. . . . And, how we teach can still be pretty unique to our craft, but our scope and sequence really need to be very much the same so the accidents of geography that can happen in schools and still do happen in schools where one student gets Mr. Smith and another gets Mr. Jones, you know, there shouldn't be a lot of difference in terms of what is delivered in each of those classrooms.
>
> So through teachers aligning their scope and sequence, building common assessments to match, student progress, sitting down as a group, analyzing performance at the student level, classroom level and in totality to talk about how collectively, that group of teachers can improve everyone's performance that leads to increased student achievement. . . . When our kids are successful, then what do we do for the kids who haven't been successful, as a team? It's not just leaving a teacher out there on their own whose students have not mastered the skills and knowledge that we expect them to but what can we do collectively, as a team, to help bring that student up.

Among the respondents in this district, the implementation of CTs as a mechanism for change seems to be challenging the default notion of the school as the unit of change and improvement. The fundamental unit of change appears to have shifted from the school to the team (perhaps to the individual teacher on the team). This move has dramatic implications for school leaders, not the least of which is that it raises the question of how much variability is encouraged or tolerated within a department or school. To foreshadow, an intriguing part of our findings is that despite the apparent encouragement of teams as the unit of change, virtually nobody among the principals we spoke with even mentioned the decision-making authority or autonomy of the CTs. Given the prominence of this topic in past research on site-based management teams, this seems a curious pattern, and one that deserves attention in follow-up work on these teams.

Design: Scope and Responsibility

As just noted, it is striking in these interviews that for many, if not most schools, CTs have become the engine of change and innovation. So as one respondent said, these teams "more clearly defined what is meant in terms of instruction, assessment, data analysis and intervention."

The vast majority of the principals talked about CTs as having a responsibility to connect teachers to one another, discuss student progress, and design interventions to help improve student learning. They also explained the role teams play in establishing a vision and goals for learning. As one respondent said, "I really look at the team as an engine of innovation for breaking us out of that factory model," and another pointed out that what's important is the "undertone of 'everybody is a leader in the school, everybody has a responsibility' . . . and we're all expected to help every child in the school."

There was considerable mention of the use of data; specifically, using common assessments was mentioned by about half the principals as an explicit responsibility of CTs. As one principal explained:

The agenda is really talking about student achievement, it is talking about student intervention. We have what we call formative and summative assessments so [teachers] look at their assessment and they see where the kids are, or how they've done and the areas that they didn't do well on. And they talk about those students and they talk about an intervention plan for those students so lots of discussion about student achievement, planning intervention, planning individual intervention made by me with each student.

On effective teams:

There is a lot of kid talk, that is a lot about children, and that talk about children could be about achievement data, it could be about positive outcomes that work with strategies, it could be about the challenges that they're still having and most of that is still about the data.

The data, one principal commented, could be "hard" data or anecdotal; there was recognition that "teacher talk" is a huge part of the puzzle. "Connecting teachers" around data was a prominent theme, mentioned by over half the principals.

So in some of the CT meetings, teachers will get up and share; "here is what we're doing on integers and my kids did well on it," so they would share with the team how he or she taught that lesson to the class.

Another important responsibility of the team is to provide an "open" forum for sharing, as one principal explained:

And so because of the unpacking and the unpacking in public, I mean there's no excuse not to know what is happening. At the same time some are exposing their weaknesses, some are exposing their strengths. And so new teachers come on board saying, "Last year during my student teaching I taught and I found a lot of success with this. And this was why." And they get deep down into why.

About half the principals noted that CTs are forums for curriculum planning, discussing pacing, and sometimes planning professional development. A similar number mentioned the team role in setting norms, though curiously at times the comment implied that CTs are critical in setting norms school-wide, not just within their team. Here, again, the "public" nature of collaboration is mentioned:

So we're like, "Okay go up to that group and see if it will work," and that would not have happened before because my grade is my grade, my class is my class, and my caseload is my caseload. Now it's *ours*. And now they're opening their doors and really kind of shifting so I have put out there to several of my high flying teachers and teams, "I want you to think outside of the box."

De-privatization of practice has been a theme in theory and research on learning communities (e.g., Kruse, Louis, & Bryk, 1994; Little & McLaughlin, 1993; Louis, Kruse, & Marks, 1996); so it is not terribly surprising that these themes come up with regard to the responsibilities of CTs. Given the focus espoused for the teams, it makes even greater sense that the scope of responsibility seems to center on promoting teacher talk as a means to improve instruction.

Design: Structure

The design elements relating to structure cover such mundane things as who serves on teams, how many teams exist in a school, and how they are organized. Nevertheless, these are important design choices for school leaders that may have a large impact on how well the teams function. All respondents provided information about these issues.

There is a great deal of consensus regarding structure, though there are notable differences by level. Elementary schools, by and large, organize their CTs by grade level. Although not all elementary principals are specific about this structure, the norm also seems to include specialists, for instance ESOL teachers, special education teachers, and coaches. In several cases, respondents made clear that these specialists are regular members on grade-level CTs, and also have their own CTs to encourage improvement in their unique areas. One school includes an administrator on each team, although this case seems to be an outlier. All three elementary principals mentioned the inclusion of instructional coaches on teams (as a resource).

Secondary principals tended to differ from elementary principals by saying that they are "following the DuFour Model. We organize by department and then divide by curriculum team." Curiously, a few principals were a little unsure about this because "sometimes they start to subdivide." An elementary principal also mentioned that she has "mini-CTs" that "pop up around areas of interest" and that may meet for a period of time "to figure out a way to get this back to the CTs in a common way." This phenomenon is interesting, representing an indicator that in these buildings, CTs have become a norm as a means to introduce change. As interests around a problem or course of action emerge, informal CTs emerge naturally as a means to scrutinize the decision and potentially influence the grade-level team. The same principal encouraged members of one CT to visit others as an agent of change:

> They were just talking the other day in the third grade team, "Could this other teacher come from another grade level?" because they heard she was doing this and such and shared with her team. Oh yeah, they liked that idea. Some teams are trying to learn about Daily Five [a system for enhancing student literacy]. I say "Well, if you want to know about that here is the teacher in our building who has really wrapped her arms around it." We've done benchmarking visits with CT teams or some members of them to go to other CTs in other schools, with the intent that they learn from that and bring something back that they could tweak to make better.

Structures that encourage articulation across teams make sense given the espoused purpose and scope of responsibilities; sharing ideas and information may facilitate decisions that promote learning.

There seems to be general agreement that teachers can serve on more than one team, which is especially prevalent in secondary schools: "Most [serve on multiple teams] because they have multiple preps so the challenge there is that for Wednesday, they're probably meeting with a different team every other Wednesday." In contrast, one secondary principal mentioned that "One of the things we have wrestled with, we have taken and bought into some research that people shouldn't be on more than two teams to be effective collaborators." Hence, in this school, they struggle with whether they ought to create teams of specialists or special educators, for fear, perhaps, of overloading them.

An interesting structural issue that came up is the question of vertical or school-wide decision making. Clearly, the prevalent decision-making structure has become the grade-level or curriculum area team. Still, several respondents talked about "vertical teams" in content areas that meet monthly or quarterly, and at least one additional principal aspired to create vertical teams. Another mentioned that it was possible to have ad hoc vertical teams to address specific issues such as a new district-mandated progress report. One principal mentioned *vertical articulation* meetings with other schools in their feeder pattern, as well. Providing some vertical decision-making structures to supplement what goes on at the grade-level or department CT speaks to the complex interconnectedness of the work of teachers in any given school. The structure also relates to the search for optimum information-sharing patterns that may promote learning among professionals across the school.

Several respondents mentioned their school-level improvement teams; and in some cases, these teams were configured from representatives of the CTs, as in this middle school:

> The CT leads are a part of what is called our leadership council, which meets every month so then our leadership council becomes more of the school decision making. So that is where there are thirty-two members on the leadership council that drive the school PLC, so then they receive additional staff development that we have to lead and manage a differentiated program.

This principal went on to say that these teachers are the "elite," the opinion leaders in the school. Thus, in these schools, the school-level improvement team provided a sort of mechanism for vertical articulation; additionally, as a forum for setting school-level goals, these structures also influence the purposes that serve as the focus of CT decision making.

Most respondents commented on the leadership role teachers play on the teams. Typical roles are facilitator, "team leader," record keeper, and in at least one case, time keeper (though this was seldom mentioned). Those who described facilitation made clear that this role is a "keeper of the process," not a position with special authority. One went a bit further:

> On the most effective teams, the team facilitator's influence stops at getting the agenda out on email. Once they arrive, her duties have ended. If she says anything it's more, "Ok, looking at the time we need to move on to this piece" or they'll also do a great job of, "It looks like we're not gonna get to all the agenda items. What do we want to prioritize out of the last three to make sure we cover and the others will be pushed to the next meeting?" It's a very facilitative piece rather than a leadership piece.

Several mentioned that the teams divide up roles at the beginning of the year (although one mentioned that initially, leaders were "hand-picked"); one said that they have gotten away from the practice of "it's my turn this year" because it seems to affect team dynamics. One principal lamented that "We haven't done a very good job of, how do you facilitate the workings of a team to strengthen each member and to strengthen the dialogue so it strengthens ultimately student learning," but another noted how the facilitative structures have changed the culture:

> Some of the structures we have put in place that have changed that mindset are that the teachers are the leaders of those teams. It's a classroom teacher who's the facilitator, who's driving unpacking of the standards, framing the lessons for the upcoming units, understanding and unpacking the state assessments so we know exactly what we know, what it means for a fourth grader to understand and be proficient . . . , all coming from the team level.

Thus, again, the team as the unit of change is reinforced; further, a culture that encourages trust-building through a relatively nonhierarchical structure seems to be reinforced.

Design: Process

Relative to other areas of design, there was less explicit mention of decision process, which is curious since this was an explicit question asked of principals (i.e., if the CTs follow a specific process, and if this is district-mandated and supported). In relation to queries about decision process, some respondents pointed to forms and recordkeeping protocols that their schools have established (e.g., agendas, check sheets), which may reveal something about formal process. In some schools, specific decision steps were mentioned or observed, for example, KidWatch (a CT member bringing a single case study about a child she is teaching to the team) and Lesson Study (a CT member sharing how he approaches a unit by demonstrating the approach in another member's classroom). In several schools the process of how decisions at the CT level factor into school-level planning and vertical articulation was mentioned.

One especially interesting process theme is the extent to which the agenda, as a formal document, drives what teams do (and in what order). One principal said, "I am excited about the agendas that they develop commonly," and another said, "First of all, an effective team . . . must have an agenda, they must have a road map, a plan . . . where all of the CT members have input." Another said, "An effective CT to me, number one, is they are organized, they have lesson plans, they have goals for the year, they have an agenda and they have someone, a facilitator for that team." The agenda appears to be both a functional and a symbolic representation of the decision-making steps teams go through each meeting. The agenda is highly structured, and it is also the primary means for communicating about the progress of the CT to the administration of the building. In most schools, each CT's agenda was also posted on a shared drive on the staff's in-house computer network.

There were other hints at formal process: for example, teams develop SMART goals quarterly; they unpack standards (meaning they strive to understand in detail how they impact the classroom); they discuss and develop common assessments; they discuss and come to consensus on common lessons and pacing; and they problem-solve and develop interventions when students are not succeeding.

> So the collaborative learning teams have to go through, it's almost like a month long process of what needs to be done throughout each week so that by the end, the results, the data is shared with the staff so the collaborative team will be able to share it.

Three respondents referred to "the DuFours' process," one mentioned "total participation techniques," another the total quality management (TQM) language of "plan, do, study, act." About a third or so referred to the process of developing norms as an important part of process, and some CTs posted norms on each meeting agenda.

> So, one of the things they do in the beginning of the year is that we ask everybody to establish their own norms. So the dynamics of a team vary year to year based on the personalities of the people and the commitment so you can even have the same people within a CT but next year because of lifestyle changes or there are various changes—maybe they took an extra course so the CTs change. We ask that they always have their norms displayed.

Several principals implied that they have common "worksheets," decision-making steps, or questions, and that the teams "need structure." However, they also discussed flexibility and the need for teams to own their own decision making. Curiously, only one principal—and only when queried—said anything about decision-making authority or autonomy, or the limits on autonomy. Two referred to the facilitator's role and conflict resolution within teams, and others mentioned the need for openness and transparency to make CTs work. To quote one,

> I'd like to see that they've developed a good chemistry, they've . . . mutual respect for each other's professionalism. I'd like to see that they've developed an openness where they are willing to share ideas and they are . . . receptive to ideas.

Some dialogue about collaboration was becoming normative or part of the culture, as it related to the time it takes for this to happen. In these cases, reading between the lines, the discussion is about de-privatizing practice.

> You have to go through that morning and storming and feeling secure and observing—fish-bowling other people's classrooms and coming back and accepting that there are other ways of making something successful. So that took us here at [this school] a really, really long time.

The same principal commented:

> It has taken us, well, this is my sixth year as principal and this is the first year where I feel like they've owned their CT. You have to get through the first phase of "Why are you making us do collaborative learning teams? You are wasting our time, we should have our personal planning, I'd get so much more done, I have things to do." You know they didn't find the value in it at

all. You had to break that barrier and once you broke that barrier, then you had to help teach them to gain trust with each other of shared lessons.

I may feel that I'm doing all the work and Scott hasn't developed any, and I do all the lesson plans and he is lazy and so then you have to be willing to sacrifice your lessons and share with each other—and then allow people to make recommendations to make things to better enrich your lesson and not feel insulted, so that is another process. Then you have to be willing to allow people to create a test based on these lessons. So all this stuff took a really long time.

This is a fascinating theme; as noted earlier, in many of the schools, the culture has changed to the point that the CT has become the primary unit of change for the school. The specifics of how a school turns that corner is hard to see based on the data we have available; this would be a worthwhile topic for longitudinal research in the future.

Design: Support

The design elements relating to support deal with the kinds of resources made available to CTs from the district and school. Overall, this support was the most mentioned topic related to design, perhaps a testament to the importance of resources in institutionalizing reform like CTs. Iterative analysis of text coded in this category yielded the following subthemes:

Administrative Support

Principals discussed a variety of ways they support CTs. First, the majority reported that either they or a delegated administrator attends team meetings, or is assigned as a liaison to CTs, more to support the teams than to hold them accountable. For example, one said, "The whole emphasis is to empower all of our staff and to develop those teacher leaders because I think those are our change agents, our forward agents, so we can keep collaborating as a school." Attendance also provides access to information for the teams that may be critical to effective decision making and problem solving.

Second, principals provide feedback and clarify expectations for the CTs in their buildings. One principal noted that "persistence and consistency" were key to creating a collaborative culture in her school, and that administrators and instructional coaches being in classrooms and in team meetings facilitates this:

I have an instructional coach for English and I have an instructional coach for math—those coaches are in the CT meetings coaching, asking questions. You say you are going to teach this, this way, share with me how this affects student achievement. So, when you have a coach and they are a kind of prompt you know, it helps you.

Some talked more about getting out into classrooms and how they involve themselves or their coaches in feedback, for instance:

We need to do rounds like a doctor; just go in, talk to them, see if there is differentiation. [We need to] come back out [and], "Did you see differentiation? What? Where is the flat-line at? What is going on?" Then we can go back in and say, "Hey Scott, we came in to see your classroom, we are seeing we are flat-lining here, here are some recommendations. Do you want me to come team teach with you, what do you want me to do so we can help these kids?" So that is what we do with this data and we meet every quarter to do this stuff.

This idea may be an important source of support; yet it may fly in the face of the overall emphasis on the team as the unit of change, depending on whether teachers see this kind of principal or coach behavior as facilitative rather than supervisory.

District-Provided Training

Surprisingly little was mentioned, specifically, about district-based training, although several principals noted that they have found district- and area-provided training for CT facilitators and leaders to be useful (and noted that more of this would be helpful to build capacity). About half mentioned district-based training with the DuFour model specifically, or sending someone to a conference about their model. But nobody mentioned district-based training in group process, per se, although perhaps the team leader and facilitator training covers this.

Grant and Other Financial Resources

One respondent discussed a grant her school had to support early development of CTs. Financial support is also suggested in terms of provision of professional development, information systems, and staffing support, though respondents did not focus on financial supports specifically.

Information

All respondents talked about using information as a resource. Many referred to the process of providing access to information through a data warehouse (e.g., data sorter, data tracker), at a rather sophisticated level:

> We have a data warehouse that has every student in it. All their common assessment scores are in there. All their [test] scores are in there. Wherever they go during our learn time is in there. If they go to the library, we capture that. What we can do is ask and answer questions around any or all of those disparate pieces of data. Their quarter grades are in there. Their interim grades are in there so that we can start to build sort of connections between all that. Show me all the kids with Ds and Fs and how they're using learn time. Show me all, tell me who's using the library. Show me who's not using the library. So, we've got that piece and we use it a lot at an admin level and leadership team level to help guide our broader work. A team is able to do it by drilling down to more specific assessment data like who can't factor a polynomial or something like that.

One noted the importance of real-time access to data: "Getting data real time so that teachers can get that in their hands and make decisions. You know, stop using the autopsy data. The [end-of-year test] scores, those kids are already gone and past." So, information is not merely an archival resource, but it is distributed to teams increasingly in real time.

Other principals talked about sharing articles, book clubs, and so on, and many referred to the county-supported formative assessment data system and its use. Many discussed the various ways they support teachers in CT's developing or creating evidence—for example, common assessments, surveys, meeting records (agendas, minutes). Schools maintain data systems and provide evidence to teams, often through an online resource and sometimes in more innovative ways. One principal talked about providing Pocket PCs to staff and students to create and amass evidence:

> Each teacher has one of these. I have one of these. So, I can show you. In the library the kids actually key in on a numeric keypad. If they go into student services they key in. It's very big brother-ish (laughs). But it actually, if you're a student, it documents what you're doing with the time.

School-Based Training

Every principal discussed this topic, and many were quite illustrative of their entire approach to adult learning. What is most telling, overall, is the handful of principals who felt that teachers' taking responsibility for professional development was something of a turning point for their collaborative cultures. One respondent was most interesting. She noted that early on, she "was pulling any apple from any tree that looked like it would taste good," until her teachers demanded focus, which she delegated to her leadership council.

School-based training comes in a variety of flavors: traditional professional development, coaching/mentoring, visits to other sites or professional conferences, book clubs, and so on. Instructional coaches, as a support and source of learning, were mentioned by at least half of the respondents. One principal noted that coaches are effective "because they teach, they're on teams so they have credibility around the work. . . . Not only do they support the work, they do the work." Similarly, administrators are engaged in visiting classes and providing coaching support.

> So everyone has an individual commitment; yours could be totally different than mine but it is a commitment to change for student progress so then we write it up there. So here is your commitment—and then we get followed back and we can say, "Ok Scott, your commitment was to do x, y, and z— how are you doing with this?" That is when the coach comes in. The assistant principal comes to the same meetings [and] the principal. "How has this changed the way students are learning?"

Quite a few principals talked about the training and development that they sponsor at the school to enrich teaching, focused on teaching strategies, content, and the like. Some discussed applying the strategy of having teachers model lessons for each other, and several mentioned the process of creating school-wide development plans through their leadership teams and CTs. One particularly innovative strategy presented was the use of lesson study:

> How we do that is "lesson study"—that is a Japanese model that was brought over to America—where your CT designs the lesson together and we pick your name out of a hat. "Oh, I'm teaching Scott's kids." So I go into your classroom, teach the lessons and the teachers don't focus on how I

teach or what I am teaching. They focus on what are the students saying and how that is happening. This is our first full year of lesson study embedment here and it is the best year to do it because they are finally owning their CT and they feel comfortable to say, "[xx] you are not pulling your load."

Some principals mentioned sponsoring school-based training for team leaders, and a few mentioned making resources available to visit other sites. Surprising to us, very little was said about training in the use of data.

Staffing Support

Two categories of staff support seem to be most prevalent: instructional coaching, and an assessment or data manager position. Not everyone mentioned instructional coaches, but a majority did, speaking glowingly about the value of the coaches who visited teams, worked with them, and often helped play a leadership role on teams.

"Data coaches" were mentioned in a few ways by about a third of the respondents. One principal noted that high schools all have district-funded assessment coaches, but added:

> What we did is we created the [school name] testing and assessment center. Every high school in [the school district] has an assessment coach. We went about it a little differently here. In most instances, those assessment coaches in individual schools are just bogged down in testing. You know they move from September [state assessments] to PSAT to one test to another test. What we did here is we staffed that with two individuals. They both teach two sections and then they kind of share some of the responsibilities of supporting the work around curriculum teams.

Another principal talked about staffing a part-time position to help with data entry and reporting; and yet another noted that school-based technology specialists are provided by the district, and often assist in making evidence available (though that is not a central part of their role). A separate type of staff support was mentioned by at least three respondents; that is, making specialists available to CTs for their meetings (ESL or reading specialists, special educators, etc.).

Overall, then, each of the school leaders interviewed recognize that the work of the CTs may require human resource support over and above what the administrative staff can provide. This finding may have interesting implications for the broader study of how leadership is distributed in schools that seek to implement CTs.

Technology Support

Tech support comes in the form of the aforementioned data warehouse or web-based database structures; the district's investment in a common formative assessment data tracking system; and for a few respondents, other tools (like the Pocket PC application referred to earlier). Many respondents crooned about their PC-based or web-based data warehouse systems, the availability of real-time data to administrators and teachers, and the way these tools have revolutionized their use of evidence. Some respondents marveled at the sophistication of the technological support provided to teachers and teams related to the distribution of data, but also lamented that this information can be a bit overwhelming at times (hence, perhaps, the investment in staff to support data use).

Time

One consistency is that the schools are devoting the time resources needed for CTs to work, largely within the school day (though some noted the need to meet outside school hours). The frequency, length of meetings, and approaches differ. On the one hand, our sample includes a school in which the principal has arranged the schedule to include common planning five days a week, and teams are expected to meet four of the five days. At the other extreme, we have a secondary school that has early release once every two weeks, and teams meet for an hour every other week. There doesn't appear to be a norm among these schools, although all but one respondent says CTs meet at least weekly.

Several respondents mentioned creative use of the master schedule: for example, one noted the difficulty of providing teams with the time needed to do their work, and expressed a need for more time; another explained that this year, some staff who would otherwise be helpful to CTs had to be excluded because scheduling got in the way of their inclusion. Overall, school leaders recognized that provision of time is both an important structural and symbolic issue to making CTs work. Across our ten schools, principals were still finding creative ways to make this investment.

DISCUSSION

This chapter presents results from a portion of a broader district-wide study of CTs. Evidence of how teams were designed and supported was gleaned from interviews with principals from ten high, middle, and elementary schools. Results describing the design of CTs in these schools were organized according to dimensions adopted from an existing frameworks used to describe decision making in general and the design of collaborative decision-making systems specifically, employing the following constructs: purpose or focus, decision-making scope, formal structure, decision-making process, and support.

Taken as a whole, the results raise some interesting questions about CTs as a reform. In sharp contrast to the pattern of findings from years of study of site-based management teams—which tended to indicate that these structures seldom focused on issues central to the improvement of instruction and often got stuck in the quagmire of ill-defined lines of decision-making authority (Bauer, 2001; David, 1989; Malen, Ogawa, & Kranz, 1990; Weiss, 1993)—in the schools we visited, the principals clearly espouse that the work of CTs is grounded firmly in what goes on in classrooms. Virtually no evidence suggested that the decision-making autonomy of teams within their grade level or subject area is problematic, as it was in much of the site-based management literature. The implementation of CTs as a mechanism for change in this district, at least, seems to be replacing the default notion of the school as the primary unit of change and improvement—with one that focuses action much more on the grade level or subject area, and at times, to the individual teacher supported by his team.

Further, a careful scrutiny of the design features of the CTs in these schools suggests that structures tend to be inclusive, often involving special area teachers and instructional coaches and occasionally being augmented by data coaches or the like. Needed evidence is made available to teams through comprehensive and relatively elaborate information systems, and the teams are supported with other vital resources like time to meet, often the nemesis of collaborative decision-making structures like CTs.

Some design areas are much less clear based on the evidence presented here, notably features related to decision-making processes and, to some degree, the scope of team authority. While it is true that respondents highlighted aspects of both of these dimensions, it was far from clear whether a well-structured decision process was endorsed or supported in these schools, save for comments on training received by aspiring or in-service team leaders. Similarly, while no respondent brought up problems relating to team authority or other aspects of decision-making scope, it is equally true that none provided a lucid definition of what that scope might include. Evidence suggests, though, that these schools are still very much working on questions related to coordination and articulation of decisions both vertically and horizontally; and some principals have invested in school-wide meeting structures to deal with these issues, but others did not mention these at all.

These issues have significant implications for school leaders. Endemic to any decentralized decision-making effort is the question of how much variability is encouraged or tolerated within a department or school. Even in a small school, CT-level decisions involving one team may have consequences for others. For instance, any decision that involves the scheduling of teacher or student time; the provision of materials, equipment or supplies; the use of facilities or space; or the allocation of human efforts involving coaches, specialists or administrators could very well affect other grade levels or subject areas directly, or set a precedent that affects other areas in the school. How these matters are coordinated is no small matter, and may severely affect the nature of school leaders' purview, or alternatively, the scope of decentralized team decision making.

As the organizational design of schools changes to make them more focused on evidence of student learning and improving student performance, so too the role of the principal shifts. When principals strive to foster high performance among CTs, they often find themselves working with teachers to understand and act upon the evidence of student learning that all are investigating. As they visit classrooms, talk with CTs, plan professional development, and decide how CTs should function, principals are becoming instructional leaders. Hence, principal instructional leadership is the type of leadership that has the greatest impact on student learning (Robinson, Lloyd, & Rowe, 2008). Furthermore, the opportunities for instructional leadership may be enhanced for principals by the cultural shifts that occur through the effort to create PLCs driven by CTs.

Finally, a degree of isomorphism (DiMaggio & Powell, 1983) is at work across schools in this district. That is, many similarities exist in design practices, particularly among schools at the same level, and particularly with regard to the purpose of CTs, the use of personnel to support CTs, and the investment of time and information-support technologies. This finding should not be terribly surprising, given that these ten schools exist in the same district. It seems likely that pressure to conform to district-adopted practices, as well as practices adopted by "high functioning" schools, would be lauded as "best practices," resulting in considerable pressure to adopt such practices (Meyer & Rowan, 1977). Yet, we also saw notable differences in practices across levels, nuances involved in implementation, that suggest that each school has adopted certain signature approaches to the work of CTs. It is impossible to tell, though, whether these differences are attributable to the maturity of CT practices across schools (i.e., clearly some schools are further along at making CTs a central part of their culture), or the result of other influences.

CONCLUSIONS

Among the conclusions we can hazard from these data is the optimistic finding that the schools we examined are focusing the work of CTs squarely on the improvement of teaching practice; leaders are devoting significant resources to enable this work to occur; and although the schools are at various stages of implementation, designs feature a significant degree of autonomy for teacher teams that provide many degrees of freedom in their decision-making and problem-solving efforts.

The most intriguing question suggested by the application of organizational theory to the design of CTs, which deserves considerable attention in follow-up work, is how leaders at the district and school level deal with the inherent variability that results from the creation of decision-making teams that enjoy the kind of autonomy espoused. Similarly, a related question might be how processes are coordinated both vertically and horizontally within and across schools. It is not hard to imagine that as any CT exercises its ability to vary practices, both predictable and unanticipated consequences on other teams and units will need to be negotiated. As examples, CT decisions may call upon limited resources (e.g., financial, material, human) that affect schedules, alter standard operating procedures, and so on. How leaders deal with these may spell the success or failure of this reform.

In sum, this study raises as many questions as it provides answers. Further work involving a much larger and diverse sample of schools would help resolve some of these, as would longitudinal work that allowed us to determine if certain design features are more or less important to the functioning of collaborative teams in our schools.

NOTE

1. This study was generously supported by the Spencer Foundation. The authors take sole responsibility for the work presented.

REFERENCES

Bauer, S. (1998). Designing site based systems, deriving a theory of practice. *International Journal of Educational Reform, 7*(2), 108–21.

Bauer, S. (2001). An initial investigation into the effect of decision-making and communication practices on the perceived outcomes of site-based management. *Research in the Schools, 8*(1), 13–27.

Bauer, S., & Bogotch, I. (2001). An analysis of the relationships among site council resources, council practices, and outcomes. *Journal of School Leadership, 11*(2), 98–119.

Bauer, S., & Bogotch, I. (2006). Modeling site-based decision making: School practices in the age of accountability. *Journal of Educational Administration, 44*(5), 446–70.

Brazer, S. D., & Keller, L.R. (2006). A conceptual framework for multiple stakeholder educational decision making. *International Journal of Education Policy and Leadership, 1*(3), 1–14.

Brazer, S. D., Rich, W., & Ross, S. A. (2010). Collaborative strategic decision making in school districts. *Journal of Educational Administration, 48*(2), 196–217.

David, J. (1989). Synthesis of research on schoolbased management. *Educational Leadership, 46*(9), 45–53.

DiMaggio, P., & Powell, W. (1983). The iron cage revisited: Institutional isomorphism and collective rationality in organizational fields. *American Sociological Review, 48*, 147–60.

78   *Scott C. Bauer, S. David Brazer, Michelle Van Lare, and Robert G. Smith*

DuFour, R., DuFour, R., & Eaker, R. (2008). *Revisiting professional learning communities at work: New insights for improving schools.* Bloomington, IN: Solution Tree.

DuFour, R., DuFour, R., Eaker, R., & Many, T. (2010). *Learning by doing: A handbook for professional communities at work* (2nd ed.). Bloomington, IN: Solution Tree.

DuFour, R., Eaker, R., & DuFour, R. (2005). *On common ground: The power of professional learning communities.* Bloomington, IN: National Education Service.

Gersten, R., Dimino, J., Madhavi, J., Kim, J. S., & Santoro, L. E. (2010). Teacher study group: Impact of the professional development model on reading instruction and student outcomes in first grade classrooms. *American Educational Research Journal, 47,* 694–739.

Glaser, B., & Strauss, A. (1967). *The discovery of grounded theory: Strategies for qualitative research.* Chicago: Aldine Publishing Company.

Kruse, S., Louis, K. S., & Bryk, A. S. (1994). *Building professional community in schools.* Madison, WI: Center on Organization and Restructuring of Schools.

Lindquist, K., & Mauriel, J. (1989). School based management: Doomed to failure? *Education and Urban Society, 21*(4), 403–16.

Little, J. W. (2003). Inside teacher community: Representations of classroom practice. *Teachers College Record, 105*(6), 913–45.

Little, J. W. (2012). Understanding data use practice among teachers: The contribution of micro-process studies. *American Journal of Education, 118*(2), 143–66.

Little, J. W., & McLaughlin, M. W. (Eds.) (1993). *Teachers' work: Individuals, colleagues, and contexts.* New York: Teachers College Press.

Louis, K. S., Kruse, S., & Marks, H. (1996). Schoolwide professional community. In F. M. Newmann & associates (Eds.), *Authentic Achievement: Restructuring Schools for Intellectual Quality.* San Francisco: Jossey-Bass.

Malen, B., & Ogawa, R. (1992). Site-based management: Disconcerting policy issues, critical policy choices. In J. Lane and E. Epps (Eds.), *Restructuring the schools: Problems and prospects* (pp. 185–206). Berkeley, CA: McCutchan Publishing Corp.

Malen, B., Ogawa, R., & Kranz, J. (1990). What do we know about schoolbased management? A case study of the literature—a call for research. In W. Clune and J. Witte (Eds.), *Choice and control in American education: The practice of choice, decentralization and school restructuring* (Vol. 2) (pp. 289–342). London: The Falmer Press.

March, J. (1994). *A primer on decision-making: How decisions happen.* New York: Free Press.

March, J., & Simon, H. (1993). *Organizations* (2nd ed.). Cambridge, MA: Wiley-Blackwell.

Maxwell, J. (2005). *Qualitative research design: An interactive approach* (2nd ed.). Los Angeles: Sage.

Merriam, S. B. (1991). *Case study research in education: A qualitative approach.* San Francisco: Jossey-Bass.

Meyer, J., & Rowan, B. (1977). Institutional organizations: Formal structure as myth and ceremony. *American Journal of Sociology, 83*, 340–63.

Murphy, J., & Beck, L. (1995). *School-based management as school reform: Taking stock.* Thousand Oaks, CA: Corwin Press.

Ogawa, R., & White, P. (1994). School-based management: an overview. In S. Mohrman, P. Wohlstetter, and associates (Eds.), *Designing high performance schools: Strategies for schoolbased management.* San Francisco: Jossey-Bass.

Robinson, V., Lloyd, C., & Rowe, K. (2008). The impact of leadership on student outcomes: An analysis of the differential effects of leadership types. *Educational Administration Quarterly, 44*(5), 635–74.

Saunders, W. M., Goldenberg, C. N., & Gallimore, R. (2009). Increasing achievement by focusing grade-level teams on improving classroom learning: a prospective, quasi- experimental study of Title I schools. *American Educational Research Journal, 46*, 1006–33.

Servage, L. (2008). Critical and transformative practices in professional learning communities. *Teacher Education Quarterly, 35*(1), 63–77.

Sharpe, F. (1996). Towards a research paradigm on devolution. *Journal of Educational Administration, 34*(1), 4–23.

Shedd, J. (1987). *Involving teachers in school and district decision making.* Ithaca, NY: Organizational Analysis and Practice.

Shedd, J., & Bacharach, S. (1991). *Tangled hierarchies: Teachers as professionals and the management of schools.* San Francisco: JosseyBass.

Simon, H. (1993). Decision making: Rational, nonrational, and irrational. *Educational Administration Quarterly, 29*, 392–411.

Talbert, J. E., & McLaughlin, M. W. (1994). Teacher professionalism in local school contexts. *American Journal of Education, 102*(2), 123–53.

Vescio, V. Ross, D., & Adams, A. (2008). A review of research on the impact of professional Learning communities on teaching practice and student learning. *Teaching and Teacher Education, 24*, 80–91.

Weiss, C. H. (1993). Shared decision making about what? A comparison of schools with and without teacher participation. *Teachers College Record, 95*(1), 69–92.

Weiss, C. (1995). The four "I's" of school reform: How interests, ideology, information, and institution affect teachers and principals. *Harvard Educational Review, 65*(4), 571–92.

Winn, M., & Keller, L. R. (2001). A modeling methodology for multiobjective multistakeholder decisions: Implications for research. *Journal of Management Inquiry, 10*(2), 166–81.

Wood, D. (2007). Teachers' learning communities: Catalyst for change or a new infrastructure for the status quo? *Teachers College Record, 109*(3), 699–739.

Yin, R. (2009). *Case study research: Design and methods* (4th ed.). Los Angeles: Sage.

Chapter Five

Influences on Teacher Sharing and Collaboration

Tanya F. Cook and Vivienne Collinson

Teachers are special people. And you know, we have to communicate with one another. We have to work together to let the kids know
that we are united. We are here to educate them, to prepare them for
the future. And sharing information, helping one another, is the best
way . . . to do that.

—Carl[1]

As teachers face the enormous challenge of reshaping education in the
twenty-first century, collaborating to integrate new technology appears to
be a wonderful opportunity for improving both teaching and learning. Computer technology imbues most facets of everyday life. However, studies
continue to indicate that change in education is not keeping pace with these
developments. Although almost all U.S. schools are connected to the Internet
and, on average, have an Internet-connected computer for every three students (Snyder & Dillow, 2012), many teachers have been slow to integrate
computers into their classroom instruction (Eteokleous, 2008; Johnson,
Schwab, & Foa, 1999; Russell et al., 2003; Van Braak, 2001). At the dawn of
the twenty-first century, Rowand (2001) found that "only one-third of public
school teachers feel 'well prepared' or 'very well prepared' to integrate the
use of computers into their teaching" (p. 4). Technology "remains primarily
a research tool, not a forum for interactive teaching, learning, communicating or collaborating" (Grunwald & Rockman et al., 2002, p. 1).

Exacerbating the challenge, schools have a long history of professional isolation and autonomy (Goodlad, 1984; Little, 1987; Lortie, 1975;
Rosenholtz & Smylie, 1984; Sarason, 1982). Teachers and leaders still

appear to have inadequate norms of collaborating to share their individual learning. However, to make full use of technological innovations and to prepare students for the future, educators must learn to integrate technology to support and extend learning in meaningful ways (Dede, 2011; Inan & Lowther, 2010; Prensky, 2006; Department of Education, 2010).

Sharing learning is a form of dissemination, which Shaw and Perkins (1992) defined as a "collaborative exchange of ideas in which differing perspectives are aired and understanding is shared" (p. 178). As such, sharing learning is a building block of collaboration and represents a precondition for the deeper and more sustained interaction that many researchers see as an ideal form of collaboration (Friedlander, 1983; Fullan, 2005; Sergiovanni, 1990). Not only is dissemination an important link between individual learning and collaboration, it is also considered a linchpin for organizational learning (Argyris & Schon, 1978; Collinson & Cook, 2007; Daft & Weick, 1984; Louis, 1994; Shaw & Perkins, 1992).

This chapter emphasizes a holistic picture of collaboration in schools; that is, a field of forces that teachers found most strongly affected their decisions to share with colleagues. These forces are examined individually and then considered together. By taking a more systemic view, school leaders gain a richer understanding of the field of forces that influence teachers' decisions to share their learning. This understanding, in turn, is likely to lead to greater success in encouraging collaboration, both in the short term and in a more sustained fashion.

SOCIAL CONTEXT: THE EDUCATORS'
ELECTRONIC LEARNING COMMUNITY

The case study in this chapter is drawn from a larger study that explored the phenomenon of dissemination among teachers involved in a project designed to help middle school teachers incorporate computer technology into classroom instruction. The study took place within the context of an early computer technology demonstration project, the Educators' Electronic Learning Community (EELC, a pseudonym). EELC was part of a five-year Technology Challenge Grant Program funded by the U.S. Department of Education. The aim of the project was to create an electronic learning community where computer technologies were used to enhance the science and social studies curriculum in middle schools and to provide professional development for teachers.

EELC provided teacher participants in three inner-city middle schools with project-designed software, in-school technical support, regular meetings with researchers, and summer institutes where teachers could enhance their learning and share their experiences. Teachers were asked to learn how to use the equipment and applications and to integrate the technology into their instruction. Although the study was conducted when this kind of technology integration was considered innovative, it is instructive because the integration of innovations and the sharing of cutting-edge learning tends to follow a pattern. Today, teachers continue to face many of the same challenges when learning to integrate technology into their instruction and when sharing their learning with others (Chen, 2008; Inan & Lowther, 2010).

A Case Study

The sample of voluntary participants for the case study included ten teachers who remained as classroom teachers in three inner-city schools throughout the initial years of the EELC project. All of the teachers had at least five years of teaching experience and half of the teachers had twenty or more years of teaching experience. Participants responded to a pre-interview survey that solicited background information, identified ways teachers had learned and shared what they had learned, and sought open-ended responses concerning forces that helped or hindered them in sharing their learning (see Collinson & Cook, 2004a, 2004b).

Participants then engaged in a semistructured interview of approximately sixty to ninety minutes. The interview explored the skills, knowledge, and insights teachers gained through their participation in the EELC project, their methods of sharing learning with one another, and the field of forces that influenced their decisions to share what they had learned. Participants also completed a postinterview survey where they rated the strength of motivating and restraining forces and then ranked the relative importance of the most influential forces. A force refers to an influence that captures participant responses with similar meanings. The forces were drawn from the pre-interview surveys and interviews. Other data sources included an EELC document review, observations, field notes, and notes taken at meetings and workshops.

Force-field analysis (Lewin, 1951) of the results of teacher rankings from the postinterview survey was used to generate a more systemic picture of the dynamic environment influencing teachers' dissemination of their learning with a view to understanding how dissemination can be encouraged. The force field generated from teacher responses indicated the strongest stimuli (motivation) and barriers (restraints) influencing sharing and collaboration.

MOTIVATION AND RESTRAINTS
INFLUENCING COLLABORATION

Teachers' decisions to collaborate with others are affected by numerous forces that can either motivate or restrain sharing. Teachers in the case study identified forty-three forces that they believe motivate dissemination and thirty-five forces that restrain it (Collinson & Cook, 2004b). In the study, dissemination included any of the ways in which teachers shared their learning with colleagues. If educational leaders—from teachers to team leaders to principals and superintendents—wish to encourage collaboration, they will need to understand the strength, distinctions, and subtlety of teacher interpretations of these forces as well as understanding which forces teachers find most strongly influence their choices.

Understanding teachers' perceptions of the strongest forces (positive and negative) is a useful tool when working to increase collaborative efforts. Figure 5.1, a force-field analysis diagram, indicates teachers' rankings of the six forces that were most important in helping them share and the five forces that were the strongest barriers to sharing. The figure does not merely present two fields of forces; it produces a more systemic picture of the dynamic environment within which teachers were making decisions about sharing their learning with colleagues.

Positive and negative influences on teacher sharing within the context of a specific school environment or culture can be understood in opposition to each other. According to force-field theory, as long as opposing fields of forces are equal in strength, the situation is in equilibrium and the status quo is preserved. Change occurs when the intensity of one field of forces is stronger than the other (Burke, 1982; Lewin, 1951; Weisbord, 1987).

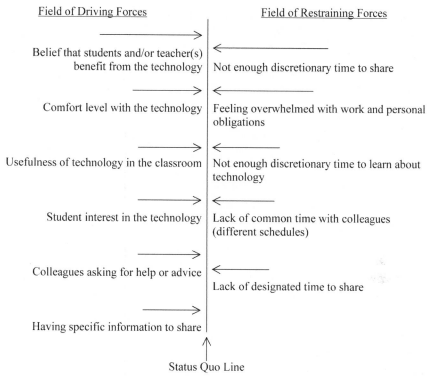

Figure 5.1. Force-field Analysis Diagram

The line down the middle of Figure 5.1 represents the status quo or current level of sharing for teachers in the project. The arrows on the left denote the driving forces that motivate teachers to increase their level of sharing. Driving forces can push "toward a positive, or away from a negative" and lead to movement (Lewin, 1951, p. 259). The arrows on the right show the restraining forces that create barriers to increasing sharing. "Restraining forces, as such, do not lead to [change], but they do influence the effect of driving forces" (p. 259). The length of each arrow indicates the strength of a given force. For example, lack of discretionary time for sharing is a strong barrier to sharing whereas having specific information to share is a relatively weak stimulus (for a more in-depth explanation of force-field analysis, see Lewin [1951]).

Force-field theory suggests that sharing would increase as motivating forces were strengthened as long as restraining forces stayed the same. For example, it is likely that this group of teachers would share more as they became more comfortable using technology in the classroom or as they became more certain of the technology's benefits to students. Force-field theory also suggests that sharing would increase as restraining forces were weakened (e.g., teachers have more discretionary time to learn or share). Considered together, driving and restraining forces create a dynamic and systemic picture.

Forces Motivating Sharing and Collaboration

In the case study, the six forces that most strongly motivated sharing can be grouped into two categories: practicality and interest at the classroom level, and teachers' levels of competence. The importance that teachers attach to practicality and interest in the classroom has a long history. More than thirty years ago, Doyle and Ponder (1977/1978) found that "the practicality ethic is a key link in the knowledge utilization chain in schools" (p. 1). Teachers who fail to see how an innovation is beneficial and useful in the classroom or how it will interest students may be reluctant to genuinely engage in individual learning, an initial step in any collaborative process.

Teachers in the case study elaborated three motivating forces in the category of practicality and interest:

1. a belief that students or teachers benefit from the innovation
2. usefulness in the classroom
3. student interest

Teachers in the case study also wanted to develop competence with the technology before sharing new knowledge and skills with others. They described three forces within the category of competence:

1. a comfort level with the innovation
2. colleagues asking for help and advice
3. having specific information to share

> *The belief that my students and I are benefiting from the project has made it easy for me to share new skills, knowledge, and insights in school and every place I go.—Irene*

Seeing benefits from the technology was the strongest stimulus to sharing for teachers in this study. The teachers repeatedly emphasized four benefits that motivated them to share what they were learning: the benefits of reaching a diverse group of students, capturing student attention, preparing students for the twenty-first century, and providing professional growth for teachers.

> You know, that's why I like this technology—it's the real reason why I like it—is because it is a different way of looking at the same old thing. And the older you get, the longer you teach, that's what you're looking for. You already know what to teach, how it works, why it does it, whatever. But you are looking for another way to improve your lesson, to excite your students, to even excite yourself.—Betty

Henry explained that if teachers see "collaboration as a key for them improving as a teacher, they'll do it. If they think they have to do it just because they have to, they won't do anything."

If I can apply it in my classroom, I will share it with others.—Henry

Just as teachers liked to know the benefits of innovations for students or teachers, some teachers mentioned usefulness in the classroom as a precondition for sharing. "It's similar to [the belief that my students and I are benefiting from the technology]. Why would I share something with someone that is not useful in the classroom?" (Karen). Betty echoed this sentiment by saying, "If I can't use it in the classroom, I have difficulty finding time for it."

Henry thought that teachers at his school were more willing to invest time in the EELC technology project than in other school improvement efforts because "with this, we see what it can do. There's buy-in . . . because they know how much it is going to impact [the classroom]." This was markedly different from his experience with other projects where

> [e]veryone's like, "Oh gee, what's this? How's it going to affect my classroom? How's it going to affect how I am as a teacher? Is it worthwhile or is it just another hoop the [school system] wants us to do?" There's initial cynicism. . . . A lot of times, you don't see a connection of how it's going to help you, and I think the project people know how it's going to help them, so they'll be more willing to share.—Henry

If you find something that works well and captures a student's attention, then you want to share it.—Karen

Student interest helped teachers share in two ways. First, student interest excited teachers. "Anything involving the television or the computer . . . gets their attention immediately. So that's great" (Donna). Student interest, in turn, helped teachers learn and then share what they had learned. As Henry observed, "We find it [integrating technology] is a way to motivate kids [and] is a way to motivate us because the kids are so interested in it. So we want to learn more and do more." Donna shared an activity that she developed "because [she] thought it was something that the kids needed to know and it was a neat way of showing them how." Second, student interest can promote sharing by generating interest and openness from colleagues. As Karen explained, when students are interested in something, "other teachers are more receptive to it."

When I am well-versed in a subject, I feel confident and comfortable in sharing what I know.—Jessie

Feeling comfortable with innovations was another motivating force for the teachers. Many felt that they were still learning the technology and were not yet ready to share. "I think when I get this thing up and rolling, it will be like duh-duh-da-duh, blow the horns and everything else in the building. I'll ask everyone to come around and see how it works or what we're working on" (Irene). Similarly, Henry said, "I think there's going to be a higher level of knowledge, insights, and willingness to share once they [teachers] get excited, once they use it."

Ellen offered a different perspective. For her, becoming comfortable with the technology motivated her to learn more, both individually and from others. The transition from learning to sharing was a "gradual process" that began with

[s]tarting to feel comfortable with what I was doing, you know, and the more I was able to do it, the more comfortable I felt doing it. And then, I don't know—it's like a search that just gets inside of you and you're just eager to share. Because if I'm eager to learn, you know, then I'm eager to share, because I find that the more I give, the more I get back from other teachers.—Ellen

If a person asks for help with a lesson and anything on EELC may help them, I share this information with them.—Betty

Some of the teachers said that colleagues' questions or requests for advice and help motivated them to share their knowledge. Collegial requests appear to convey recognition of expertise and represent a source of satisfaction for the recipient:

> Some of the teachers at [another school] were having trouble [with the technology] and so they sent me an e-mail message asking me for instructions. . . . And I was really amazed that they sent the e-mail to me because I felt, "Wow! Wow!" There's [the school system coordinator] and then they have somebody at their school who's a coordinator. And it made me feel that, "Wow," you know, "I'm glad they think they can ask me something." And it made me feel so good. So I sent them a message with all the steps.—Ellen

However, the teachers seemed to respect a tacit norm of "ask and I'll gladly help" (Irene). Carl explained that "most of the time, I would wait for somebody to ask" before offering to share. Donna also noted that often when she shares, it is because "I have been asked by peers or instructed to do so."

If I have located some information that is informative, relevant, or interesting to a unit of study, I want to share.—Jessie

Teachers in the study were motivated to share when they had specific information, such as "something interesting or a new way of doing something" (Donna). In particular, they shared information with colleagues who taught the same subjects or grade levels. For instance, Ellen said, "I taught chemistry last year, so a lot of the sites that I was able to use when I taught chemistry, I saved on a disk and I shared that with Betty so that she could use that with her chemistry classes this year." Karen commented, "A lot of times, Jessie and I will, if we find a website that looks interesting, we will share with each other because we both teach sixth grade science."

Forces Restraining Sharing and Collaboration

All five of the strongest forces restraining sharing among teachers—not enough discretionary time to share, feeling overwhelmed, not enough discretionary time to learn, lack of common time with colleagues, and lack of a designated time to share—are related to a single category: lack of time. This is hardly surprising. In the literature on school reform and restructuring, time has long been identified as one of the strongest barriers to change (Cambone, 1995; Gandara, 1999; Kruse, Louis, & Byrk, 1995; Little, 1987). Fullan and Miles (1992) observed that "every analysis of the problems of change efforts that we have seen in the last decade of research and practice has concluded that time is the most salient issue" (p. 750).

Although an understanding of teachers' interpretations of time is a logical first step in creating more appropriate and worthwhile time for learning and change, few studies have explored what teachers mean when they say, "I don't have enough time." This section elucidates the five strongest barriers to collaboration for teachers in the case study (these and additional aspects of time were elaborated in Collinson & Cook, 2001).

> *I don't have time to communicate with other teachers, . . . especially not with teachers outside the building, at another place.*—Michael

Not enough discretionary time to share was the strongest force restraining sharing. Discretionary time is unscheduled time that individual teachers can spend however they choose. Teachers drew a distinction between discretionary time to share and discretionary time to learn, and found both to be in short supply. Irene explained that for her, "time for discussions and explorations with other staff members" is one of the biggest barriers to sharing with other teachers. "We really don't have . . . much time to share. There is no time for you . . . as a science teacher to go into another science teacher's room who's teaching the same thing, the same grade level, or whatever, and see how they're doing" (Betty).

Teachers also noted that there is rarely time for any in-depth or sustained sharing. "Whenever I catch Ellen, it's either, 'I got to hurry up and maybe question her,' or vice versa. It's, like, always on the go" (Carl).

> When we're exposed to things, we share. It's no good keeping it all to yourself. You've got to share it. So we just do the best we can with that. [But] like I said, there's really no time to do that. . . . You're pulled in a million different ways to try to do a good job.—Betty

Donna commented that planning periods, one of the few times of the day when teachers are not with their classes, are filled with other obligations.

In the EELC schools, sharing occurred "on the fly" or on a "catch-as-catch-can" basis.

Curriculum demands and classroom management issues are overwhelming at this point.—Jessie

Feeling overwhelmed by everything that needs to be done is similar to the previous force (lack of time to share). However, for some teachers in this study, feeling overwhelmed went beyond the school schedule and involved new demands relating to a potential state takeover of their schools or personal obligations. Two distinguishing features characterized this force: a sense of pressure and a level of unease. Feeling overwhelmed also revealed the multilayered nature of time; namely, simultaneous pressures from the schools and district, and sometimes from home.

Feeling overwhelmed can make teachers less receptive to new information and insights. As Jessie observed, "A lot of times, people don't want to do more than what they have to do. It's already a huge burden to begin with." The teachers' many comments about feeling overwhelmed underscored how too many concurrent initiatives or pressures can overwhelm teachers and thereby derail ongoing teacher interest, learning, and collaboration.

Because there is such a lack of time, you're limited as to what you learn or what you share with someone else.—Donna

Many of the teachers in this study indicated that they do not have enough discretionary time to learn about the technology on their own before sharing with colleagues. Lack of discretionary time to learn, as a restraining force, is a counterbalance to two of the strongest motivating forces for sharing: feeling comfortable with the technology and having something specific to share. The tension of these opposing forces was reflected in teachers' comments. Donna explained that she needs time to learn because "even though I am better than many coworkers, I have not reached that comfort level [with the technology]. . . . If you have the time, . . . you can also learn more on your own and [then] share it." Likewise, although Irene was "really enthusiastic" about the technology and "sure when I get this thing up [and running], Honey, everybody's going to know!," she said, "I really haven't had time to share too much of anything, because I really haven't done anything."

Michael's experiences indicated how reducing this force may encourage teachers to continue to learn and share.

> During the summer, I had the time to sit down and relax and be calm and work and work and work on it [integrating the technology into instruction], and that really, really motivated me. Then I had the chance to talk with the other project people in the building. You know, we shared and shared. "What do you have in your module?" "What do you have in this?" "What do you have in that?" And it really kept me going, going, going!—Michael

Having time to learn, especially time to learn with colleagues, was something that Irene found "very, very, very helpful." She was a strong advocate for meetings where the EELC teachers could learn from each other.

> *We don't really get to see each other because of different floors, different routines, and different schedules.—Nancy*

Lack of common time with colleagues presented a different challenge to sharing and collaboration. Irene clearly delineated lack of common time from lack of discretionary time. Because of block scheduling, she used to have a double planning period every day.

> So the teacher that's teaching down the hall and around the corner, when I'm free I could help her or could share with her, but she's got her class and vice versa. That's the kind of time I'm talking about. We don't have sharing time. . . . Like, this year, we have more time than we've ever had, but we don't have common time. [With the current schedule], I could go in and maybe sit in on her class, but after I did, when will I talk to her about what I saw?—Irene

A compounding facet of lack of common time with other teachers was a lack of information about when other teachers were free to meet. Some of the teachers mentioned that they have difficulty sharing because they do not know each other's schedules.

> We used to get a master schedule where we knew everybody's schedule. But they don't do that anymore. . . . So your whole day is just scheduled in for you, and it's just like you go in[to] your little cubby hole and do whatever you're going to do, and when it's over, you go out. Down on the first floor, they don't know what the second floor is doing, the third floor is doing. You know, that kind of thing. Anybody you ask—"When are you

free?" "I'm free first period"—it's not a problem with us. But you will not be given a sheet with that on it.—Irene

"You just don't see people, because they're all on different time schedules. They eat lunch at a different time, they meet at a different time. So it's really hard to share" (Betty). "Basically, [the only time] they can do it is before or after school" (Henry).

We don't come together enough so we are not able to share enough.—Ellen

Lack of a designated time to share may further restrain collaboration and may reflect how little time is organized for groups of teachers to spend together.

> We can all learn from each other, but there has to be a [designated] time set up and a process where we can collaborate, basically. I really don't think it's going to happen through osmosis as much as you'd like it. There are teachers all over the building, and even though we're in this project, if there was a set-up time [when] we could meet for the specific purpose of helping each other out with the technology, I think we'd learn the most. . . . There are no opportunities as a staff during the day or [during] professional development to share best practices.—Henry

One teacher mentioned another closely related problem: a lack of time to focus on one thing. Karen explained that for her, time to learn and share meant having uninterrupted time with another teacher.

> To have quality time, meaning—this is what I mean by time—where I don't have to do any other busy work during that time. Because right now, during my planning period, not only are you checking papers, you are printing lesson plans, you're calling parents, you're just doing all these different things all at once. . . . So it is just a structured block of time that you can devote purely to one thing.—Karen

Considering the Forces Holistically: Influencing Sharing and Collaboration

"Instead of picking out one or another isolated element within a situation, . . . it [is] advantageous, as a rule, to start with a characterization of the situation as a whole" (Lewin, 1951, p. 63). Viewed holistically, the force-field diagram (Figure 5.1) reveals that time is a precious commodity for teachers and that, in general, they are going to spend time sharing only those things that they feel comfortable with and that they believe will interest students and help them learn. In this case study, the driving forces were generally internal and related to teachers' professional judgments and personal dispositions.

Conversely, the restraining forces were generally external and related to the structure of the school day. This suggests that it may be easier to encourage sharing by working to reduce restraining forces (issues of time) before working to increase driving forces (practicality, interest, and competence). Making more time for sharing and collaboration by increasing discretionary time to learn and share, reducing pressures to help teachers feel less overwhelmed, creating more common time, or providing designated opportunities to share is likely to be the strongest and fastest path to encouraging sharing and collaboration in the short term.

Lewin (1951) suggested that lessening restraining forces is like clearing stones from a river rather than narrowing the river's banks. Clearing stones allows the river to take its natural course as existing forces drive the water forward more swiftly. Narrowing the river's banks can also increase the river's velocity, but doing so increases pressure and forces the water forward. In schools, reducing or removing barriers to change (clearing the stones) releases pressures that restrain change. Sometimes, however, principals or superintendents mandate change (narrowing the river's banks) without reducing restraining forces that would ease the change. For example, they may evaluate teachers on how much they ask colleagues for help or advice (increasing pressure for change) without creating time for collaboration (reducing a pressure restraining change).

Heath and Heath's (2010) explanation of shaping the path to help make a change process easier is a useful elaboration of Lewin's metaphor.

> If you want people to change, you can provide clear direction . . . or boost their motivation and determination. Alternatively, you can simply make the journey easier. Create a steep downhill slope and give them a push. Remove some friction from the trail. Scatter around lots of signs to tell them they're getting close. (p. 181)

Although shaping the path by reducing restraints is often an effective way to begin a change process, change always stems from driving forces, so boosting teachers' positive motivation also helps make the journey easier. For example, the forces of practicality, student interest, and usefulness are positive and powerful influences on teachers' decisions to share.

These motivating forces accentuate the critical importance of providing teachers with a practice-based rationale for a given reform rather than simply explaining the reform and supplying implementation information. This study suggests that teachers need to understand why to do it, not just how to do it. That is, teachers benefit from seeing how an innovation is relevant for students before they spend time on it, and they are more likely to remain engaged in collaborative endeavors when relevance is determined through shared understandings that are tested in the classroom.

Structuring time for individual learning and reflection can also boost motivation, making the journey easier. Individual learning helps teachers feel comfortable with innovations and gives them the opportunity to find and develop meaningful content to share with their colleagues. The comments of teachers in this study suggest that not all learning can or should be collective. If their comments hold true for other groups of teachers, then some teachers' need for individual learning should not lead researchers to assume that sharing does not occur or that a particular setting is professionally isolated. Some teachers may need time as learners to figure out things on their own and to test new ideas or approaches in their classroom in preparation for collective learning.

Deeper and more inclusive collaboration in schools eventually requires a more careful examination of underlying attitudes and norms that shape teacher's expectations. Whereas initial efforts to boost sharing and collaboration by making more time for teachers may work well for some teachers, others who lack a disposition for sharing may not seize collaborative opportunities. Attitudes that restrain dissemination appear to be pervasive and well-known to the teachers:

> Attitudes. Attitudes. That's always going to be something that's going to keep anybody from doing things. Attitudes . . . like "I don't need to do this" or "What makes you think that she knows what she's doing?" or "I've been doing [it] this way for so long and I'm tired of them always trying to do something different,". . . or "That child will never learn anything," or "I can't do anything with their parents," [or] "It's not my job to do this." You know, "I don't need to go to a workshop" or "I don't need to do this."—Jessie

Sustaining Sharing and Collaboration

In some cases, making time for increased collaborative efforts may have a snowball effect: the more teachers share and learn, the more they want to share and learn. For Ellen, collaboration began at the school level, but as she learned to learn with colleagues, her collaborative interests spread beyond the school.

Ellen started her own web page for teachers, served as teacher/technology advisor to a local television station, and had a wide collegial network, but said that she had to learn to collaborate.

> At one time, . . . I would keep things to myself. I wasn't a person that would, you know, share a lot. And it seems that through the EELC project, I've been able to share more. I guess it's given me an opportunity to have a closer relationship or connection with other teachers, especially teachers that I'm not used to being with all the time, because it brings me in contact with teachers that are not directly here in the building. . . . I've been able to verbalize things to them, and after doing that, now I'm able to do more as far as verbalizing the type of things I do and being able to share that information more openly. . . . I first had to overcome my fears and take the plunge. . . . It took time, patience, and determination. Soon I was able to build up my confidence, and although I lacked the expertise that others may have had, I made use of the tools I had and gradually began to grow.—Ellen

Once Ellen learned and her collaborative gestures were well received or reciprocated, the self-sustaining nature of collaboration allowed her to flourish and learn even more (also see Collinson, 2012).

> The thing that motivates me to share what I've learned is my own desire to learn from others. When I share what I've learned, it opens the door for others to communicate their own experiences, ideas, and problems, and we begin to learn from each other.—Ellen

Unlike the other teachers in the study, Ellen found that the strongest barriers to dissemination were negative attitudes of colleagues, defensiveness from peers, and difficulty changing habits. She ranked only one aspect of time (feeling overwhelmed) as one of the five strongest barriers to dissemination. Because Ellen is such a strong collaborator, her responses hint at the possibility that lack of time may only be an initial barrier to sharing. There may be stages of barriers to sharing, with the first stage relating to time to share and the next stage relating to attitude. As suggested by Maslow's (1954) hierarchy of needs, there may be levels where the conditions for sharing need to exist before it is possible to determine whether a disposition for sharing exists.

THE PROMISE OF LEARNING TO
LEARN TOGETHER

The comments and insights of the ten EELC teachers reveal the challenges and possibilities inherent in influencing teacher dissemination. They help us consider the forces, both individually and systemically, that most strongly influenced the teachers' decisions to share with colleagues and to envision building traditions of sharing and collaboration that include all educators. This group of teachers underscored the importance of respecting teachers' need for interest and practicality, boosting teachers' feelings of competence, removing time barriers, and addressing underlying attitudes to influence teacher collaboration. Given the small sample, this collection of forces influencing teacher dissemination offers multiple pathways for future action and further research. Interconnections among beliefs, practicality, individual learning, competence, time, school structures, attitudes, and norms also merit exploration. A better understanding of how to influence teacher collaboration has potential to benefit teachers and, through teachers, to enrich students, schools, and society. Only as teachers learn to learn together can the full promise of collaboration, and ultimately organizational learning, be realized.

NOTE

1. Pseudonyms are used throughout.

REFERENCES

Argyris, C., & Schon, D. A. (1978). *Organizational learning.* Reading, MA: Addison-Wesley.

Burke, W. W. (1982). *Organizational development: Principles and practices.* Boston: Little, Brown & Company.

Cambone, J. (1995). Time for teachers in school restructuring. *Teachers College Record, 96*(3), 512–43.

Chen, C.-H. (2008). Why do teachers not practice what they believe regarding technology innovation? *Journal of Educational Research, 102*(1), 65–75.

Collinson, V. (2012). Leading by learning, learning by leading. *Professional Development in Education, 38*(2), 247–66.

Collinson, V., & Cook, T. F. (2001). "I don't have enough time": Teachers' interpretations of time as a key to learning and school change. *Journal of Educational Administration, 39*(3), 266–81.

Collinson, V., & Cook, T. F. (2004a). Collaborating to learn computer technology: A challenge for teachers and leaders. *Leadership and Policy in Schools, 3*(2), 111–33.

Collinson, V., & Cook, T. F. (2004b). Learning to share, sharing to learn: Fostering organizational learning through teachers' dissemination of knowledge. *Journal of Educational Administration, 42*(3), 312–32.

Collinson, V., & Cook, T. F. (2007). *Organizational learning: Improving learning, teaching, and leading in school systems*. Thousand Oaks, CA: Sage.

Daft, R., & Weick, K. (1984). Toward a model of organizations as interpretation systems. *Academy of Management Review, 9*(2), 284–95.

Department of Education. (2010). *Transforming American education: Learning powered by technology* [National Educational Technology Plan 2010]. Washington, DC: Author.

Dede, C. (2011). Reconceptualizing technology integration to meet the necessity of transformation. *Journal of Curriculum and Instruction, 5*(1), 4–16.

Doyle, W., & Ponder, G. A. (1977/1978). The practicality ethic in teacher decision-making. *Interchange, 8*(3), 1–12.

Eteokleous, N. (2008). Evaluating computer technology integration in a centralized school system. *Computers and Education, 51*(2), 669–86.

Friedlander, F. (1983). Patterns of individual and organizational learning. In S. Srivastva (Ed.), *The executive mind* (pp. 192–220). San Francisco: Jossey-Bass.

Fullan, M. (2005). *Leadership and sustainability: System thinkers in action.* Thousand Oaks, CA: Corwin Press.

Fullan, M., & Miles, M. B. (1992). Getting reform right: What works and what doesn't. *Phi Delta Kappan, 73*(10), 745–52.

Gandara, P. (Ed.). (1999). *The dimensions of time and the challenge of school reform*. Albany: State University of New York Press.

Goodlad, J. I. (1984). *A place called school: Prospects for the future*. New York: McGraw-Hill.

Grunwald Associates, & Rockman et al. (2002). *Are we there yet?* Alexandria, VA: National School Board Foundation.

Heath, C., & Heath, D. (2010). *Switch: When change is hard*. New York: Random House.

Inan, F. A., & Lowther, D. L. (2010). Factors affecting technology integration in K–12 classrooms: A path model. *Educational Technology Research and Development, 58*(2), 137–54.

Johnson, M. J., Schwab, R. L., & Foa, L. (1999). Technology as a change agent for the teaching process. *Theory into Practice, 38*(1), 24–30.

Kruse, S. D., Louis, K. S., & Byrk, A. (1995). An emerging framework for analyzing school-based professional community. In K. S. Louis & S. D. Kruse (Eds.), *Professionalism and community: Perspectives on reforming urban schools* (pp. 23–44). Thousand Oaks, CA: Corwin Press.

Lewin, K. (1951). *Field theory in social science: Selected theoretical papers.* D. Cartwright (Ed.). New York: Harper & Row.

Little, J. W. (1987). Teachers as colleagues. In V. Richardson-Koehler (Ed.), *Educators' handbook: A research perspective* (pp. 491–518). New York: Longman.

Lortie, D. (1975). *Schoolteacher: A sociological study.* Chicago: University of Chicago Press.

Louis, K. S. (1994). Beyond managed change: Rethinking how schools change. *School Effectiveness and School Improvement, 5*(1), 2–24.

Maslow, A. H. (1954). *Motivation and personality.* New York: Harper & Row.

Prensky, M. (2006, December–January). Adopt and adapt: 21st century schools need 21st century technology. *Edutopia,* 43–45.

Rosenholtz, S. J., & Smylie, M. A. (1984). Teacher compensation and career ladders. *The Elementary School Journal, 85*(2), 149–66.

Rowand, C. (2001). Teachers and computers: Teacher use in public schools. *Education Statistics Quarterly, 2*(2), 72–75.

Russell, M., Bebell, D., O'Dwyer, L., & O'Connor, K. (2003). Examining teacher technology use: Implications for preservice and inservice teacher preparation. *Journal of Teacher Education, 54*(4), 297–310.

Sarason, S. B. (1982). *The culture of the school and the problem of change* (2nd ed.). Boston: Allyn & Bacon.

Sergiovanni, T. J. (1990). *Value-added leadership: How to get extraordinary performance in schools.* New York: Harcourt Brace Jovanovich.

Shaw, R., & Perkins, D. (1992). Teaching organizations to learn: The power of productive failures. In D. Nadler, M. Gerstein, & R. Shaw (Eds.), *Organizational architecture* (pp. 175–92). San Francisco: Jossey-Bass.

Snyder, T., & Dillow, S. A. (2012). *Digest of education statistics, 2011.* Washington, DC: National Center for Education Statistics.

Van Braak, J. (2001). Individual characteristics influencing teachers' class use of computers. *Journal of Educational Computing Research, 25*(2), 141–57.

Weisbord, M. (1987). *Productive workplaces: Organizing and managing for dignity, meaning, and community.* San Francisco: Jossey-Bass.

Chapter Six

Teaming to Break the Walls of Isolation

Collaboration in Elementary Grade Level Teams

J. John Dewey and Sharon Conley

One key step to teacher professionalism is collaboration (Cooper & Brown, chapter 1, this volume). This chapter begins with a look at collaboration at two elementary school sites.[1] The following chapter (chapter 7) considers collaboration at secondary school campuses. Each of the two chapters begins with the same model of work group effectiveness but employs different methodological approaches. Through the consideration of collaboration in these chapters, we seek to explore what lessons can be learned and applied to the formation of teacher teams more generally.

One approach to collaboration as a work enhancement strategy (Crow & Pounder, 2000; Pounder, 1998, 1999) is the creation or refinement of the practice of organizing teachers (e.g., those who teach at particular grades) into *grade level* teams. Several key questions will be considered in this chapter, including:

1. How do school leaders create an organizational context for grade level teams?
2. How do teachers perceive the quality of their training and support in their efforts to be collaborative?
3. What are some positive outcomes of these school structures?

In this chapter, we report on a qualitative study of how teachers perceived collaboration within their grade level teams in two California elementary schools. We explore their perspectives through the lens of a prominent work group effectiveness model (Hackman & Oldham, 1980). We follow the lead of Crow and Pounder (2000), who used the model to frame their qualitative inquiry of middle school teacher teams. We find that four qualities enhance teacher collaboration in teams: a supportive organizational context, appropriate structural/design features, healthy interpersonal processes, and the perception that the group is effective in accomplishing its goals.

Initially we lay out a theoretical framework for considering the work group effectiveness of teacher teams in schools. We then present findings from interviews of teacher team members who are participating in grade level teams at two California elementary school sites. The interviews illustrate the larger school organizational context (including administrative support), the way the group is designed, and member interactions that all influence the group to be effective (or not). We suggest that there are processes by which teachers in grade level teams may become more effective and satisfied with their work, as well as processes that influence organizational change and growth more broadly.

A MODEL OF WORK GROUP EFFECTIVENESS

Hackman and Oldham's (1980) model of work group effectiveness has been widely used to study teams both within and outside of educational settings. According to these authors, self-managing work groups are "intact (if small) social systems whose members have the authority to handle internal processes as they see fit in order to generate a specific group product, service, or decision" (p. 164). Furthermore, self-managing groups are considered high functioning if they meet the following three criteria: (1) the output of the work group is of sufficient quality and quantity; (2) the group experience satisfies the needs of its members; and (3) the social process enhances the capability of the team to work together on subsequent tasks.

In addition, there are some initial conditions that set up a group and its ability to work together. These three criteria are: a supportive organizational context, appropriate structural or design features, and healthy interpersonal processes. With regard to *organizational context*, for a group approach to work design to have a lasting effect—and not simply become a quick fix to perceived organizational problems—the organization as a whole should be hospitable to changes in work practices.

For example, managers, or in the case of schools, principals, must be ready and willing to implement enhanced supervisory practices that support teachers through adequate training and development. School principals thus have an essential role to play in providing an organizational context that supports the design of work groups: managerial practices have to be altered to ensure that the effects of group design persist. By contrast, with unsupportive management conditions, "New behaviors tend to extinguish, and the organization persists pretty much as it was before the work was redesigned" (Hackman & Oldham, 1980, p. 142).

A supportive organizational context also provides rewards and recognition for the members of a group. A formal reward system, informal "recognition" (p. 195), setting performance objectives, highlighting possible constraints, and providing feedback are all important forms of support (Hackman & Oldham, 1980). Zander (as cited in Hackman & Oldham, 1980), in his book *Motives and Goals in Groups*, suggested that when a group receives feedback about its progress toward achieving an objective, goal-directed effort is enhanced. In addition to providing rewards and recognition, management should attend to enhancing the knowledge and skill levels of group members by providing necessary training and/or technical consultation.

Second, three features of the way teamwork is structured or designed (*design features*) also influence work group effectiveness. These are (1) the design of the group task, (2) the composition of the group, and (3) group norms that support the performance process. Successful group outcomes are dependent on the extent to which the group is motivated, a feature that can be enhanced by, for example, providing sufficient autonomy to assume responsibility for carrying out the work and opportunities to work on high-level tasks.

The composition of the group reflects, for instance, the extent to which members can bring "high levels of task-relevant expertise" (p. 174) to the group's work (Hackman & Oldham, 1980). This might require that the group has an appropriate balance of experienced and newer teachers or types of teaching expertise. Finally, group norms reflect the way that the group establishes expectations for its own work and develops a mutual understanding of how decisions will be made and conflict handled. "The advantage to a group in having clear norms about performance strategies is that the need to manage and coordinate group member behavior on a continuous basis is minimized" (p. 180).

Design features, however, may not affect performance across all circumstances; the success of a group depends "jointly on the demands of the work itself, the characteristics of the people, and the properties of the broader organizational context" (Hackman & Oldham, 1980, p. 189). Although many positive aspects accrue from self-managing work groups, teams are not always technologically or motivationally appropriate; moreover, design features may be relatively difficult to create, support, and manage (Hackman & Oldham, 1980). Finally, *healthy interpersonal processes* help ensure that positive patterns of interaction exist, coordination is sufficiently well developed, a balance of input exists among group members, talents and skills are brought to bear on the group task, and the overall performance of the group is enhanced by the sharing of knowledge and experience (Hackman & Oldham, 1980).

TEAMING AND TEAMWORK IN SCHOOLS

Teacher teaming has been envisioned as a mechanism for school change and for breaking down the isolation of the individual classroom teacher, thereby meeting the goals of a professional-oriented model of reform (Conley & Muncey, 1999; Cooper & Brown, chapter 1, this volume).[2] Teacher teaming as a reform emphasis can also be traced in part to a renewal of interest in the "middle-school paradigm" (Clark & Clark, as cited in Scribner, Sawyer, Watson, & Myers, 2007, p. 71), which envisions teams as a central component of middle school organization. Teacher teaming focuses on changing teachers' roles through new organizational configurations, clusters of teachers designated as teams (Conley & Muncey, 1999).

In the general organizational literature, Senge (1990) suggested that teams are essential to the development of organizational vitality and productivity. "Teams, not individuals, are the fundamental learning unit in modern organizations. Unless teams can learn, the organization cannot learn" (p. 10). Evidently, contemporary understandings about organizational development have also influenced educational policy and practice. Educational practitioners and researchers recognize increasingly that the active involvement of individuals at each level of the educational system is necessary for substantive change and organizational revitalization to occur (Spillane, Halverson, & Diamond, 2001).

In education, several studies have examined interdisciplinary teams at the middle school level (e.g., Crow & Pounder, 2000), and others at the high school level (e.g., Scribner et al., 2007). However, fewer studies have investigated elementary school grade level teams. As recently as 2008, a doctoral dissertation by Rosanne L. Kurstedt entitled, *A Study of Fifth-Grade Teachers' Grade-Level Meetings: The Complexities of Teachers' Group Work* observes, "The grade-level meeting, a prevalent form of peer collaboration, remains largely unexplored" (p. 1) in K–6 education. Yet increasingly, observers call for teachers to work with and learn from others on an ongoing basis—the sharing of skills, ideas, and knowledge that are likely salient sources for organizational learning (Collinson & Cook, 2007). Furthermore, enhancing understanding about elementary teachers' work in teams appears crucial for leveraging and in-stitutionalizing the core message of collaboration as a work enhancement strategy (Pounder, 1999).

In a recent re-examination of work design theory in educational set-tings, Mayrowetz, Murphy, Louis, and Smylie (2007) maintained that educational researchers must attend not only to issues of work motivation, as emphasized by Hackman and Oldham's (1980) model, but also to such organizational concepts as sense-making in organizations and organi-zational learning. For example, they posed the questions, "What does it mean to 'make sense' of change as radical as a redesigned workplace or job?" (p. 83); and, how can teachers learn how to become change agents in their organizations and exercise leadership such as "providing and selling a vision" (p. 80), potentially progressing beyond the traditional repertoire of teacher knowledge and skills?

In the current study, using Hackman and Oldham's (1980) framework of work group effectiveness, and combining other insights into the contextual features of group design and processes, we explored teachers' views of work groups in action. The following two questions guided our study: What are teachers' perceptions of the organizational context, design features, inter-personal processes, and effectiveness of their grade level teams? What are significant barriers to and positive outcomes of these teacher teams?

METHOD

To conduct this study, we collected interview data from teachers in four grade level teams in two K–6 elementary schools. The schools were located in two neighboring suburban California school districts in a medium-sized community. Team members from two grade level teams (K–1 and 5–6) at Manzanita school and two grade level teams (K and 5/6) at Ponderosa school participated in this study. (All school and teacher names are pseudonyms.) Within these districts, grade level teams had been in place on an informal basis for some time. However, a recent shift in district perspective was that it was essential for the districts' schools for teachers to meet to collaborate. In addition, a renewed emphasis had been placed on teaming overall in the schools.

One administrator described a refocusing of the grade-level teaming effort around the concept of a professional learning community (PLC). She stated that previously, elementary teams primarily addressed logistical matters but that "under the new structure of teaming there is more focus on adjusting instruction to the needs of students at grade level." To explore these newly focused and perhaps formalized teams, the study used interviews allowing us to examine teachers' perspectives and insights about their experiences.

Interview questions probed specific dimensions using Hackman and Oldham's (1980) classic model as follows:

- *Supportive Organizational Context*: Rewards and objectives for performance; availability of task-relevant training and technical consultation; clarity of task requirements and constraints.
- *Design Features*: Design of the group task; team composition; group norms about performance process.
- *Interpersonal Processes*: Coordinating team efforts and fostering commitment; weighing inputs and sharing knowledge; implementing and inventing performance strategy.
- *Work Group Effectiveness*: Member satisfaction; perception of teams fostering enhanced capability in teaching and/or in the ability to collaborate in the future.

The research followed several steps. First, we contacted the elementary districts based on their articulation of efforts to enhance teaching and learning through the use of collaborative grade level teacher teams. The districts were geographically accessible to the researchers and had a history of collaborative working relationships with the local university where the researchers were working. Based on consultation with district administrators as well as prior school contact, one elementary school was chosen from each district for participation in the study.

Next, in spring 2010, we scheduled meetings with the principals of each school to obtain permission for school personnel to participate in the study and to discuss potential grade level teams for inclusion. We asked principals to present the study to teachers at a staff meeting and request volunteers to contact the lead author for interviews. Principals then forwarded us the names of the volunteers as well as their contact information.

We then selected grade level teams—two from each school—based on teachers' willingness to be interviewed. Not all teachers were interested in participating; however, we were ultimately able to interview all but two team members (one each from two of the four teams). Study participants are displayed in Table 6.1, as well as their corresponding schools and team grade levels. We also interviewed one superintendent and the two school principals, as well as made use of school websites and documents such as accountability reports. We recorded and transcribed the interviews and then analyzed the data with particular attention to the aspects of work group effectiveness described in Hackman and Oldham's (1980) model.

In the next sections, the schools and teams are first described. Following those descriptions, the findings are then organized with respect to the model. Drawing on Crow and Pounder's (2000) study of middle school teams, we divide the key findings into organizational context, design, interpersonal process, and work group effectiveness.

Manzanita and Ponderosa Schools

Manzanita School, with a student enrollment of approximately 230, employed about twenty-five teachers. Nine percent of the students received free or reduced-price lunches, 6 percent were English learners,

Table 6.1.　Teachers Interviewed by School and Team

School	Team	Teachers Interviewed
Manzanita	A–K/1	3–Mandy, Jen, Leah
Manzanita	B–5/6	3–Dan, Steve, Lucy
Ponderosa	C–K	4–Kara, Patty, Lynne, Theresa
Ponderosa	D–5/6	4–Bev, Natalie, Cindy, Stacey

and 4 percent were identified as having disabilities (California Department of Education, 2010; system documentation). A stated goal of the school was "to continue . . . [our] efforts to close the achievement gap between our highest performing and lowest performing students . . . through focused grade level collaboration" (school documentation). Further, the school's accountability report indicated that teachers were to "meet in . . . grade level[s] . . . to conduct data analysis to identify areas of need." In 2009–2010, the district indicated that a strategic plan was in place to identify "our instructional priorities and needs as we strive to improve our high-performing district," maintaining that "Students and staff will benefit from a defined focus for our team effort to serve students and families" (district documentation).

In Manzanita, Team A was a K–1 grade level team comprised of four teachers, each assigned a K or a K–1 combination class. Although Mandy and Jen were early on in their careers (the former having recently completed her credential and in her first teaching position), Leah and Helen had worked together for ten years. The group did not have an assigned team leader but Mandy served more broadly as the "lower elementary [grades K–2] team leader." Like its counterparts throughout the district, the team met each Thursday afternoon for up to two hours, focusing much of its work on lesson planning, discussing individual student needs, and sharing curricular ideas, with additional focus as needed in the areas of assessment and testing outcomes. Interviewees described the team as having established a strong work ethic that positively influenced both school and student outcomes.

Manzanita School's Team B was a 5–6 grade level team also comprised of four teachers (Dan, Steve, Tom, and Lucy), all with over twenty years teaching experience at the upper elementary level, including one in her retirement year. All had worked at the school for at least ten years, mostly at different grade levels, but two had worked together at the same grade level for twelve years. Interviewees indicated a comfort among the members, as well as a high degree of assuredness, confidence, and good humor. In the Thursday meetings, the team focused its work on curriculum and lesson planning, student academic intervention, and logistical planning (setting up field trips, events, calling parents, etc.). Because the school employed specialists in art, music and technology, the team spent part of its time scheduling groups of students for these programs. Further, as some students moved between the classes and grade levels for certain subjects, this also required (logistical) coordination. There was also a social aspect to the team; "We try to check in as far as how we're doing in life. We spend time talking about our personal lives" (Dan).

Ponderosa School, slightly larger than Manzanita, had a student enrollment of approximately 300 and employed approximately 30 teachers. Fifteen percent of its students received free or reduced-price student lunches. Ten percent were English learners, and 3 percent were identified as with disabilities (California Department of Education, 2010; system documentation). The school's district had called for teachers to team at grade levels and its strategic plan called for providing "monthly grade-level release time at each school site to develop a community of lifelong learners" (district documentation). To facilitate the pursuit of these goals, teachers at Ponderosa worked in grade level teams described as "work[ing] together to analyze and improve student achievement and discuss research-based strategies" (school documentation).

Ponderosa School's Team C was a K grade level team comprised of four teachers: Kara in her second year of teaching, Patty in her fifth (second at Ponderosa), Lynne in her sixth, and Theresa in her fifteenth (ninth at Ponderosa). There was, therefore, a good balance of experienced and novice teachers, with two members (Lynne and Theresa) having worked together for many years. The team met twice weekly during two forty-five-minute sessions and twice per month for another hour. The team focused on aligning mathematics and language arts across the classrooms, monitoring adherence to state standards, curriculum planning, creating rubrics and assessments, and addressing the individual needs of students. The team also worked on strategic planning initiatives that "come down from the district" (Patty).

Ponderosa School's Team D was a 5–6 grade level team consisting of four relatively experienced teachers. Bev taught for seven years before coming to Ponderosa, and has been in the school for twelve years. Natalie has taught fifth and sixth grade students for more than twenty years and has been in the school fifteen years. Cindy has been teaching in the district for twenty-five years, with fifteen at Ponderosa. The least experienced, Stacey, was in her fifth year (having also worked in two previous schools for two years each). All team members exuded an assuredness that comes with the level of experience they possess. In this respect they had certain similarities to Manzanita's 5–6 team, who were also characterized by their depth of knowledge and experience.

Meetings focused primarily on curriculum, the school's writing program, rubrics, assessments, scheduling, and the strategic planning initiative from the district. In addition, coordination occurred with the special education teacher. The team sometimes divided itself by grade level to focus on grade-specific issues. The team was characterized by their experience and expertise, or as Stacey describes it, "cooperation, a good knowledge of teaching, and a willingness to share ideas."

FINDINGS: FOUR QUALITIES OF TEAMING

We organized our results according to four aspects of Hackman and Oldham's (1980) model of work group effectiveness: supportive organizational context, design features, healthy interpersonal processes, and work group effectiveness (Crow & Pounder, 2000). See Table 6.2 for an overview of each team. In the paragraphs that follow, we illustrate *one* model element for each team as an illustration of model application (see Enomoto & Conley, 2012).[3] Specifically, Manzanita Team A demonstrated a *supportive organizational context*, Manzanita Team B *design features*, Ponderosa Team C *healthy interpersonal processes*, and Ponderosa Team D *work group effectiveness*. Each is viewed as the most illustrative example of each type based on the data, but as shown in Table 6.2, all of these components occurred in each team to varying degrees.

A Supportive Organizational Context: Manzanita School's Team A, K–1

Themes in Team A related to a supportive organizational context included time for planning, flexible performance objectives, principal support, autonomy in team operation, task constraints, some conflict with other duties, recognition, and the need for additional training. Primarily facilitating the work of Team A was the time provided by the school district and administration; team members identified the Thursday planning time as critical. Further, when asked about performance objectives, one team member, Jen, noted that the team's weekly "agenda" was fairly open unless specific

Table 6.2   Hackman and Oldham's Organizational Context, Design Features, Interpersonal Processes, and Work Group Effectiveness

Team	Supportive Organizational Context	Design Features	Healthy Interpersonal Processes	Work Group Effectiveness
Team A K/1 Manzanita	Time provided for planning, flexible performance objectives, support from the principal, latitude in operation, task constraints, conflict with other duties, recognition, need for more training	Focus on planning and student intervention, homogeneity in attitude, strong work ethic, experience of teamwork, knowledge of standards and curriculum content	Even participation, level of cooperation, advanced comfort level, balance of skills, proximity of work space, no conflicts, perception of other teams as dysfunctional	Effective, reach consensus quickly, students exceed standards, improved student discipline, enhanced communication skills, sense of well-being among members
Team B 5/6 Manzanita	Time provided for planning, use of specialists, support from the principal, recognition, latitude in operation, creative freedom, occasional time constraints, need for more training	Focus on aligning content with standards, planning and intervention, experience of teamwork and good mix of personalities, creativity, flexibility, ability to handle conflict	Comfort level, 'synergy', camaraderie, concern for personal as well as professional matters, no conflict, individual vs. team dynamics can be hindrance, acknowledge not all teams highly functional, some conflict with other teams	Effective in accomplishing goals, improvements in student learning and behavior, teaching performance, improved consistency, enhanced professional commitment, sense of well-being

(continued)

Table 6.2 (*Continued*)

Team	Supportive Organizational Context	Design Features	Healthy Interpersonal Processes	Work Group Effectiveness
Team C K Ponderosa	Time provided for planning, support from the principal, recognition, specific meeting agendas, less latitude, occasional time constraints, extraneous requirements, perception of being micromanaged	Focus on adherence to standards, Open Court [a], rubrics and assessments, balance of experienced and novice teachers	High degree of comfort working together, sharing of ideas, one member more dominant, general helpfulness, balance of responsibilities, friendship	Effective, reach consensus quickly, improvement in teaming process, enhanced coordination, camaraderie, progress seen in reading results, more efficient student assessment
Team D 5/6 Ponderosa	Time provided for planning, support from the principal, recognition, specific meeting agendas, less latitude, time constraints, e.g., need to spend time planning lessons for substitutes, increased workload, in-service training provided	Focus on curriculum, writing program, rubrics and assessments, experienced team members, high level of knowledge and professionalism, flexibility, some degree of disconnect with administration	Communication, cooperation and collegiality, friendship, strong degree of comfort, openness and adaptability, even participation, balance of skills, few significant conflicts, slight difference in degree of participation	Effective, make decisions quickly, output meeting principal expectations, improved student writing, improved student learning, discipline, teacher effectiveness, enhanced sense of commitment, solidified collegiality

[a] Open Court is a structured reading program.

school-wide or district-wide issues needed to be addressed. She continued that the team was focused "adequately" on the needs of students and their development. She states, "The common thread is making sure all the students are learning the skills they need to learn, but other than this common thread, we don't have an agenda."

Team members also recognized the support of the principal in facilitating their work. The principal encouraged members to work together productively to "carve out the weekly planning time" and monitor the results of student assessments. According to Jen:

> [District and site] administration [are] constantly bringing instructional strategies and teaching to the forefront of our work: how we are reaching students, questioning us, asking to see our assessments, monitoring our progress, [monitoring] how much the students are learning and what sort of intervention [is needed]. If [students] do need intervention, they're willing to help us find some strategies.

The K–1 team enjoyed a considerable amount of autonomy in how it operated. As Leah states, "We have pretty much all the freedom we want as long as we are meeting on a weekly basis to talk about student instruction with a focus on intervention and [how students can master California content] standards." Welcoming the freedom it was given to operate, the team found this to be one of the elements that most facilitated their work. As another team member, Mandy, mentions, the district had fortunately not imposed a structured reading program such as Open Court:

> We're lucky we don't have a program like Open Court. [Our district has] let us use a few different programs or we can use what we want to accomplish the same goal. We've actually created our own assessments, and no one's told us exactly what we need to do. I feel like if something isn't working for us, we're able to go and figure out something else.

The team felt task constraints, however. These included a lack of time available to meet, furthered by a need to be on various committees and to perform assigned duties outside of the classroom (e.g., parking lot duty, district committees, school committees, and weekly staff meetings). As Leah states, time was "rather limited for the amount of organization that has to happen. On top of planning, we also have to do other things that our principal requires." In regard to recognition, members indicated that the team was given verbal acknowledgment for their efforts by the principal and by some of the parents, and were seen by other teams in the school to be a "functioning" team. However, training for work on teams was viewed as a shortcoming, partly attributed to budget constraints. Leah felt the team could benefit from district training about students with special needs, such as autism. Jen too saw the need for training, commenting:

> As far as training that helps us work as a functioning, collaborative team with a focus on student instruction, it has been very few and far between. [It] is kind of a hit-or-miss drive-by [district] staff development [without much] follow-up or progress monitoring.

Jen also believes there could be a stronger school-wide effort to strengthen the functioning and dynamics of teacher teams.

> The principal is an advocate of [PLCs], and likes to consider us one. . . . But I don't think teams come together with the whole school and talk about student instruction with the detail that is supposed to happen for a [PLC].

She also states that there was variation in team effectiveness across the school:

> I haven't witnessed a lot of team building exercises going on. I don't think everyone brings up the issues of a dysfunctional team to the management. I think lots of teams just continue functioning in a poor environment and don't try to seek out help.

Design Features: Manzanita School's Team B, 5–6

Themes in Team B related to design features included focused tasks (e.g., aligning content with standards), experience as collaborators and a good mix of personalities, creativity, flexibility, and norms for handling conflict. With regard to tasks, Team B spent the majority of its time developing curriculum, planning units of study and coordinating different groups of students across a variety of subject areas. When asked about the expertise needed to carry out the group's work (team composition), members noted that they drew on their considerable experience as individuals and collaborators to ensure that elementary school fifth and sixth grade content standards were met and that all students achieved at the highest possible level.

The team experience resulted in a natural and smooth way of operating, described by Steve as "synergy." Both he and Dan mentioned the significance of the "camaraderie" of the group. Dan emphasizes the ease with which they worked together: "Certain roles get assumed over the years, so naturally our own personalities have drive toward certain things and that's why it's a good mix. We don't necessarily have to contrive [roles]; we've figured [them] out over time." Steve comments on the sense of momentum that facilitated the accomplishment of goals within the team:

> You get that synergy going and you get ideas. You have an idea and bounce it off someone else. [Then] they have an idea and it kind of grows and builds. You get an energy going, an enthusiasm amongst the team that helps you accomplish whatever goal you have.

When team members were asked what skills they felt they brought to the teamwork process, they emphasized flexibility, creativity, and willingness to accept each other's ideas. Dan remarks, "The creative side is really important. You're given a static curriculum but you have to make it come alive in a way that the students will be more motivated." Lucy states, "I can usually see some creative side to the picture. I'm always looking for that angle. I can look at the scope of something and synthesize it, see how we're going to approach it." Steve explains that "flexibility" was key, characterizing it as "not having a real set way of doing things, being open to new ideas, [and] a willingness to not always have it the way you want it to go." Without flexibility, he opines, "you're probably not going to be able to work together."

Further, interviewees described the level of cooperation within the group as "on the highest level." Yet when asked about group norms, some indicated they had not adopted any formal method of apportioning roles or responsibilities, nor any leadership positions. When organizing groups of students by subject or rotation, the team divided up teaching responsibilities, such as planning a science or social studies unit. Otherwise the team employed a more informal approach to the division of labor. Steve explains it in this manner:

We don't have individual responsibilities to a great degree, no. I would say, it's more just coming together usually, and asking, "How can we accomplish this? How can we meet the needs of this group of students? How can we put on this event?" . . . It's not like you have assigned roles—you're going to take care of this and I'm going to take care of that. We're just going to work on it together and accomplish it together. That's the norm in my experience.

When asked about the appropriateness of group performance strategies, team members emphasized that they dealt with conflicts that arose without difficulty. As Lucy states: "We have little blips here and there, philosophical things or maybe a discipline issue that's a tiny flare up and it's gone. [Conflict] never becomes an issue." Dan says that he "can't remember a time when we've argued about something." Yet members recalled past difficulties in other teacher teams to which they had belonged, which they attributed to "miscommunication." Steve recalls:

There have been a few instances [in other teams] I can think of through the years. Usually it puts a strain on the collaborative effort. It kind of shuts [us] down for a while until the parties have gotten over it and are ready to move on, back to meeting the needs of the kids.

Healthy Interpersonal Processes: Ponderosa School's Team C, K

Themes in Team C concerning healthy interpersonal processes included a high degree of comfort of members working together, sharing of ideas, some member dominance, general helpfulness, fair division of responsibilities, and even friendship. When asked about interpersonal behaviors within the team, Team C members agreed that they were "on the same page" with many aspects of their work. Further, there was a high degree of comfort when it came to sharing teaching knowledge and strategies, and in developing new ideas and approaches. As Patty says, "I think everyone is definitely very open about sharing anything they have, not just work but their strategies." Lynne highlights the central role of personality in the team process:

Having worked in a number of grade level teams, personality is a huge factor. You can get a lot done with people you see eye-to-eye with and of like mind. It really is helpful to have a team that is efficient and works well.

One member was identified as being "verbose" at team meetings. She recognized that she did most of the talking at meetings but stated: "I don't know if that necessarily translates to power or influence." Patty felt that this did not derail the process:

> There might be people who tend to maybe talk more than other people, but overall there's not somebody who is really strong and opinionated and wants to take over, or someone who doesn't want to say anything. I think we all play our part.

Another team member, Lynne, illustrated the balance of the team as follows:

> One person is extremely organized; she is very linear and good at planning ahead. Two of us are quite good at a more creative approach. One other person is willing to do just about anything. There are a lot of different personalities on this team. I think we bring strengths as far as our own personal teaching style and [willingness] to share [strengths] without being threatening.

Overall, the team benefited from very positive interpersonal processes characterized by helpfulness and a fair division of roles and responsibilities: "We all tend to work really well together; nobody feels like they're doing more or less" (Patty). According to Kara, this sentiment also appears to be shared by the principal, who "thinks that our team works really well together, and is always talking about how she wants to keep the team intact." Patty suggests that working well together stemmed partly from members being able to relate well both as friends and as colleagues:

> It's just because we are so close. Part of it's just the proximity [of space], we have [a shared] door right there. I mean it's not all about work. I'll go in there and talk to Lynne about whatever. That's the good thing too; we do stuff occasionally on a personal level. We talk work but then we are also just close in general.

Work Group Effectiveness: Ponderosa School's Team D, 5–6

Themes characterizing Team D's work group effectiveness included: making decisions quickly, output that met principal expectations, improved student writing, enhancement of student learning and discipline, teacher effectiveness, enhanced sense of commitment, and solidified collegiality.

Team D considered itself effective in achieving its goals, with each member expressing that the team made decisions and developed strategies quickly. This was seen as important because it prevented meetings and debates from going on too long. Cindy says, "I'm a fast, efficient person, and they are in the same mindset. I want to cut to the chase and get to it." Stacey states, "We've accomplished the things we've needed to accomplish." Bev also suggests that decision making was a fast process, and indicated the reason for this:

> It takes very little time. Most of the time we agree. There have been a few things where three people feel one way and one feels another, or two and two, but when everybody expresses their opinions and has some evidence to back it up then everyone sees eye to eye. We've never had any friction. Never.

Examples given by team members to demonstrate accomplishing targets centered on the use of rubrics and products derived from the use of the school's writing program. "I think that the rubrics [for student writing] we've put out, or discussion notes, anything that we're expected to turn in to the principal, I feel has been as complete as she's required" (Cindy). Stacey expresses a similar viewpoint, suggesting that the time invested in developing writing rubrics had paid dividends:

> Just looking at some of the finished products we had talked about, in [student] writing, we spent a lot of time on that. And seeing what the students were able to accomplish, based on some of the planning that we'd done, being able to look at that with the rubrics.

Team members felt in general that working together had enhanced student learning, discipline, and their own effectiveness as teachers. Improvements in these areas derived from the ability to share and evaluate current practices as a group, share ideas, and analyze strengths and weaknesses. All members stated that they would continue working as a part of a teacher team. Bev states, "I think [teaming is] vital. I know that I am a better teacher by having a team because the others help me. I feel strongly that multiple heads are better than one." Stacey states, "Yes, because we're all so busy with our teaching that [teaming] forces us to sit down as a group, to brainstorm. A lot gets accomplished."

DISCUSSION AND CONCLUSIONS

We began this chapter with three key questions: (1) How do school leaders create an organizational context for grade level teams? (2) How do teachers perceive the quality of their training and support in their efforts to be collaborative? (3) What are some of the positive outcomes of these school structures? Collaboration in the teams and schools we studied was far from a straightforward process, somewhat different from the more formalized description of teams provided in the method section. By contrast, teaming could best be understood as a continuous process that is never finished. In light of this complexity, Hackman and Oldham (1980) de-emphasized straightforward cause-effect relations in their model, choosing instead to emphasize how one can *create conditions* that will support high team effectiveness. They stated:

> By creating a motivating group task, a well-composed group, and group norms favoring open discussion of performance strategies, we believe, the *chances* are increased that group members will invest themselves in their work and perform it relatively well. Moreover, we expect that under such conditions group members will find the group experience more satisfying than frustrating and that group processes will be relatively healthy and constructive. (p. 189)

Although our study is only of two schools, there are lessons that can be learned that may apply more broadly.

How Do School Leaders Create an Organizational Context for Grade Level Teams?

Just as students need preparation to engage in group work, so do teachers also need preparation and support to work as a team in a school. This study provided a snapshot of what may need to be built into the process of collaboration and the role principals play in supporting that collaboration.

Hackman and Oldham (1980) suggested that for work group design to have a lasting effect, managers must engage in enhanced supervisory practices that support employees. The present study suggested that the two elementary school principals enhanced the success of teaming along the lines of Hackman and Oldham's (1980) recommendations. This finding also appeared consistent with related literature on principal-teacher relationships (Fullan, 2007; Smylie, 1992; Smylie, Conley, & Marks, 2002).

In this study, teachers' perceptions were that the principals worked diligently to create a collaborative culture among the teaching staff and to enhance what interviewees described as the concept of a PLC. Notably, this level of support could be understood as influencing all three areas of Hackman and Oldham's (1980) requisites for successful group work: a supportive organizational context, design features, and healthy interpersonal relationships. For example, principals' encouragement of members working together productively, "carving out weekly planning time," and monitoring student progress may enhance team self-direction and assumption of significant tasks.

However, what appear to be positive changes can come with unintended consequences. In Team A, the Thursday planning time provided by the district was critical for the team's work; however, time constraints were also an issue. A lack of time available to meet was furthered by a need to be on various committees and to perform assigned duties outside of the classroom. Time, according to one interviewee, was "rather limited for the amount of organization that has to happen. On top of planning we also have to do other things that our principal requires." Principal attentiveness to time constraints, perhaps through continual monitoring of available time—and the balance of teamwork with other duties—would appear critical in supporting the team's success in accomplishing its goals (Crow & Pounder, 2000).

Principals may also create a supportive organizational context by providing formal and informal recognition to teams for their efforts. In Team D, for example, members acknowledged that they received such recognition from the principal. In this team (although not elaborated in our case description), both Stacey and Bev point out that the principal had begun to visit classrooms more frequently, and planned to display in the school's weekly bulletin examples of good practice that she had observed. Stacey states, "I feel like our principal's very supportive of what we do and compliments us frequently. When she walks through our classrooms and sees what we're implementing, she'll just jot down a note or catch us in passing."

How Do Teachers Perceive the Quality of Their Training and Support in Their Efforts to Be Collaborative?

Team D indicated that significant training was provided at the district level in the form of in-service support. As Cindy states, "I went to an in-service this summer over the writing project that is part of our school." There have also been two district training sessions held at the school on the subject of differentiated instruction that supported the work of this team. Yet in Team A, members indicated a need for more training concerning the purposes and dynamics of teaming as a strategy for improvement.

Although the team viewed itself as high performing and effective, members cast themselves as a model team surrounded, at times, by some dysfunction among other teams in the school. It may be that teaming, as suggested by Hargreaves and Macmillan (1995), introduces issues related to team insularity that then lead to communication problems between a team and others at the same school (see also Mayrowetz et al., 2007, p. 86).

Furthermore, teachers in our study stressed skills involved in teamwork that were often built over a long time. As Collinson and Cook (2007) in their book *Organizational Learning* suggested, leaders must attend to human relations, facilitating a social system in which human beings are a linchpin to "interact to construct their learning and learn from each other" (p. 62). "Attending to human relations" (p. 62) involves three core assumptions:

1. Learning depends on interpersonal knowledge (e.g., communication skills, respect and compassion, conflict management).
2. These skills contribute to a supportive environment for organizational learning.
3. Collaboration is vital to collective learning, inquiry, and dissemination of knowledge.

Building such a social system in a school needs consistent nurturing and refinement over time. Preparation for being a supportive team member does not stop at training but must be ongoing and continuous. In Team B, members spoke of team roles being "assumed over the years" and having "figured out roles over time." Providing attention to such issues appears likely to promote and accelerate the process of team building and the dissemination of organizational learning. In addition, this observation raises an interesting question about high turnover schools; might such schools with many new teachers define formal roles initially rather than let them emerge more informally?

What Are Some Positive Outcomes of These School Structures?

When teams in this study worked well together, they produced tangible outcomes that they believed met or exceeded standards within the school. In concert with Hackman and Oldham's (1980) model, however, we found that team members' notions of effectiveness went beyond the idea of producing a concrete product. Although Team D members could identify the improvement of student writing rubrics as a result of the groups' work together, they also spoke of less tangible outcomes such as team commitment, satisfaction, and building collegiality. Teachers felt more effective in their teaching and believed that they had grown as professionals. Among the comments that illustrated these notions were:

- "Having reliable people who are supportive motivates me to spread my wings and do a lot more things on this campus for the students than I would if I was working alone."—Dan
- "I wouldn't ever really prefer to work alone. I really like the idea of being able to be a team, the opportunity to share and exchange. It's the only way to work. I can't see myself as 'the island' all alone. I just would not thrive on that kind of insular kind of environment. It would be very stagnant for me."—Lucy
- "I've been at schools before where you don't work as closely. Having a team, . . . you feel a sense of somebody keeping you on track and basically helping you with all the work you need to get through. It's a nice feeling knowing that you're part of something and that you're working towards something and everybody's collaborating [and you're getting great results]."—Patty

These perspectives suggest that the value of teaming for participants in the two schools is in the regular interaction that generates discussions around teaching and learning and encourages supportive practices. Teaming, then, engenders a sense of collective responsibility, which has been shown to have a positive relationship with teacher learning and efficacy (Conley, Fauske, & Pounder, 2004; Mayrowetz et al., 2007; Pounder, 1999), as well as with gains in student engagement and achievement (Louis, Marks, & Kruse, 1996). As Shiu and Chrispeels (2004) discovered, elementary teams are powerful sites for *in-situ* learning and professional development. The transformative power of teacher teaming is evidenced in the responses of the teachers in this study, and is present in related literature on teaming (Garcia, 2008).

In this study, elementary teachers appear to have a natural disposition for collaboration. The way in which this proclivity can be harnessed can be facilitated by the context and design variables negotiated and implemented by school administrators. The yield of these teams with respect to student learning and other outcomes appears strongly related to the development of the teams and their ability to engage in critical evaluation and analysis of current practices.

CONCLUDING REMARKS

A final note can be made about elementary teams in particular. Although as noted in this volume (Bair, chapter 2, this volume; Cooper & Brown, chapter 1, this volume), the norm has been for teachers to often work independently, this study joins a growing literature base that mirrors results of studies of more established (e.g., middle schools) teaming initiatives (Crow & Pounder, 2000). Teacher teaming along with principal involvement appears to yield tangible and intangible results, thereby benefitting student learning and teacher professionalism.

The ease of collaboration found in the teacher teams in this study may be a feature common to elementary schools, which are smaller than secondary schools and less organizationally complex. In addition to differences in structural features, elementary schools also have significant cultural and functional differences. Elementary schools may be seen as a more nurturing environment, where teachers have parent-like relationships with students (Cooper & Brown, chapter 1, this volume). Students are almost always in one room together, and usually have fewer teachers, as opposed to high schools, where there are "multiple sites of community" (Louis et al., 1996, p. 765), and where subject matter affiliation may lead to segmentation between teachers. Elementary schools, then, might be viewed by practitioners as having inherently advantageous structural and cultural conditions that lead to advanced levels of collaboration and community building. Attempting to replicate these conditions is a consideration for secondary school administrators and their district partners, and several have been tried.

Meanwhile, some strategies that might be considered by systems seeking to further enhance elementary school teaming at grade level include the following:

- Administrators should consider that work enhancement occurs as a consequence of teaming; however, there is sufficient literature to illustrate that the team process can detract from organizational goals (Zeichner, 1991). Principals, therefore, should consult with their teaching staff before taking steps to implement a teaming strategy.
- Not only should teachers feel empowered by their principals and district administrators, they should also be provided with sufficient resources, including time, training, and recognition and rewards to be able to be their most effective.
- As teachers pursue collaborative endeavors, there is a need for principals to be involved in norm setting, to support teamwork, and to help direct it toward positive outcomes. The role of the principal "strongly influences the likelihood of change" (Fullan, 2007, p. 95).
- Principals also play a key role with regard to recognition and rewards, although this tends to be an area of organizational support that is less developed. Principals should consider the value of intrinsic rewards, and act to implement visible recognition for those who perform in teams. Supports for release time (e.g., substitutes) could be accomplished at the district level and in union-negotiated agreements.
- Principals should also attend to the continuity and length of experience of team members. Principals and the organization will likely benefit from keeping teams intact for as long as possible, and from maintaining consistency in goals and support structures.

- Principals have a critical role to play in fostering a greater understanding of the teaming process; however, they should be careful to avoid a top-down approach to teaming.

NOTES

1. The authors thank Justin Smith and Susan Zink for their comments on earlier drafts of this chapter.
2. Two other mechanisms in professional-related reform included teacher leadership and action research (Conley & Muncey, 1999).
3. Enomoto and Conley (2012) similarly utilized different case studies to each illustrate a single model component of routinized action in organizations.

REFERENCES

California Department of Education (2010). *Data Quest*. Retrieved January 2, 2010, from http://data1.cde.ca.gov/dataquest/

Collinson, V., & Cook, T. F. (2007). *Organizational learning: Improving learning, teaching, and leading in school systems*. Thousand Oaks, CA: Sage.

Conley, S., Fauske, J., & Pounder, D. G. (2004). Teacher work group effectiveness. *Educational Administration Quarterly, 40*(5), 663–703.

Conley, S., & Muncey, D. E. (1999). Teachers talk about teaming and leadership in their work. *Theory into Practice, 38*(1), 46–55.

Crow, G. M., & Pounder, D. G. (2000). Interdisciplinary teacher teams: Context, design, and process. *Educational Administration Quarterly, 36*(2), 216–54.

Enomoto, E., & Conley, S. (2012). *Accreditation as routinized action*. Paper presented at the annual conference of the University Council on Educational Administration, Denver, CO.

Fullan, M. (2007). *The new meaning of educational change*. New York: Teachers College Press.

Garcia, C. D. (2008). *The relationship of team learning and teacher learning through collaboration and their effects on teacher behaviors*. Santa Barbara: Unpublished doctoral dissertation, College of Education, University of California, Santa Barbara.

Hackman, J. R., & Oldham, G. R. (1980). *Work redesign*. Reading, MA: Addison Wesley.

Hargreaves, A., & Macmillan, R. (1995). The balkanization of secondary school teaching. In L. S. Siskin & J. W. Little (Eds.), *The subjects in question: Departmental organization and the high school* (pp. 141–71). New York: Teachers College Press.

Kurstedt, R. L. (2008). *A study of fifth-grade teachers' grade-level meetings: The complexities of teachers' group work.* New York: Unpublished doctoral dissertation, College of Education, Fordham University.

Louis, K. S., Marks, H. M., & Kruse, S. (1996). Teachers' professional community in restructuring schools. *American Educational Research Journal, 33*(4), 757–98.

Mayrowetz, D., Murphy, J., Louis, K. S., & Smylie, M. A. (2007). Distributed leadership as work redesign: Retrofitting the job characteristics model. *Leadership and Policy in Schools, 6,* 69–101.

Pounder, D. G. (1998). Teacher teams: Redesigning teachers' work for collaboration. In D. G. Pounder (Ed.), *Restructuring schools for collaboration: Promises and pitfalls* (pp. 65–88). Albany, NY: SUNY Press.

Pounder, D. G. (1999). Teacher teams: Exploring job characteristics and work-related outcomes of work group enhancement. *Educational Administration Quarterly, 35*(3), 317–48.

Scribner, J. P., Sawyer, R. K., Watson, S. T., & Myers, V. L. (2007). Teacher teams and distributed leadership: A study of group discourse and collaboration. *Educational Administration Quarterly, 43*(1), 67–100.

Senge, P. (1990). *The fifth discipline: The art and practice of the learning organization.* Garden City, NY: Doubleday.

Shiu, S., & Chrispeels, J. H. (2004). An analysis of the habitual routines and effectiveness of collaborative teacher grade level teams in an elementary school. *Journal for Effective Schools, 3*(2), 81–94.

Smylie, M. A. (1992). Teachers' reports of their interactions with teacher leaders concerning classroom instruction. *The Elementary School Journal, 19*(1), 85–98.

Smylie, M. A., Conley, S., & Marks, H. M. (2002). Exploring new approaches to teacher leadership for school improvement. In J. Murphy (Ed.), *The educational leadership challenge: Redefining leadership for the 21st century* (One hundred and first yearbook of the National Society for the Study of Education, Part 1, pp. 162–88). Chicago: National Society for the Study of Education.

Spillane, J. P., Halverson, R., & Diamond, J. B. (2001). Investigating school leadership practice: A distributed leadership perspective. *Educational Researcher, 30*(3), 23–28.

Zeichner, K. M. (1991). Contradictions and tensions in the professionalization of teaching and the democratization of schools. *Teachers College Record, 92*(3), 363–79.

Chapter Seven

Collaboration in Middle School Departments

A Work Group Effectiveness Perspective

Sharon Conley and Frank C. Guerrero

In this chapter, we begin with Hackman and Oldham's (1980) work group effectiveness model but shift the focus from elementary teams (chapter 6) to middle school departments.[1] This chapter uses survey data from department team members in five California middle schools to analyze individual team members' perceptions of their work in departments. We specifically examine the design of the group work, their organizational context, and the team's task and interpersonal processes. Further, we explore which of these features are related to members' perceptions of department outcomes such as improvements in teaching and learning and commitment to the team. Indeed, learning about members' perceptions might provide a further basis for designing middle school departments to enhance positive outcomes for school personnel and students.

WORK GROUP ENHANCEMENT

As noted throughout this volume, one recommendation called for as part of reform and restructuring efforts is the enhancement of teacher collaboration. This suggestion has perhaps been a renewed goal in the context of the accountability movement, in which public education is defending itself from state takeover, probation, reconstitution, and/or loss of accreditation (Mintrop, 2003). To reinvigorate underperforming schools, teacher collaboration has been considered as a means of school improvement. One means of facilitating collaboration has been *work group enhancement* (Conley, Fauske, & Pounder, 2004; Crow & Pounder, 2000; Pounder, 1998, 1999; Smylie, Conley, & Marks, 2002). *"Work groups* [emphasis added] or teacher teams are designed to increase members' responsibility for the group's performance and outcomes, creating work interdependence and opportunities for self management" (Pounder, 1998, p. 65). An enhancement strategy focused on work group design emphasizes members employing interpersonal and group decision-making skills and exerting enhanced control over a broad array of work-related issues (Crow & Pounder, 2000; Pounder, 1998).

Perhaps the clearest example of a work group enhancement strategy is the creation of interdisciplinary teams in middle schools that organize work around students rather than work in traditional departments. Pounder and colleagues have carried out a series of studies that have applied Hackman and Oldham's model of job design (chapter 6) in analyzing these collaborative structures (see Conley et al., 2004; Crow & Pounder, 2000; Pounder, 1998, 1999).

However, work group enhancement strategies could also make use of the subject department grouping. This focus on departmental work groups may be of interest for three reasons. First, departments appear to be fundamental work units in secondary schools (middle and high schools) (Keedy & Robbins, 1993; Mayrowetz, Murphy, Louis, & Smylie, 2007). Therefore, they appear a logical starting point in assessing how to change the workplace culture from one of isolated teachers to teacher collegiality (Keedy & Robbins, 1993).

Second, for schools with administrations that have elected not to form interdisciplinary teams, strengthening departments is another way in which group work at the school site might be improved. Third, the leaders of these departments—department chairs—can be instrumental in channeling "content-specific goals, directions, and reforms [viable for] staff development" overall (Keedy & Robbins, 1993, p. 185). Moreover, teachers at a school may find their department leaders "accessible and credible because they possess subject-centered expertise and they teach [in adjacent classrooms] or down the hall" (p. 186).

However, as of 1993, Keedy and Robbins observed that although "the department is the logical focal point for . . . instructional improvement," collaborative work arrangements that have been facilitated by departments were "largely ignored by researchers" (p. 185). This chapter examines middle school teachers' perceptions of their departments in two California districts focused on enhancing department work efforts as a means of school improvement. Survey items were designed to capture not only the design features of these teams, but also their perceived organizational context (e.g., training and consultation) and their task and interpersonal processes (Hackman & Oldham, 1980). Thus, we used Hackman and Oldham's (1980) work group effectiveness model as a conceptual lens for examining teachers' perceptions of their departments.

FRAMEWORK: DEPARTMENTS AS WORK GROUPS

Hackman and Oldham's (1980) work group effectiveness model is perhaps the most widely applied in studies of work teams (Dewey & Conley, chapter 6, this volume). According to this model, departments would be considered work groups for three reasons. First, departments are *real groups*, or "intact social systems, complete with boundaries, interdependence among members, and differentiated member roles" (p. 4) (e.g., department chair, department members) (Hackman, 1990).

Second, departments have a *task* to perform, or an outcome for which members have collective responsibility, notably, the curriculum and the teaching of a subject area within a secondary school. Third, departments operate in an *organizational context*; that is, they "manage relations with other individuals or groups in the larger social system" (p. 4) such as other departments and the school administration (Hackman, 1990). For example, in a case study of professional community in an urban high school, among the forums promoting collaboration were cross-department course offerings including "a humanities course team-taught by the art teacher and a colleague from social studies" (King & Weiss, 1995, p. 92).

Notably, the subject of boundaries has recently been the focus of debate in some literature. Some scholars (McGregor, 2003) highlighted the *communities of practice* concept, whereby teaching practice is "created by members of the grouping through the making of *meaning* [emphasis added] together, which . . . brings into existence the community" (Wenger, 2000, as cited in McGregor, 2003, p. 114). In this context, "Departments are likely to intersect and overlap to varying degrees with communities of practice in different contexts, but they may not be the same" (McGregor, 2003, p. 118; see also Johnson, 1990; McLaughlin & Talbert, 1990). Communities of practice were likely to occur organically, including formal or informal communities of practice that draw teachers outside the boundary of a department or even a school (McGregor, 2003; see also Collinson, 2012). Indeed, this type of interaction has been seen most clearly in interdisciplinary teams where members are setting aside—or ignoring—department boundaries (Pounder, 1999).

However, a focus on the bounded department remains important because of the shared curriculum and content. In addition, department teams may potentially form more readily than communities of practice. For example, when new teachers enter the school, they become members of departments "imposed by formal organizational structures" (McGregor, 2003, p. 118; see also Johnson, 1990). Thus, because of the hierarchical structure, departments may be a more straightforward setting in which to examine groups. Similarly, departments appear more likely to include a broad membership focused on a subject area as opposed to that of a more specialized interdisciplinary group. A study of department groups, therefore, offers insight into a predominant area where teacher communities form and where the potential to generate sharing appears to be strong (Cook & Collinson, chapter 5, this volume).

WORK GROUP EFFECTIVENESS

Before identifying major aspects of team design and functioning believed to contribute to overall team effectiveness, it is necessary to specify what is meant by work group effectiveness. This discussion draws on chapter 6 as well as Conley et al.'s (2004) and Conley and Christensen's (2011) descriptions of Hackman and Oldham's (1980) work group effectiveness model. Work groups are effective, according to this model, if they produce outcomes that are both high in quantity and quality; that is, enough work is produced that is sufficiently worthwhile—or, put another way, if the "group's productive output meets the *standards* of quantity, quality, and timeliness of its product of the people who receive, review, and/or use that output" (Hackman, 1990, p. 6). In education, teaching and learning outcomes are expected to have the greatest effect on the work group's overall effectiveness or outcomes.

Additional aspects of work group effectiveness include the extent to which members are *committed* to their particular group and desire to *continue* participating on it, that is, "the degree to which the process of carrying out the work enhances the capability of members to work together interdependently in the future" (Hackman, 1990, p. 6). In this study, these aspects were incorporated in the outcomes of team cohesion, or the degree of affective attachment a team member has to the department, and team commitment, the extent to which a member wants to keep working with the department and help it reach its goals.

Thus, group effectiveness should be judged on the noted criteria and not assessed by mere output alone because results do not provide the clearest picture, or reveal the "whole story" (p. 6) of the group's effectiveness (Hackman, 1990). As Hackman and Oldham (1980) noted, a group could perform a specific task extremely well but would not be considered effective if the group burns itself out in the process. "The same thinking would apply if a group alienated or de-skilled its members in the course of carrying out its work" (Hackman, 1990, p. 6). Indeed, as a "high-involvement" (p. 159) strategy for improving human resource management, effective work group design shares a critical commonality with participation, job enrichment, and workplace democracy strategies: the intention of empowering members and giving work more significance, thereby contributing to commitment and satisfaction (Bolman & Deal, 2003).

Hackman and Oldham's (1980) model also identified four major contributors to work group effectiveness: design features, organizational context, task and interpersonal processes, and enabling conditions. First, initial or "set-up" *design features* of the group refer to the design of the group task. These teamwork features include a motivating structure for the group task (i.e., where the work to be done in the department requires cooperation and a high level of skill), task autonomy, and a mix of individuals with a full complement of knowledge and skill that can be expected to enhance team effectiveness.

Second, the *organizational context* includes rewards for good performance and available training and consultation. For example, in a business setting, a reward could be a team bonus; in an education setting, there might be special recognition of a department by the principal at a meeting. In addition, charting new territory in a team task (e.g., disaggregating and analyzing student data) might require new information, skills, or knowledge; the organization could meet this requirement by providing opportunities for training and consultation. For instance, in California, the assignment of a state-approved consultant to struggling schools (District Assistance and

Intervention Team [DAIT]) is an intervention that Hackman and Oldham (1980) would consider a source of training and consultation.

Third, *task and interpersonal processes* include coordinating team actions and fostering commitment to the team's work; knowledge sharing and contributions of all department members; and implementing, as well as inventing, performance strategies in advance of accomplishing the task. One can envision that advanced coordination, for example, could help reduce or eliminate unanticipated problems when the parties concerned (e.g., math department members) have had the opportunity to provide input and identify possible pitfalls (e.g., in proposing master scheduling for the subject area to administration).

And finally, some related but conceptually distinct team characteristics, according to Hackman and Oldham (1980), are *enabling conditions* or intermediate criteria of work group effectiveness. Viewed as most closely related to how well a team ultimately accomplishes its task, enabling conditions can be expected to affect work group effectiveness directly (Hackman, 1990). For the present study, the enabling condition was knowledge/ skills applied, or the amount of knowledge and skill group members brought to bear on the work of the team.

SURVEY METHOD

A descriptive and correlational study was designed to describe select work group effectiveness variables and their interrelationships. In particular, we used a survey method to explore the relationship between the independent variables (design features, organizational support, task and interpersonal processes, and enabling condition) and the dependent variables (team commitment, standards met, etc.) based on Hackman and Oldham's (1980) work group effectiveness model. The instrument was examined using the following fourteen variables:

Design Features

- Motivating structure of the task
- Task autonomy
- Mix of expertise

Organizational Support

- Rewards/recognition
- Training

Task and Interpersonal Processes

- Coordinating efforts
- Weighting/balancing
- Implementing strategies
- Inventing strategies

Enabling Condition

- Knowledge/skills applied

Work Group Effectiveness

- Teaching and learning
- Team commitment
- Team cohesion
- Standards met

The scale items measuring each of these variables are in Appendix 7.1.

Instrumentation

We adapted Conley et al.'s (2004) instrument used in their study of interdisciplinary teams to a middle school department context. The survey reported in the 2004 study was developed utilizing findings from Crow and Pounder (2000), Pounder (1999), and specific variable scales and survey items used, respectively, by Hackman and Oldham (1980) and Vinokur-Kaplan (1995) in their related studies of work groups in other organizational contexts. In the current study, in cooperation with three middle school teachers who were not part of the current study's schools, several items from the instrument were altered to fit more closely the circumstances of middle school departments.

Most items were measured on a six-point scale ranging from one, *very inaccurate*, to six, *very accurate*. Teachers responded to items tapping several of the research constructs (i.e., design features, organizational context, task and interpersonal processes, enabling condition, and work group effectiveness). Teachers also reported information about the department in which they participated most often, including estimating the percentages of time they spent on particular activities, how long department members had been working together, and whether aspects of the group's work together had changed. In addition, teachers were encouraged to write on the survey itself any additional comments and/or context they felt useful or important. While not an expansive source of survey data, these comments provided an opportunity to address the limitations of survey methods by providing greater freedom of expression to respondents.

A reliability analysis (Cronbach's alpha estimates) revealed that twelve of the fourteen study variables had alpha coefficients of 0.67 or higher, suggesting acceptable reliability; however, for one variable (team cohesion), the Cronbach's alpha was lower (0.51). A final variable, implementing strategies, had a reliability of 0.44; therefore, we chose to use one item, "I am comfortable sharing my ideas on teaching strategies with my work group/department" instead of a scale for that variable.

Sample and Data Collection

Five middle schools in southern coastal California were selected for participation in this study. The schools were located in two adjacent urban districts chosen on the basis of proximity to the research team's location and prior district contact. The districts served approximately 25,000 students in two neighboring moderately sized cities. Demographics within the two districts were seen as diverse, with 54 percent to 81 percent of students eligible for free or reduced-price student lunches and 57 percent to 89 percent minority students. In addition, both districts employed a teacher collaboration focus for their school improvement efforts. One district encouraged a collaborative focus in each school's "Single Plan for Student Achievement." One school, for example, emphasized "teacher collaboration [to] establish policies, discuss school operations, and identify staff development and delivery options" (system documentation). The second district emphasized collaboration in school board policy statements directing schools to "provide resources for collaboration, planning, and professional development for all staff" (system documentation).

Initially, district administrators (the superintendent or assistant superintendent) were contacted by telephone or e-mail for permission to participate in the study and to make suggestions of middle school principals who could be contacted. Five middle school principals were nominated by district administrators and agreed to participate: three in one district (District A) and two in the other (District B). Two middle schools in District A and one middle school in District B were designated by the state as in program improvement (PI) status for not meeting adequate yearly progress (AYP). The other two schools (one from each district) did not receive Title I funds and were not formally designated as in PI status but were nonetheless struggling to meet school improvement goals (superintendent communication).[2]

Once permissions from the principals were acquired, the survey and a letter explaining the study and requesting participation were distributed to teachers from the five schools in their mailboxes or in faculty meetings, depending on principal preference.

One hundred and twenty teachers returned the survey, approximately 60 percent of the original sample. Response rates for the schools ranged from a low of 18 percent to a high of 78 percent. Low response rates in two of the schools may have been due to data collection very late in the school year and the involvement of many teachers in preparing eighth grade students for graduation. Further, the method of depositing the surveys in mailboxes may have also contributed to lower response rates.

Three-quarters (75 percent, or eighty-four) of the respondents were female and one quarter (25 percent, or twenty-eight) were male (eight teachers did not respond to the question about gender). The sample was also fairly experienced, with 59 percent having ten or more years of service in their current district. Teachers were asked to designate the departments in which they participated, as well as the *one* subject area department that they were involved in most regularly (i.e., language arts, math, social science, science, physical education, electives). Forty-six percent of the respondents reported that they were in departments with five or fewer members, with the remainder (54 percent) indicating that departments had over five members.

The majority of respondents (56.7 percent) indicated that their department ments had been working together with largely the same members for over five years. The second largest category (18.3 percent) reported working with the same members for two to three years. In addition, one-half of respondents reported that most members of their department shared a common preparation or consultation period. Further, teachers reported, on average, spending about one-quarter of their time planning curriculum (content, curriculum standards, alignment) and instruction (27 percent), as well as discussing assessment (rubrics, grading, results) and academic goal setting (27 percent).

They spent about one-fifth of their time coordinating/organizing team management issues (agenda setting, scheduling, division of responsibilities) (21 percent) and discussing learning needs/problems of individual students (19 percent). However, because they indicated that about one-quarter of their time was spent on "other activities" not accounted for by the above response categories (26 percent), the survey did not appear to capture fully the variety of areas in which department members were engaged.

Finally, forty-six teachers responded to an open-ended question asking them about the rationale they were provided for having department members collaborate. Responses were grouped around four concepts:

1. a principal requirement or administrative mandate (e.g., "the principal's request," "principal instructions," "mandated communication")
2. benefits to students, teaching, and learning (e.g., "helps kids," "better teaching," "best practices to support student learning")
3. analysis of student data (e.g., "data analysis," "analysis of student benchmarks," "[analyze] school improvement data," "data analysis meetings")
4. faculty collaboration and sharing (e.g., "informal meetings to discuss strategies and behaviors," "share successes and challenges," "[develop] common themes," "collaborate around test scores," and "collaborate on the best ways to support students" "meet re: department concerns")

Limitations

This study was limited to middle school teachers employed in two California districts. The data in this study were primarily restricted to self-report survey data. Although two interviews were conducted with teachers as part of the study, there was no observational data of the work of department teams.

It was beyond the scope of this study to collect data on how principal and department heads viewed the dynamics of departments, as well as to observe the work of departments. Despite these limitations, the data provide insight into middle school teachers' perceptions of the structure of their department, their organizational context, the interpersonal processes of the teams, and department outcomes.

RESULTS

Design Features

The California middle school teacher respondents in this study rated their departments as having moderate levels of the design features (see Table 7.1). Put another way, they indicated, on average, that it was between "slightly" (four) and "mostly accurate" (five) that the work of the department required cooperation, required members to use high-level skills, and was designed in such a way that there were opportunities to contribute to students' educational experience or learning (*motivating structure of the task*). Similarly, teacher ratings were between "slightly" and "mostly accurate" that the department had discretion in structuring and monitoring its work and provided opportunities for the use of professional autonomy or discretion (*task autonomy*). In addition, teacher ratings indicated that "most" (close to five) people in their department had strong instructional, interpersonal, student assessment, and classroom management skills (*mix of expertise*).

Regarding open-ended responses, on one item about the motivating structure of the task ("cooperation needed to do the work"), a language arts department teacher characterized this aspect as changing "a great deal" in the recent past. He elaborates: "I have known these people for four years and have seen an enormous positive change [in group cooperation]." However, one social studies teacher characterizes group cooperation in his department as having not changed: "None; if anything, it has shown who in the department is doing their job and who isn't."

Table 7.1. Mean Scores for Key Variables for the Sample of Middle School
Teachers (*N* = 120)

Variables	Mean	SD
INDEPENDENT VARIABLES		
DESIGN FEATURES		
1. Motivational Structure of the Task	4.36	.87
2. Task Autonomy	4.69	.96
3. Mix of Expertise	4.91	1.13
ORGANIZATIONAL SUPPORT		
1. Rewards/Recognition	1.85	.92
2. Training	3.22	.96
TASK AND INTERPERSONAL PROCESSES		
1. Coordinating Efforts*	2.66	1.22
2. Weighting/Balancing	3.58	1.26
3. Implementing Strategies	4.96	1.11
4. Inventing Strategies	4.38	1.12
ENABLING CONDITION		
1. Knowledge & Skills Applied	3.87	1.28
DEPENDENT VARIABLES		
WORK GROUP EFFECTIVENESS		
1. Teaching & Learning	4.37	.99
2. Team Commitment	5.10	.98
3. Team Cohesion*	1.89	1.13
4. Standards Met	5.04	1.01

*Low values are associated with high levels of this variable.

Organizational Context

Teachers rated their organizational context somewhat differently depending on whether questions were about rewards/recognition as opposed to training and technical assistance. Teachers rated receiving formal and informal *recognition and rewards*, on average, as between "never/almost never" (one) and "infrequently" (two). They rated *training* and assistance, by contrast, as between "sometimes" (three) and "often" (four) (see Table 7.1).

Indeed, the organizational context of the departments garnered the most open-ended comments on the survey, mostly about training and other forms of assistance provided by the organization. Some comments noted the importance of assistance in the area of computer technology. According to a math/science teacher, for example, "We were provided substitutes to work at the district [level] on exploring technology to be used in the classroom. We [also] had technology training during the summer."

A social studies teacher attributed improvements in the area of support and training to "everything [having to do with] support [in the area of] technology." Correspondingly, a language arts teacher states that, "Extensive support is available regarding new (or, at least 'new' to me) computer technologies upon request. It is available from peers, technology support staff, . . . and from the district offices."

Still other teachers pointed to improvements in the organizational context as focused on upgrades in the areas of the curriculum, learning, and assessment. A science teacher department head, for example, notes,

> We now have pacing calendars [delineating skills related to a particular curriculum to be acquired over a particular period of time] in place for seventh and eighth grades. We now have a set of common assessments [defined goals relating to learning and assessment] and a working data management system to review the results of these assessments.

Another math teacher echoes the importance of the "pacing calendar" and "six common assessments," in combination with the frequent ("two to three times per month") department meetings. Further, a math/science teacher states, "We go to conferences such as the California Math Council in Palm Springs." And, according to a (language arts) teacher, training on both "data collection and assessment" and on the "*inside* [internal to the department] curriculum" had improved the available training and support. Finally, another science teacher offers that, "Training for *new* curriculum has been good."

A department head in the electives area (art teacher) provided different examples of improvement on "outside advice and assistance the department seeks and receives." She attributes progress to "a professional learning community [focused] department," as well as "department heads who also belong to the leadership team, [thereby] fostering better communication." Another teacher states, "Staff members meet during collaboration time to discuss any support they need." An additional teacher, however, was critical of help provided by a (former) department head, stating: "Our department chair was re-assigned [recently] providing us with a more organized department chair who facilitates our meetings more appropriately."

Finally, three teachers responded to questions about organizational context by downplaying this factor in the context of other aspects. A science teacher ranked organizational context factors as having "changed little" since his school was declared as being in PI status, attributing lack of progress to a "top [down] system of management." A social studies teacher pointed out that providing recognition to the department was "not a top priority in the school." She notes that "there is very little support showing any positive recognition of the department and the activities we have organized for the school!" Taking a different tack, a math teacher downplayed the importance of organizational context factors and organizational rewards by emphasizing instead the "intrinsic motivation of the teachers to want what is best for their students and community."

Task and Interpersonal Processes

Teachers' perceptions were moderate, on average, concerning the task and interpersonal processes characterizing their departments. Perceptions were between two ("disagree") and three ("slightly disagree") on average that there was difficulty *coordinating their efforts* with other department members. Furthermore, teachers rated between three ("slightly disagree") and four ("slightly agree") that their efforts and responsibilities were evenly distributed in the department (*weighting/balancing*). In addition, teachers rated close to five ("agree") that they were comfortable sharing ideas on teaching strategies with their department (*implementing strategies*). Finally, they rated between four ("slightly agree") and five ("agree") on average, department creativity and innovation in developing new ways to do its work, including through the innovative use of technology (*inventing strategies*) (see Table 7.1).

As to the open-ended questions, one teacher emphasized the aspect of interpersonal processes dealing with "coordinating work with other department members." He notes that he had never seen people in the department "fail to reach consensus" but if they did, they "would immediately seek outside assistance rather than turn on each other in any way." This same teacher focuses on the "creative use of technology" to accomplish the department's work, stating that these efforts were "still in the process of 'becoming,' but that they were definitely coming."

Intermediate Effectiveness

Teachers' perceptions appeared moderate, on average, concerning the intermediate effectiveness criterion of knowledge and skills applied to the work. Teachers rated between three ("some") and four ("many") members of the department applying knowledge and skills to the group's tasks by, for instance, sharing instructional methods and engaging in group problem-solving processes, as shown in Table 7.1. However, none of the open-ended comments were directed toward addressing this intermediate effectiveness criterion.

Work Group Effectiveness

Teachers' perceptions also appeared moderate, on average, concerning the work group effectiveness of their departments. Perceptions were between four ("slightly agree") and five ("agree") that the department's problem solving and instructional strategies had promoted effective teaching and learning and favorable student behavior in the school (*teaching and learning*). In addition, teachers' ratings were close to five ("agree") that they would like to continue to make an effort to help the department fulfill its goals (*team commitment*). Furthermore, teachers' ratings were close to two ("disagree") that teachers, if given a chance, would change to another department (team cohesion). Finally, their ratings were close to five ("agree") that their department usually met standards (e.g., accountability, timeliness) expected in the school as a whole (*standards met*) (see Table 7.1).

Regarding the open-ended questions, one special education teacher summarizes: "I feel our schedule/staff has always worked well together regardless of [the school being in PI] status." And, according to another language arts teacher: "There is an inspiring intensity within an easy-going atmosphere where teachers must grow and improve daily." One physical education teacher qualifies her response of "slightly agree" that department strategies had promoted effective teaching and learning, stating that it was true "for [just two department] teachers."

She further indicates that she wanted to keep working with "just one [other] teacher" in the department, and that her commitment to the department was because of that teacher. (Earlier, she had noted that she and the other teacher "spent time on planning curriculum, discussing assessment, and organizing department issues" but that two others "sit and listen and don't really follow through.") Another social studies teacher remarks,

> Much of the dissatisfaction my department feels is due to one employee who doesn't participate in meetings, doesn't attend all meetings, and is not an effective teacher. [He] resents any suggestions to improve [his] classroom management and teaching skills.

Correlation Analyses

In this section, we turn to our analysis delineating relationships among the design features, organizational context, interpersonal processes, and the intermediate effectiveness criterion on the one hand and our four work group effectiveness variables (teaching and learning, team commitment, team cohesion, and standards met) on the other. Table 7.2 provides the correlations among these variables.

The relationships between teaching and learning and the design features, organizational support, interpersonal processes, and intermediate effectiveness criterion were highly significant. The same was generally true when correlating team commitment, team cohesion, and standards met with these variables. However, team commitment, team cohesion, and standards met were unrelated to rewards/recognition (Table 7.2). This finding indicates that there was no relationship between the extent to which the department received formal and informal recognition for its efforts and the extent to which members were committed to working with the department, felt attached to the department, and believed the department met performance standards.

Further, standards met was unrelated to two of the three design features (i.e., motivating structure of the task, task autonomy) and both organizational support variables (Table 7.2). This indicates that there was no relationship between the extent to which the department had motivating tasks, exercised independence and professional autonomy, received rewards and recognition, and had training and assistance available—and the extent to which teachers believed the department met performance standards in the school. What *was* related, however, included the perception that department members were strong in such areas as interpersonal and instructional skills (mix of expertise), did not have difficulty coordinating their work (coordinating efforts), and had developed new and innovative ways to achieve the group's goals (inventing strategies).

Regression Analyses: Predicting Work Group Effectiveness

A series of regression analyses were conducted to determine which, if any, design features, organizational support, interpersonal processes, and enabling condition variables were good predictors of the four aspects of

Table 7.2. Correlations among Teachers' Perceptions of Design Features, Organizational Support, and Task and Interpersonal Processes and Dependent Variables (N=120)

Variable	1	2	3	4	5	6	7	8	9	10	11	12	13	14
1. Motivating Structure of Task	—													
2. Task Autonomy	0.29**	—												
3. Mix of Expertise	0.21*	0.45**	—											
4. Rewards/Recognition	0.11	0.13	0.19*	—										
5. Training	0.24**	0.13	0.23*	0.28**	—									
6. Coordinating Efforts	-0.33**	-0.18	-0.45**	-0.12	-0.19*	—								
7. Weighting/Balancing	0.18	0.14	0.47**	0.30**	0.12	-0.56**	—							
8. Implementing Strategies	0.46**	0.24**	0.26**	0.13	0.15	-0.36**	0.07	—						
9. Inventing Strategies	0.30**	0.23*	0.43**	0.14	0.24**	-0.59**	0.44**	0.34**	—					
10. Knowledge & Skills Applied	0.39**	0.32**	0.64**	0.33**	0.38**	-0.46**	0.50**	0.38**	0.59**	—				
11. Teaching/Learning	0.55**	0.25**	0.36**	0.23*	0.29**	-0.47**	0.34**	0.36**	0.55**	0.62**	—			
12. Team Commitment	0.46**	0.39**	0.44**	0.02	0.25**	-0.59**	0.25**	0.54**	0.59**	0.50**	0.57**	—		
13. Team Cohesion	-0.28**	-0.26**	-0.44**	-0.11	-0.23*	0.46**	-0.34**	-0.28**	-0.37**	-0.45**	-0.44**	-0.56**	—	
14. Standards Met	0.09	0.15	0.43**	-0.00	0.14	-0.61**	0.40**	0.14	0.54**	0.36**	0.39**	0.45**	-0.37**	—

*Correlation at .05 level (2-tailed).
** Correlation at .01 level (2-tailed).

work group effectiveness. In Tables 7.3 through 7.6, for each dependent variable, we present the results of a regression analysis identifying the significant predictors of that outcome.

As seen in Table 7.3, two variables were good predictors of teaching and learning. A strong predictor of the perception that the department's strategies had promoted effective teaching and learning and favorable student behavior was *knowledge/skills applied*—that the teams' members knew and shared instructional methods and curriculum development strategies, demonstrated understanding of subject matter outside their area of expertise, and engaged in systematic group problem-solving processes (ß = 0.40, p < 0.01). A second significant predictor of teaching and learning was *motivating structure of the task* (ß = 0.35, p < 0.01). Together, the model including these variables explained 51 percent of the variance in our teaching and learning variable.

As seen in Table 7.4, three variables were good predictors of team commitment. *Coordinating efforts* was a strong predictor of teachers' desires to continue as a member of the team and put in effort to help the department meet its goals (ß = –0.33, p < 0.01). A second significant predictor of team commitment was *inventing strategies*, reflecting the creative use of technology and other new ways to communicate and achieve goals (ß = 0.29, p < 0.01). Together, the model including these variables explained 52 percent of the variance in team commitment.

As seen in Table 7.5, a single variable, *coordinating efforts*, was a good predictor of team cohesion, an outcome reflecting attachment to the department and not desiring to change to another (ß = 0.26, p < 0.05). The model including this variable explained 24 percent of the variance in team cohesion.

Finally, as shown in Table 7.6, three variables were good predictors of standards met. *Coordinating efforts* was a strong predictor of teachers'

Table 7.3. Regression Analysis: Variables Best Predicting Teachers' Perceptions of Teaching/Learning ($N = 120$)

Variable	B	SE B	Beta	t value	p
Motivating Structure of the Task	0.41	0.09	0.35	4.35	0.000
Knowledge & Skills Applied	0.31	0.08	0.40	3.71	0.000

Note. $R = 0.743$; $R^2 = 0.552$; *Adj.* $R^2 = 0.509$; $SE = 0.690$; F *ratio* $= 12.691$.
$p = 0.000$.

Table 7.4. Regression Analysis: Variables Best Predicting Teachers' Perceptions of Team Commitment ($N = 120$)

Variable	B	SE B	Beta	t value	p
Coordinating Efforts	−0.27	0.08	−0.33	−3.59	0.000
Inventing Strategies	0.25	0.08	0.29	3.17	0.002

Note. $R = 0.746$; $R^2 = 0.557$; *Adj. R^2* = 0.519; *SE* = 0.674; *F ratio* = 14.812. $p = 0.000$.

Table 7.5. Regression Analysis: Variables Best Predicting Teachers' Perceptions of Team Cohesion ($N = 120$)

Variable	B	SE B	Beta	t value	p
Coordinating Efforts	0.24	0.11	0.26	2.24	0.027

Note. $R = 0.549$; $R^2 = 0.301$; *Adj. R^2* = 0.242; *SE* = 0.980; *F ratio* = 5.074. $p = 0.000$.

Table 7.6. Regression Analysis: Variables Best Predicting Teachers' Perceptions of Standards Met ($N = 120$)

Variable	B	SE B	Beta	t value	p
Mix of Expertise	0.18	0.09	0.21	2.15	0.034
Coordinating Efforts	−0.31	0.08	−0.37	−3.83	0.000
Inventing Strategies	0.27	0.09	0.30	3.05	0.003

Note. $R = 0.657$; $R^2 = 0.432$; *Adj. R^2* = 0.406; *SE* = 0.771; *F ratio* = 17.131. $p = 0.000$.

perceptions that the department typically met the standards of account-ability, timeliness, quantity and quality expected school-wide (ß = −0.37, p < 0.01). A second significant predictor of standards met was *inventing strategies*, and a third, *mix of expertise* (ß = 0.30, p < 0.01 and ß = 0.21, p < 0.05, respectively). Together, the model including these variables explained 41 percent of the variance in standards met.

DISCUSSION AND CONCLUSIONS

In contrast to the punitive focus of some reform measures (see Daly, 2009), the current research focuses on the potential of department teams to not only promote work effectiveness but for the group experience to be personally satisfying to members (Kruse, Louis, & Bryk, 1995). The

findings in this chapter provide information for school leaders in analyzing the needs and dynamics of the "bounded" department, fundamental
units in the organizational makeup of schools (Keedy & Robbins, 1993).
With three of the schools in this study assigned to PI status by the state
department of education, teams had become a central component of strategies for improvement in the districts under study (Mintrop, 2004). Our
survey findings from five middle schools in two urban California districts
revealed important relationships among several design, organizational
support, interpersonal process, and enabling conditions with perceptions
of work group effectiveness.

One notable finding was that the *motivating structure of the task*
emerged as a strong predictor of our work group effectiveness measure of
teaching and learning. This design feature deals with whether the "team
task [is] clear, consistent with a group's purpose, and high on . . . motivating potential" (Hackman, 1990, p. 10). It also deals with department
work as not being seen as comprised of individual efforts but as a group
of teachers undertaking "joint work" and "interdependence" (Mayrowetz
et al., 2007, p. 79). It seems reasonable that when teachers view the work
of these curriculum-focused departments as primarily requiring group
(rather than individual) efforts—and see the group as having significant
and challenging work to do—they would also view departments as poised
to make significant teaching and learning improvements in the school.

Second, we found that *coordinating efforts* and *mix of expertise*
emerged as two strong predictors of standards met, a key aspect of work
group effectiveness. Our mix of expertise measure involved asking teachers about the number of people in their department with strengths in such
areas as instruction, interpersonal relationships, and classroom management. Not surprisingly, the more teachers perceived members within their
departments as having these needed skills, the greater the perception that
school-wide standards were being met.

The finding regarding the importance of *mix of expertise* appears to
have implications for practice. Unlike other kinds of teams (such as
middle school interdisciplinary teams), choosing members of middle
school departments appears somewhat "set" in a school; how then does
one obtain the right mix of people? Perhaps a principal (or department
head) could attend to knowing the strengths and weaknesses of each staff
member in a particular department. When weaknesses, such as a lack of

members with strong interpersonal skills, for example, are identified, the school leader might then initiate training in interpersonal effectiveness or make use of consultants (such as DAIT) for that team.

In addition, a department head might assign novice teachers to pair with more experienced or effective teachers or "buddies" within a department to enhance knowledge and skills. Were student disciplinary effectiveness a skill that was found lacking, for instance, a principal might assign a teacher perceived to be strong in disciplinary procedures (even from a different department) to act as a mentor to a novice teacher in the department or provide training as well.

Further, our broader finding indicated that teachers' perceptions that a department's work has been successful is influenced by both (a) members having requisite skills and (b) members being able and willing to coordinate their efforts. Problems encountered with coordinating a department's efforts may reflect an underlying difficulty with discretionary time as suggested in other chapters (e.g., Cook & Collinson, chapter 5, this volume). In addition, norms of equality, autonomy, and privacy that have traditionally existed in schools may contribute to a perception of coordination difficulties (Keedy & Robbins, 1993).

Interestingly, *coordinating efforts* not only emerged as a significant predictor of the belief that a group had met standards, but also that members were committed to working together and continuing their membership in the department. That is, coordination of efforts was important not only for influencing perceptions of quantity, quality, and so on, of group output but also for teachers' finding the group experience to be satisfactory and worthwhile. Group coordination might satisfy needs—not only by helping reduce or eliminate problems in a department's work (such as scheduling classes) but also by enhancing efficacy and trust (Tschannen-Moran, 2001) and providing a mechanism for department input into higher-level administrative decisions (Bauer, Brazer, Van Lare, & Smith, chapter 4, this volume).

Third, we found that perceptions of rewards provided to departments in the form of formal or informal rewards in recognition of department work was not high. A mean of 1.85 for the variable *rewards/recognition* corresponded to between 1 "never/almost never" and 2 "infrequently," indicating that department members perceived these rewards as rarely available. This finding is consistent with related research (e.g., see Conley et al., 2004; Muncey & Conley, 1999; Pounder, 1999). As Conley et al. (2004) noted:

> With regard to the supportive organizational context variable of teacher work groups in schools, the performance evaluation and rewards systems that exist in schools are not designed for a group emphasis (other than whole school recognition). Furthermore, schools have notoriously limited reward systems of any type. (p. 670)

Rewards and recognition that might be considered by school leaders may include: announcing team accomplishments in faculty meetings; providing team of the year (similar to outstanding educator awards) district-wide; publishing accomplishments in the local newspaper; providing high priority for field trip or outside activity funding or scheduling; and including the activities of departments in back-to-school night for parents. In addition, stipends to support the department's work could be considered, such as providing team members stipends when tasks are particularly challenging or short term in nature. Funds could also be budgeted that are targeted for departments to choose needed materials.

Finally, it is interesting that task autonomy did not emerge as a significant predictor; however, autonomy was significantly correlated with three of four outcomes in the study. This finding may correspond to Mayrowetz and colleagues' (2007) observation that a team may be highly autonomous from administrative oversight in "determining the focus and nature of its work" (p. 79) but still be accountable to the administration in meeting its goals. Further, administration must coordinate the work of several groups within the school (Mayrowetz et al., 2007). In Hackman and Oldham's (1980) model, autonomous work teams should be accorded sufficient discretion to accomplish their work. Our mixed findings about task autonomy may reflect the importance of coordination over simple discretion and autonomy within a school (Mayrowetz et al., 2007; Shedd, 1988).

To conclude, school leaders might pursue a variety of strategies involving a mix of the dimensions found in Hackman and Oldham's (1980) model, thus providing a way for administrators to do "more than delegate tasks or relinquish authority; [but also] . . . manage the boundaries among several workgroups [and help to] . . . coordinate that work to maintain coherence" in the school (Mayrowetz et al., 2007, p. 70). Hopefully this chapter has taken a step toward illustrating a variety of mechanisms for making progress in this area.

NOTES

1. The authors appreciate assistance from Bruce S. Cooper, Justin Smith, and Nicole Wellman on earlier versions of this chapter.

2. Title I of the Elementary and Secondary Education Act (ESEA) provides financial assistance to local educational agencies (LEAs) and schools with high numbers or high percentages of children from low-income families (Department of Education, n.d.).

REFERENCES

Bolman, L. G., & Deal, T. E. (2003). *Reframing organizations: Artistry, choice, and leadership.* San Francisco: Jossey-Bass.

Collinson, V. (2012). Leading by learning, learning by leading. *Professional Development in Education, 38*(2), 247–66.

Conley, S., & Christensen, M. (2011). Administrative teams. In B. S. Cooper & S. Conley (Eds.), *Keeping and improving today's school leaders* (pp. 29–52). Lanham, MD: Rowman & Littlefield.

Conley, S., Fauske, J., & Pounder, D. G. (2004). Teacher work group effectiveness. *Educational Administration Quarterly, 40*(5), 663–703.

Crow, H. M., & Pounder, D. G. (2000). Interdisciplinary teacher teams: Context, design, and process. *Educational Administration Quarterly, 36*(2), 216–54.

Daly, A. J. (2009). Rigid response in an age of accountability: The potential of leadership and trust. *Educational Administration Quarterly, 45*(2), 168–216.

Department of Education (n.d.). Improving basic programs operated by local educational agencies (Title I, Part A). Retrieved from: www.ed.gov/programs/titleiparta/.

Hackman, J. R. (1990). *Groups that work (and those that don't).* San Francisco: Jossey-Bass.

Hackman, J. R., & Oldham, G. R. (1980). *Work redesign.* Reading, MA: Addison-Wesley.

Johnson, S. M. (1990). The primacy and potential of high school departments. In M. W. McLaughlin, J. E. Talbert, & N. Bascia (Eds.), *The context of teaching in secondary schools: Teachers' realities* (pp. 167–84). New York: Teachers College Press.

Keedy, J. L., & Robbins, A. D. (1993). Teacher collegial groups: A culture-building strategy for department chairs. *Clearing House, 66*(3), 185–88.

King, J. A., & Weiss, D. A. (1995). Thomas Paine high school: Professional community in an unlikely setting. In K. S. Louis & S. D. Kruse (Eds.),

Professionalism and community: Perspectives on reforming urban schools (pp. 76–104). Thousand Oaks, CA: Corwin Press.

Kruse, S. D., Louis, K. W., & Bryk, A. S. (1995). An emerging framework for analyzing school-based professional community. In K. S. Louis & S. D. Kruse (Eds.), *Professionalism and community: Perspectives on reforming urban schools* (pp. 23–42). Thousand Oaks, CA: Corwin Press.

Mayrowetz, D., Murphy, J., Louis, K. S., & Smylie, M. A. (2007). Distributed leadership as work redesign: Retrofitting the job characteristics model. *Leadership and Policy in Schools, 6*, 69–101.

McGregor, J. (2003). Collaboration in communities of practice. In N. Bennett & L. Andersen (Eds.), *Rethinking educational leadership: Challenging the conventions* (pp. 113–30). London: Sage.

McLaughlin, M. W., & Talbert, J. E. (1990). The contexts in question: The secondary school workplace. In M. W. McLaughlin, J. E. Talbert, and N. Bascia (Eds.), *The contexts of teaching in secondary schools: Teachers' realities.* New York: Teachers College.

Mintrop, H. (2004). *Schools on probation: How accountability works (and doesn't work).* New York: Teachers College Press.

Muncey, D. E., & Conley, S. (1999). Teacher compensation and teacher teaming: Sketching the terrain. *Journal of Personel Evaluation in Education 12*(4), 365–85.

Pounder, D. G. (1998). Teacher teams: Redesigning teachers' work for collaboration. In D. G. Pounder (Ed.), *Restructuring schools for collaboration.* Albany: State University of New York Press.

Pounder, D. G. (1999). Teacher teams: Exploring job characteristics and work-related outcomes of work group enhancement. *Educational Administration Quarterly, 35*(3), 317–48.

Shedd, J. B. (1988). Collective bargaining, school reform, and the management of school systems. *Educational Administration Quarterly, 24*(4), 405–15.

Smylie, M. A., Conley, S., & Marks, H. M. (2002). Exploring new approaches to teacher leadership for school improvement. In J. Murphy (Ed.), *The educational leadership challenge: Redefining leadership for the 21st century* (One hundred and first yearbook of the National Society for the Study of Education, Part 1, pp. 162–88). Chicago: National Society for the Study of Education.

Tschannen-Moran, M. (2001). Collaboration and the need for trust. *Journal of Educational Administration, 39*(4), 308–31.

Vinokur-Kaplan, D. (1995). Treatment teams that work (and those that don't): An application of Hackman's group effectiveness model to interdisciplinary teams in psychiatric hospitals. *Journal of Applied Behavioral Science, 31*, 303–27.

Wenger, E. (2000). Communities of practice and social learning systems. *Organization, 7*(2), 225–46.

APPENDIX 7.1. SCALE ITEMS FOR SURVEY MEASURES

Variables

Design Features

Motivating Structure of Task *(Cronbach's alpha coefficient = .77)*

1. The work of the department requires a lot of cooperation among people.
2. The department's work can be done adequately by each person working alone-without talking or consulting much with each group member. (Reverse scored)
3. The work of the group requires members to use a high number of complex or high level skills.
4. The department's work requires the group members to do many different things, using a variety of their talents.
5. The group's work is not very significant or important in the broader scheme of things. (Reverse scored)
6. The work of the department is designed so that members have very few opportunities to contribute significantly to students' educational experience or learning. (Reverse scored)
7. Just doing the work required by the department provides many chances for members to figure out how well the group is doing.

Task Autonomy *(Cronbach's alpha coefficient = .67)*

1. The work of the department is designed in a way that gives members much opportunity for independence and use of professional autonomy or discretion.
2. My department has much discretion in structuring and monitoring its own work.
3. In my department, I feel free to suggest new steps for instructional strategies that meet students' needs.

Mix of Expertise *(Cronbach's alpha coefficient = .95)*
How many people in your department would you say . . .

1. Have strong instructional skills?
2. Have strong interpersonal skills?
3. Have strong student assessment skills?
4. Have strong classroom management skills?

Organizational Support

Rewards/Recognition *(Cronbach's alpha coefficient = .81)*

To what extent do you think your department receives the following types of rewards in recognition for its efforts?

1. Formal recognition from the school
2. Formal recognition from the public
3. Informal recognition from the school
4. Informal recognition from the public

Training *(Cronbach's alpha coefficient = .79)*

1. My department seeks assistance or advice from others (for example, other teachers, administrators, outside experts) in conducting its work.
2. As a department member, I personally seek assistance or advisement in doing my department-related work.
3. When my department can't reach a decision, it turns to other resources for help (for example, other departments, administrators, outside consultants).

To what extent are the following persons, groups, or other resources available to your department to provide special training or consultation?

1. State consultant (DAIT) (if applicable)
2. Staff (union) representatives

3. School administrators
4. Other departments in your school

Task and Interpersonal Processes

Coordinating Efforts *(Cronbach's alpha coefficient = .75)*

1. It is difficult for us to find times to meet.
2. Sometimes coordinating my work with other department members is more trouble than it is worth.
3. It is difficult to communicate with other members as much as I need to.

Weighting/Balancing *(Cronbach's alpha coefficient = .70)*

1. Only a few department members do most of the team's work. (Reverse scored)
2. The department's work responsibilities are evenly distributed among its members.
3. There is a low degree of participation on the part of some members of the department. (Reverse scored)

Implementing Strategies

1. I am comfortable sharing my ideas on teaching strategies with my work group/department.

Inventing Strategies *(Cronbach's alpha coefficient = .87)*

1. We creatively use technology (e.g., email, shared calendars) to communicate and to coordinate our efforts.
2. My department is creative in developing new ways to achieve the team's goals.
3. My department is innovative in developing new ways to do its work.

Enabling Condition/Intermediate Effectiveness Criterion

Knowledge & Skills Applied *(Cronbach's alpha coefficient = .95)*

How many department members would you say do the following when the group is working?

1. Know and share with the department a variety of instructional methods?
2. Know and share with the department a variety of curriculum development strategies?
3. Demonstrate an understanding of subject matter outside their own areas of expertise?
4. Engage in systematic group problem-solving processes?

Work Group Effectiveness

Teaching and Learning *(Cronbach's alpha coefficient = .94)*

1. My department's problem-solving strategies have promoted effective student learning, effective teaching, and favorable student behavior.
2. My department's instructional strategies have promoted effective student learning, effective teaching, and favorable student behavior.

Team Commitment *(Cronbach's alpha coefficient = .70)*

1. Given the way my department works together now, I would prefer not to continue to be a member in the future. (Reverse scored)
2. I would like to keep working together with most of the members of my department.
3. I am willing to put in a great deal of effort to help my department fulfill its goals.

Team Cohesion *(Cronbach's alpha coefficient = .51)*

1. If I had a chance, I would change to another department.
2. I feel little commitment to my department.

Standards Met *(Cronbach's alpha coefficient = .96)*

My department usually meets the standards of:

1. accountability expected by the school as a whole.
2. timeliness expected by the school as a whole.
3. quantity expected by the school as a whole.
4. quality expected by the school as a whole.

Chapter Eight

Professional Learning Communities Using Evidence

Examining Teacher Learning and Organizational Learning

Michelle D. Van Lare, S. David Brazer, Scott C. Bauer, and Robert G. Smith

Teachers should use evidence of students' learning to inform instruction. This resounding directive appears throughout current scholarship, practitioner literature, and federal policy (Ikemoto & Marsh, 2007; Means, Chen, DeBarger, & Padilla, 2011). Concurrently, school and district leaders are grappling with how to make evidence use a common practice within their schools. One response has been the creation of collaborative structures to facilitate teachers' use of evidence and instructional dialogues. The notion of collaborative structures, or professional learning communities (PLCs), has been popularized (e.g., DuFour, Eaker, & DuFour, 2005) to the extent that PLCs are now at the center of contemporary school reform.

Leaders in the PLC effort argue the promising connections between the use of evidence, teacher collaboration, and increased student achievement. As the PLC movement roars ahead, research must continue to investigate these claims, exploring how such teams use evidence of student learning and how teachers learn through the use of evidence (Coburn & Talbert, 2006; Moss, 2012).

The purpose of this chapter is twofold. First, we aim to examine a central function of PLCs: the processes through which teachers use evidence. That is, we want to know how teachers within collaborative structures make sense of evidence to build connections between evidence and classroom instruction. Second, we anchor our examination guided by the explicit goal of PLCs' examination of classroom evidence: learning. We ask what the processes we have captured might mean for teacher learning and for organizational learning, both targets in this current school reform movement.

Although the amount of scholarship on data use in schools has increased recently, only a small portion of this work captures processes through which teachers analyze evidence of student learning (e.g., Oláh, Lawrence, & Riggan, 2010). Recently, Little (2012) characterized the scholarship describing and analyzing the processes of evidence use as underdeveloped and called for more work examining the microprocesses that shape teachers' practices. Recent research depends heavily on survey or interview data, but few studies portray the small movements that teachers make within discussions of evidence. Capturing these movements, or actions, is essential as we attempt to build a more holistic understanding of how teachers are using evidence and how expectations within and external to the PLC shape their practices.

This chapter positions data use in the very specific structures of PLCs; therefore, our analysis of PLCs offers a significant contribution to the literature base on collaborative structures. PLCs have been studied and written about, but generally this work has occurred in an isolated manner and is uninformed by related theory. Additionally, much of the recent PLC literature is advocacy for a particular model (e.g., DuFour, 2004; DuFour, DuFour, Eaker, & Many, 2010; DuFour et. al., 2005) and tends not to acknowledge the theoretical roots of procedures that are promoted as "best practices" for improving teaching and learning.

The academic literature focused on PLCs is more helpful for understanding what happens when teachers collaborate, but it tends to be characterized by a lack of connections between current concepts of PLCs and the theoretical literature on teacher learning and organizational learning (Servage, 2008). Thus, what we know about PLCs tends to be how advocates believe they should function and how researchers perceive them, largely disconnected from the organizations (school and districts) in which they are embedded.

This chapter takes a step toward grounding empirical, field-based research in theory about how teachers learn and how organizations function. PLCs are rarely, if ever, considered in their nested organizational contexts—in schools within school districts (Horn, 2010; Little, 2003; McLaughlin & Talbert, 2001). The result is that the term *professional learning community* has evolved to mean a specific design of teacher collaboration with rules regarding the use of time, language, and protocols. Much of the current literature constricts our understanding of what teachers do to facilitate their own learning and exercise teacher leadership in an effort to improve student performance, because of an overemphasis on "best practices" that too narrowly define PLC work. By avoiding advocacy and contextualizing PLC processes and outcomes, we may be able to enrich research into teacher collaborations and their results. This kind of fieldwork has strong potential to expand how researchers understand the enactment of PLCs in educational contexts.

RESEARCH QUESTIONS

We focus our study using the following research questions:

1. How do PLCs use evidence of student achievement to inform classroom actions?
   a. How is evidence generated and represented within PLCs?
   b. How do teachers analyze evidence?
2. To what extent is organizational learning resulting from teachers' use of evidence in PLCs?

The questions we pose are answered from the perspective we explain in the next section. We have based this research on theoretical domains to guide our understanding of teacher learning within collaborative structures and organizational learning.

CONCEPTUAL FRAMEWORK

We frame our investigation of PLCs using theoretical constructs drawn from sociocultural learning and organizational learning. The conceptual framework developed here is, broadly speaking, a hypothesis we test with the data that we have collected and analyzed. We should note that we use the term *learning* in a neutral sense. What is learned may or may not be healthy for the organization and may or may not have a positive effect on teaching and learning.

Teacher Learning and Sociocultural Learning Theory

We begin by focusing on the processes of teacher collaboration within PLCs and draw from sociocultural learning theory, considering the PLC as a community of practice (Lave & Wenger, 1991; Wenger, 1998). The term *practice* encompasses both what teachers *do* as well as the social and historical context that "gives structure and meaning" (p. 47) to what they do (Wenger, 1998) and is the central unit of analysis to capture learning. Wenger (1998) defines learning as a change in participation within a community.

To capture possible changes in participation, we rely on Horn's (2010) work on teacher engagement. Horn's (2010) comparative case study of two communities of math teachers conceptualizes the patterns through which teachers present and examine problems of practice: *replays* and *rehearsals*. Both practices are ways in which teachers represent their classroom actions. *Replays* are renderings of past events that tend to be specific, perhaps a blow-by-blow retelling of teacher and student interactions within a classroom. *Rehearsals* are renderings of what teachers envision happening, or believe could happen, based on past experiences. *Rehearsals* might be more generalized and could include a teacher predicting how his students would react to new content. Both work as platforms through which teachers may identify, clarify, normalize, and understand their teaching practice. The ideas of replays and rehearsals help to explain how practices that exist within isolated classrooms are brought into the collective enterprise of the school community.

Horn's (2010) argument is that through these representations of practice, teachers may extend representations of practice by probing for clarification, offering more information, or brainstorming causes of any problems. Extensions present teachers an opportunity to *revision* their practice. Through these discussions, teachers are continually repositioning themselves and their practices, finding new visions of their practice. Portraying teacher learning within collaborative discussion, Horn's (2010) work theorizes that the dialogue pattern of representations, extensions, and revisioning creates platforms for teacher learning.

Organizational Learning

In this section, we draw from two distinct threads of theory on organizational learning as a way to describe possible pathways for learning within and among PLCs.

PLCs tend to be discussed in a manner largely divorced from their organizational contexts (e.g., DuFour et al., 2005; Mintrop, 2004). Such a separation seems ill-considered because PLCs exist in part as a result of larger organizational forces and influences from outside the formal organization of schools and districts. Furthermore, PLCs themselves behave as organizations (Schein, 2010), albeit small ones, with highly permeable boundaries. They are nested within schools, which are nested within school districts. Their work is further nested inside state and national policy in the form of accountability mandates and potential or real consequences stemming from student achievement. We remove PLCs from their theoretical isolation to expand understanding of how they are influenced, and why they make certain kinds of choices.

Organizational Learning Embodied in Routines

PLCs by definition are assumed to exercise substantial volition. In current visions of PLCs, teachers are expected to use information or evidence (currently commonly described as student data), to interpret what they find, and to act on their interpretations (DuFour et al., 2005; Osterman & Kottkamp, 2004). Organizational conditions may limit PLCs' decision-making discretion for several reasons: for example, the need for consistency and predictability in implementation. A common instrument for maintaining consistency and predictability within organizations is organizational routine.

Organizational routines are a common response to bounded rationality (March, 1994; March & Simon, 1993) and reduce the need for decision making in complex or ambiguous circumstances (Allison & Zelikow, 1999). We believe that teaching tends toward routinization because teaching and learning are complex and difficult to understand (Bidwell, 2001) and because the effects of teachers' efforts are ambiguous and only vaguely known over a long span of time. Routinized behavior is further encouraged by the PLC advocacy literature that purports to present best practices (DuFour et al., 2010; DuFour et al., 2005). Justification for following routines is rooted in the notion that they represent the best way of improving student achievement.

Levitt and March (1988) explain that routines capture organizational history and experience in ways that allow them to be carried forward into contemporary organizational work. This type of phenomenon is easily observed in the current pursuit of "best practices" in teaching and learning. The term *best practices*, borrowed from business and engineering, suggests an optimal method of, for example, teaching reading to third graders whose first language is not English. But knowing what works best is complicated, given that variable inputs are organized into the domains of content knowledge, students, and pedagogy that constitute pedagogical content knowledge (PCK). Thus, what is actually occurring in the application of best practices may be the implementation of routines that are believed to be effective in similar situations (O'Day, 2009).

Adoption of routines has a less certain outcome when one considers the possibility that teachers may adapt them in unexpected ways. Teachers' tendencies to ignore and change reform-minded directives have been well documented (Cuban, 1993; Tyack & Cuban, 1995). Feldman and Pentland (2003) explain that this happens because of the bidimensional nature of routines. The ostensive aspect of routines refers to their intent from whoever created the routine. The performative aspect of routines, in contrast, describes how they are shaped or adapted by those who are expected to carry them out—teachers, in our case. Thus, best practices as organizational routines are likely to look different in different classrooms and settings (Conley & Enomoto, 2009; Spillane, 2012).

Organizational learning via routines is one possible path, but not the only one. Argyris (1999) and Argyris and Schon (1978) wrote theoretically and empirically for decades about a different form of organizational learning. We now turn to their model not as an alternative to Levitt and March (1988), but as an additional lens for discovering what PLCs do.

Organizational Learning as Double-Loop Learning

Argyris and Schon (1974; 1978) begin from a point not too distant from Levitt and March (1988)—the difference between aspirations and outcomes. Employing different language, Argyris and Schon (1974; 1978) explain that what organizations aspire to do may be detected in vision or mission statements. They call these *espoused theories*—what the people within organizations say they want. Actions taken are inferred by Argyris and Schon (1974) to stem from implicit theories in use that organization members understand as the ways in which they should perform their roles.

Addressing mismatches between theories in use and espoused theories is made difficult because organization members may behave as though the gaps do not exist in an attempt to maintain individual, group, and school legitimacy (Argyris, 1999; Argyris & Schon, 1974). Reluctance to admit a gap between espoused theories and theories in use is part of the larger problem of "undiscussables," the issues that people simply do not talk about. Worse, undiscussables can be self-sealing—no one talks about issues that no one discusses (Argyris, 1999).

Governing values (Argyris & Schon, 1978) or governing variables (Argyris, 1999) are similar to the rules that are followed within organizations (March, 1994). An obvious governing variable in many schools is that PLCs meet regularly to discuss student achievement outcomes. Another potential governing variable that links to our earlier discussion of learning through routines is that PLCs will apply best practices in situations where learning is determined to be deficient. Argyris (1999) maintains that organizational learning that brings espoused theories in line with theories in use requires changing governing variables. He and Schon (1974) refer to this as *double-loop learning.*

Clearly distinct from learning through routines, double-loop learning suggests that PLCs would or should explore gaps between espoused theories and theories in use, opening up undiscussables, and ultimately altering governing variables. No routine way exists to do this and such a mission for PLCs strongly implies that they would have substantial autonomy and decision-making power. If governing variables are to be addressed, then the school as a whole would need to be amenable to change.

The practices of a community characterized by organizational learning, as envisioned by Argyris (1999) and Argyris and Schon (1974), are more likely to be drawn into double-loop learning efforts that question the status quo. The search for solutions will be a more ambiguous process that may not readily accept routine behaviors or solutions.

METHODS

This study employs a predominantly qualitative methodology because our research questions are focused on learning how PLCs function in a natural setting. We used a qualitative case study design (Merriam, 1998) that involved our team of researchers spending time in school settings, working to capture the processes and the context of the phenomena under study.[1]

Roll out of this research project started in January 2012. Data collection continued until the end of the school year in June 2012.

Research Setting

The Heritage County Public Schools (HCPS)[2] constitutes a large suburban school district on the East Coast. One of the wealthier districts in its state, HCPS has pockets of poverty and is ethnically and linguistically diverse. Twenty-five percent of the district's students receive free or reduced-price meals. More than half of the district's students are identified as nonwhite, with the largest ethnicities being Asian, Hispanic, or African American. Thirteen percent of the district's student population is enrolled in English speakers of other languages programs, and a roughly equal percentage of students receive special education services.

In an effort to make the administration of the school district more manageable, HCPS is organized into eight areas, each led by an assistant superintendent with a minimal staff. An area is a geographical location that typically includes three high schools and their feeder middle and elementary schools. The areas are meaningful units for supervision, dissemination of services and resources, approval of budget and staffing, and support in the form of professional development. Nevertheless, many services are centralized at the district level. The superintendent and his administrative team are clearly in charge of the articulation and implementation of policy as determined by the board. These administrators take an active role in explaining how PLCs are intended to work.

This district has engaged teachers in PLCs at least since the current superintendent was appointed nine years ago. Some early adopters developed PLCs several years before, but implementation of the strategy was not widespread until a clear mandate was perceived during the past three years. At this point, it appears that all schools have PLCs in place, although they function in different ways and in varying degrees of fidelity to what the district intends. The area assistant superintendents understand that it is their job to ensure that PLCs are at work in their schools and that they are helping to improve student achievement.

One significant area to which the district has devoted resources is a test question bank and repository that is capable of generating tests, storing student data, and identifying standards and elements being tested. The district program is available to teachers across the system, and some grades and content areas are mandated to use this test bank and repository for at least two student assessments a year.

Participants

With the assistance of a central office assistant superintendent and her director of professional development, we identified four of the eight clusters with adequate stability and a strong interest in PLC implementation that would give our research team the endorsement it would need to improve the likelihood of school and individual participation in the study. After interviewing the director of professional development to learn about PLC policy and intentions generally, we interviewed all four of the area superintendents who were recommended. During these discussions, we asked the area superintendents to identify as many schools as they could that they believed would be interesting places to study PLC work. We kept this question purposely ambiguous, hoping to capture a range of PLC practices.

The research team gathered basic background information on all of the schools named by the assistant superintendents and created first and second choices of schools at each level (i.e., elementary, middle, and high school). Our intent was to create a purposeful sample that would represent a wide range of schools in the district, based on student demographics and assistant superintendents' brief descriptions of the extent to which PLCs were being implemented in the named schools. We eventually collected data from ten schools.

Principals at each of the participating schools were study participants (see Table 8.1). In addition to interviewing them about their perceptions of PLCs generally and in their schools, we asked them to identify specific PLCs within their schools that they believed would be helpful in our research. Similar to the assistant superintendents, we left this choice question as ambiguous as we could, hoping for a variety of PLCs (two or three in each school). A selection of teachers from the identified PLCs made up the last set of participants in this study.

Table 8.1. Participants and Observations

Category of Participants	Number of Participants
Central Office	5
Building Principals	10
Teachers	18
Instructional Coaches	3
PLC Meetings Observed	20 (over 45 hours)

Data Collection

Our original intent was to interview principals and teachers, based on the guidance received from area assistant superintendents. Shortly after the school district approved this research, however, the assistant superintendent in charge of research strongly suggested that we interview the director of professional development because of her first-hand knowledge of PLC implementation. She, in turn, encouraged us to interview the area assistant superintendents for similar reasons. We followed this advice by first creating an interview protocol that was based largely on the principal interview protocol we had already created. Both sets of questions asked about the purpose and structure of PLCs. Each interview lasted approximately thirty minutes.

Principals were usually interviewed alone, but some chose to involve one or more assistant principals in these interviews that focused on the purposes of PLCs and how PLCs were structured and supported (by both the district and principals). In the first portion of the interview, we probed to understand how principals perceive effective PLC work, evidence of student learning, and PLCs' use of such evidence. In the second portion of the interview, we focused on how principals have structured the PLCs themselves (e.g., how individuals get included in one PLC or another and how time is made available) and how they were supported with resources such as professional development.

We then moved on to teacher interviews. Similar to principals, we interviewed teachers for approximately thirty minutes, asking a somewhat different set of questions. We inquired about teachers' actual experiences because they were involved in their PLCs on a much more consistent basis than anyone else we interviewed. We heavily emphasized the use of evidence guided by our research questions.

As we interviewed teachers, we observed PLCs in action, often interviewing and observing on the same day, providing an important triangulation vehicle. Instead of simply relying on what administrators and teachers told us about how PLCs work, we had the opportunity to see how their stated beliefs aligned with their actions and to ask questions prompted by observations.

Data Analysis

Qualitative data were analyzed using two different kinds of data codes. Our first set of analyses was based on codes derived from the conceptual framework for this study (Maxwell, 2005; Merriam, 1998). For this analysis, several of the conceptual areas were used as codes: evidence, replays, rehearsals, extensions, revisions, and routines. These were applied to interview transcript texts and field notes from observations. We maintained a coding list that included working definitions to obtain greater coding consistency within the research team.

As we read interview transcripts and field notes and engaged in coding, new ideas and themes emerged. Thus, we added codes (Maxwell, 2005; Merriam, 1998) to our coding list and were able to probe the data more deeply. These codes included unpacking standards, generating evidence, boundary crossing, reflecting on group processes, and setting goals.

Coding is a mechanism for sorting the qualitative data, but it also provides a means of identifying themes across participants and sources (Maxwell, 2005). We calibrated our coding using anchor transcripts and repeated discussions among research team members to identify and clarify important themes that could be identified as a result of coding and sorting.

All coding was accomplished on qualitative software (NVivo). Once completed, we generated reports according to code and continued constant comparison by looking for themes within codes. These themes then became an organizing scheme for our findings.

Validity Threats

The greatest threats to the validity of our findings come from researcher bias and school district interests. Our research team of six individuals (four faculty and two doctoral graduate research assistants) helped to protect against individual bias by means of more than one individual coding any given data source and the need to come to agreement about what we were finding. Researcher bias was further mitigated by conducting member checks as findings emerged, but this also presented a new validity threat.

For purposes of access, we collaborated with district and school building leaders for sampling decisions, leading to some bias in which teachers and PLCs we chose as participants. Therefore, this study is not indicative of the variety across the entire district. However, even within this sample, we have found variance because many leaders suggested we observe a variety of PLCs.

FINDINGS

Our analysis focuses on the research questions we posed previously, and the findings are organized here according to these questions. We begin by investigating the processes at work within the collaborative teams by delving into the subquestions of our first research question: *How do PLCs use evidence of student achievement to influence classroom actions?* We then offer findings on what we saw as evidence of teacher learning and organizational learning within these collaborative structures.

How Is Evidence Generated and Represented within PLCs?

Although teachers discussed evidence in multiple ways, several sources for data were prioritized both in interview data and in team observations. First were common assessments, which are discussed further in this section. Second were standardized tests such as the Developmental Reading Assessment (DRA). Following these, teachers most often named exit tickets, anecdotal notes, and student work as possible sources for evidence.

Common Assessments

Teachers named "common assessments" as a primary source for evidence of student learning. Common assessments most often took the form of multiple-choice tests, sometimes with open-ended questions, assessing the content and discrete skills taught within an established amount of time. Assessment items were generated by several sources, although most common were tests created in the district's test question bank.

This source allowed teachers to use previously created tests, choose questions from the bank to create a test, or generate their own questions to add to the bank. Teachers were able to give tests through online portals or through pen and paper. If teachers used the online portal, student scores were stored, offering the possibility of the generation of data reports over time. In some content areas and grades, the district mandated that two or four tests had to be given in the 2011–2012 academic year.

Often, common assessments were a combination of test questions generated at the district level and by teachers within the teams. For example, when asked, "What kind of data do you think is most helpful in providing evidence of student learning?" one elementary special education teacher responded as follows:

T: I think our common assessments . . .

R: Your school creates or the district creates?

T: We do both. We give the district ones so we have [a test bank] that the district makes but even next week we are giving the [test bank] but we're adding on questions to it. [The test bank] is thirty-five questions and we're adding another fifteen, so the kids will have a little bit of a longer test to take. So both, they have two that they are required to take and then one other, so that is not enough assessment so we make a lot of our own too.

Collaborative discussions about what test questions should appear on common assessment was a practice we observed across schools and PLCs.

We also see in our data some outliers, teachers who questioned the utility of common assessments. One example of this was a ninth grade math teacher who explains,

There are a lot of tests. I feel like we do a hell of a lot of tests, which I am not exactly happy about, but like I said, the quarterly common assessments. We also do, I am sure you have heard about, the county [test banks], which we don't stress about. We let our kids do them, and they are not always very successful which is funny because our [State] scores are awesome compared to the [test bank] scores and where the county is in relation to that. I think a lot of it is just getting a pulse for our kids and we talk about that too. . . . We

do warm-ups, our kids have homework every day, and . . . I guess I personally feel like a good gauge is just how my kids feel, like how they react, how
they are listening taking notes and all that stuff for me. That is as useful as
a test report.

This teacher focused on several sources and questioned the usefulness of the district-level tests ("we don't stress about"). She explained
that students "are not always very successful," which she viewed as a
misalignment to the state standardized test, perhaps undermining the
district tests' validity. In this case, the tests were not teacher created, but
instead, teachers used the tests as designed at the district level. Although
the district test offered a "pulse for our kids," this teacher named valid
sources of evidence that she and her students generate, such as warm-ups,
homework, and "how kids feel." As in this case, limited data suggest that
when teachers did not choose test items, common assessments became
less significant to them as evidence of student learning.

How Do Teachers Analyze Evidence?

Work within PLCs was significantly varied across the district, and as
a result, describing a singular process of analysis is problematic. Despite these differences, replays and rehearsals were consistent patterns
in teacher collaborative discussions. Our analysis has identified five
purposes for teachers' use of replays and rehearsals. These include understanding the following: (1) what should be taught; (2) student assessments; (3) students' thinking on assessments; (4) linking instruction to
student performance; and (5) how instruction might change. These five
purposes are explained here.

Understanding What Should Be Taught

The language some teachers used when describing how they work to
understand what they are expected to teach was "unpacking standards."
When asked to describe their work within PLCs, one instructional coach
explains, "We unpack all of our standards, our benchmarks, and our indi-
cators so we come to a real common clarity around what it is exactly kids
need to know and need to know how to do." We observed several teams

examining the standards in an upcoming unit and interpreting standards through collaborative discussion. In these discussions, teachers would rehearse the instruction, naming specific lessons or activities they planned to do in their classrooms.

Understanding Assessment

Teachers also spent time working to understand the assessments they were giving students. In some conversations, teachers evaluated assessment items, naming them "good" or "bad." Evaluations were used to decide whether to include items in common assessments or to explain why students struggled with certain items. One example of this category took place in a meeting of seventh grade civics teachers (teachers are identified as T1, T2, T3, T4, T5).

T1: One thing that I wanted to share real quick, before we jump to that too, on the econ [in the district test bank], look at this question. . . . This is the headline, it describes "President assigns interstate highway belt." Ok, choices are a public service, individual initiative, state program and public good. This is a straight [test] question directly from the bank, this is a horrible question.

T2: Horrible.

T1: But what is really amazing to see though is the correct answer they're saying is a public good not a public service and they argue that the kids argue, "Well the highway is a public services because . . ." but I did have some kids that think it was an individual initiative.

T3: Did they know what initiative meant?

T1: No, evidently not. That is almost equally split forty-eight to forty between public service and good. It is a good question to teach that, if that is the only thing you're doing.

T2: Don't they usually when they are talking about that though, they are usually talking about public goods and services. They don't separate them so that is, that is a terrible question.

Teachers identify this question as "horrible" and explicate why (e.g., "they don't separate [goods and services]"). These evaluations were often accompanied by short rehearsals in which teachers would estimate how students would understand an item or, as is seen in this case, in short replays illustrating how students interpreted items on an assessment. These episodes were closely related to the next category.

Understanding Student Thinking on Assessments

Much of the observational data captured teachers working to understand what students were thinking when performing on an assessment. Teachers highlighted where students' thought processes might lead them to perform poorly on assessments. To explain their analysis, teachers replayed classroom discussions or conversations with individual students. For example, the following is an excerpt from a meeting of first grade teachers. One teacher begins this vignette by summarizing student results on a common assessment on time.

> T1: Yeah, just analyzing the data it really came out as there are three areas the kids need help in. There is, so there are three little intervention groups. One of them is just timed to the half hour it is actually knowing that the hour hand goes in between the two hours and the other group is actually reading the half hour clock and the last group, the third group would be they have a hard time with the a.m. and p.m. and scheduling. Of just, when do you brush your teeth, 2 a.m. or 6 a.m.? Just kind of knowing the sequential order of the day with a.m. and p.m.

> T2: Yeah, I think that is a good point because I am doing mine within the school day identify a.m. and p.m. because p.m. is later and a.m. is early, it is like the morning. But if it is something outside of the school day they have a lot more trouble putting that into some context.

> T3: I had one say p.m. that they ate dinner. I mean 2 p.m. because they can't conceptualize.

> T4: Well p.m. is later . . .

> T3: I know but right, what is 2 p.m.?

In this episode, T1 outlines the three problems students had on the assessment. T2 and T3 react to one of these categories and offer very short replays to demonstrate the problems their students are having with a.m. and p.m. These replays are limited but indicate that teachers are working to understand how student thinking relates to the results they are seeing on assessments.

Understanding How Instruction Links to Student Performance

The next category signifies a process through which teachers work to connect classroom instruction to how students are performing on assessments or understanding material. As an example, the following dialogue was taken from a sixth grade meeting in which teachers were discussing math (T1, T2, T3, T4). One teacher asked the group, "So how did your kids do on coordinate plane?"

T2: So far, it has been good. I mean what else, once they started doing it by themselves like the crawling and then walking. And then one of my kids decided it didn't matter on which sides you put positive and negative so we had that conversation. "Well I'm putting positive on this side, and you're putting positive on that side you can't just switch them right?" One of my girls goes, "Well, mine is the opposite." "Well, why is yours the opposite? Why put negative on this side, why not that side?" I said that actually matters.

T3: That is the number line.

T4: I have one that did the same thing he goes, "Is it ok if I do the negative here, and the positive there?" and I'm like "no!"

T1: Well I had a kid go, "Is it always x, y?" because I said, "Every time you have the ordered pair x, y" and then I say, "It is always think alphabetical order."

In this short excerpt, teachers use replays ("And then one of my kids . . .") to give evidence of their students' thinking or misperceptions. Teachers then give examples of instructional actions ("always think alphabetical order") to demonstrate how instruction responds to student thinking. In this example, teachers name what they have done to correct students' misperceptions. In very limited examples, some teachers name instructional actions that might have contributed to students' misperceptions.

Understanding How Instruction Might Change for Different Results

The last category that we identified is the processes through which teachers articulate how changes in instruction might improve student performance. In an interview, one sixth grade teacher described an example of how her team responds when they have identified content students have struggled with on an assessment. She explained that the team attempts to identify one strategy that is more effective based on student performance on an assessment.

> The perfect example is the question we just had on a previous test . . . there is one where the kids had to put the fractions in order, like order them from least to greatest and they weren't allowed to use a calculator. . . . Two of the teachers actually used a strategy where there was a certain strategy where you count the jumps to one, and we taught that to them and our students did relatively well compared to the other two groups who didn't use that strategy. So that is something that we would discuss tomorrow and make sure that everyone understands how the strategy works and then go back and teach our students how to do it.

The teachers have identified an interesting strategy that they assume led to improved results. According to the interview, teachers will use replays to make sure that "everyone understands how the strategy works," and the teachers will incorporate the change in their classrooms.

The replays and rehearsals found in these excerpts are isolated and short. Although teachers are representing their classroom practices in these episodes, it is difficult to characterize the learning happening in each because these do not include extensions or revisions. In the following section, we examine a longer episode that captures an example of a revision. In this excerpt, we see all five purposes for replays and rehearsals overlapping as teachers begin to revise their practice.

To illustrate, we have chosen a vignette of one episode of a second grade team meeting. In this case, teachers are looking at a multiple-choice question that asks students to identify a possible contraction for this sentence: "They would not run in the mud" and presented three options for the answer, including "wouldn't" and "won't." (Teachers are labeled T1, T2, and so on to T8.)

> T7: I had one of my students circle C for won't, but she did her BES [best effort strategy] and she said, "will + not = won't." So, she just didn't look at the *would not*, so she knows won't, which is interesting because I think I mentioned the won't thing like one time.
>
> T6: Yeah, because it's irregular.
>
> T7: Right, because we decided not to really focus on that.

T1: And, if my kids missed it, four of my kids circled "won't" and it's the one that also makes sense in the sentence. "They won't run in the mud. They wouldn't run in the mud."

T2: They would not; they will not—syntactically correct.

T3: Maybe for next time, we might want to leave this [test question] out, just because it is so tricky.

T6: I think the key is learning from this will force you to change . . . or check into the way you're teaching this, because if you say, "What word will re-place it? What word could also fit there?" then, yeah, there is more than one choice. But, if you are really teaching them the BES like you said (motioning to T7), "Ugh, she just didn't notice would" then they should get it.

T8: And, it would be good when we unpack and frame it to make sure we talk about irregulars and maybe strategies for how to teach irregulars. You know, because I don't think we explicitly discussed it when we unpacked and framed contractions. The irregular ones?

T1: We talked about "won't," as one, because that is the only one we're expected to teach.

T8: Alright. Yeah.

T1: But, thinking about what [T6] just said, that is how I taught it.

T6: That's what I mean—that might be how we taught it. [Other teachers agreeing.]

T1: That's how I taught it—with what makes sense, but you need to think what is another correct way to write would not, so I think that makes a huge difference.

T6: Right, just check into your teacher language with how are you teaching it because that is one strategy, but that won't always work. And so . . . the other thing is, too, if this [the assessment] is for our purposes, it's not a [state test], so doing this like a [state test] with it being really hard shows us, so next time we have to plan our teacher language better. I don't think . . . if the students are confused, they're confused for a second . . . sorry. That helps us plan our teaching, though. So, I think it's good to leave it, kind of hard.

T4: As a question, approaching it as the question, rather than the students, it's a good one so it has that.

Teachers: Right, yeah.

At the start of this exchange, T7 and T1 name the answers their students gave for the test item and articulate *student thinking on the assessment*. T3 moves the discussion from *understanding student thinking* to *understanding assessment*, questioning whether the test item is "good" and should be kept. T6 quickly responds by arguing that the question is helpful and moves the discussion towards *understanding how instruction links to student performance* ("check into the way you're teaching this"). At this point, T8 addresses how the group "unpack[ed] and frame[d]" this content, moving the focus to *what should be taught*. Next, T1 moves the conversation back to *understanding how instruction links to student performance*, declaring "that is how I taught it!" Finally, T6 finishes this episode by focusing on teacher language or how *instruction might change student performance*. Teachers articulate the connections between teaching, assessment, and student thinking, ultimately envisioning a change in instruction.

In her explanation of learning within teacher teams, Horn (2010) argues that through extended replays and rehearsals that lead to revisions of practice, members of the community are "repositioned" within the community of practice (Lave & Wenger, 1991). We suggest that this episode illustrates a revision as teachers reconsider pedagogy previously unexamined. However, our second question is concerned with what organizational learning is evident in these episodes.

To What Extent Is Organizational Learning Resulting from Teachers' Use of Evidence in PLCs?

In the previous dialogue, we believe a connection exists between the assessment and teachers' revision of practice because we see that these five processes overlap within the episode. Therefore, teacher discussion links assessment with student thinking and with instruction. Although this dialogue demonstrates these connections, our next question asks for evidence of organizational learning, and our discussion is guided by Levitt and March's (1988) concept of routines as discussed in our conceptual framework.

Routines

Routines act as guiding forces that focus and narrow the work of teachers within collaborative teams. The drive for teachers to use evidence to inform instruction has generated numerous routines, shifting teaching practices in ways not yet examined. For example, the creation and use of common assessments shape the discussions of student learning, creating routinized patterns for how learning is identified and translated into action. For discussion purposes, we use the episode of second grade teachers as an example.

Teachers analyzed isolated questions on assessments to try to decipher student thinking in relation to specific content material. The first step in their analysis was to walk through how a student engaged in the *procedure* of answering the test question. At the start of this episode, T7 identifies one student who did not answer the question correctly. She describes the student's thinking or process when answering that question:

> I had one of my students circle C for won't, but she did her BES and she said, "will + not = won't." So, she just didn't look at the *would not*, so she knows won't, which is interesting because I think I mentioned the won't thing like one time.

In this description, the teacher identifies what the student knows ("will + not = won't") and concludes a procedural problem that led to the student missing the question ("she just didn't look at the *would not*").

Through continued discussion, teachers move beyond procedure to questioning how students understand contractions. T6 explains how teachers' instruction might have changed the way students interpreted the question.

> I think the key is learning from this will force you to change . . . or check into the way you're teaching this, because if you say, "What word will replace it? What word could also fit there?" then, yeah, there is more than one choice. But, if you are really teaching them the BES like you said (motioning to T7), "Ugh, she just didn't notice would" then they should get it.

T6 prompts the teachers to question how well students understand contractions, and, with this move, the routine of the test continues to frame the discussion. This response offers an "if-then" pattern consistent with the structure of the test: if teachers teach "best effort strategies," then students should be able to answer this question correctly or "they should get it."

As a result of these patterns, when teachers revise instruction, it is often focused on discrete tactics and very small movements in teaching. T6 summarizes the discussion by saying "Right, just check into your teacher language with how are you teaching it because that is one strategy, but that won't always work." Teachers are focused on tactics to be able to identify correct answers, particularly identified best practices ("best effort strategy"), and their analysis of students' thinking leads them to discrete movements ("teacher language") that should support students in improved performance on assessments. The discussion continues to be shaped by the language of tests, as student learning is diagnosed through the lens of assessment.

DISCUSSION AND CONCLUSIONS

Teacher discussions that focus on micro-movements within the classroom provide evidence of specific ways teachers intend to change instruction. This mode of classroom organization offers potential designs for future empirical work to capture what changes are made as a result of teachers' use of evidence, and the effect on student achievement. Our data captured multiple examples of how teachers envisioned changes.

However, we believe the discussion of organizational learning demands larger questions about the nature of these potential changes. The evidence implies that teachers are focused on solving short-term dilemmas, and we have little evidence of teachers using collaborative structures to uncover undiscussables or question governing variables (Argyris & Schon, 1974).

Implied but not really discussed when we addressed learning via routines are some important assumptions. Two of the most prominent are that PLCs and schools within the same district should look more similar than different and that risk should be minimized (Bauer, Brazer, Van Lare, & Smith, chapter 4, this volume). Similarity and risk aversion are pursued more confidently as seeking "best practices," especially if they are reputed to be "research based." We in no way intend to imply that such an approach is warranted or that administrators would know better than anyone else what practices are most appropriate in a variety of classrooms and circumstances. We only mean to convey that these are potential messages to PLCs and teachers. Nevertheless, if tacit assumptions within the school's organizational culture include the credibility of best practices and the need to maintain isomorphism as a means to legitimacy, then learning via routines seems more likely.

A very different set of assumptions might begin with the idea that classrooms and schools are inherently unique, rendering the notion of best practice and routinized problem solving largely irrelevant. To address contextually based needs requires that teachers be given the latitude to investigate root causes of the problems they experience and share in PLCs (Bauer & Brazer, 2012). Teachers would still be largely powerless in the face of their challenges unless an additional assumption is that they can experiment with promising solutions that appear to mitigate or eliminate root causes (Osterman & Kottkamp, 2004). Doing so might make classrooms, grade levels, or schools look different from one another, so an additional important assumption would be that variation is acceptable.

NOTES

1. This study was generously supported by the Spencer Foundation. The authors take sole responsibility for the work presented.

2. All proper nouns used in this paper are pseudonyms. The information in this paragraph was gathered from the school district's website. To protect the anonymity of the district and research participants, no citation is given.

REFERENCES

Allison, G., & Zelikow, P. (1999). *Essence of decision: Explaining the Cuban missile crisis* (2nd ed.). New York: Longman.

Argyris, C. (1999). *On organizational learning* (2nd ed.). Malden, MA: Blackwell Business.

Argyris, C., & Schon, D. (1974). *Theory in practice: Increasing professional effectiveness.* San Franciso: Jossey-Bass.

Argyris, C., & Schon, D. (1978). *Organizational learning: A theory of action perspective.* Reading, MA: Addison-Wesley.

Bauer, S. C., & Brazer, S. D. (2012). *Using research to lead school improvement: Turning evidence into action.* Thousand Oaks, CA: Sage Publications.

Bidwell, C. E. (2001). Analyzing schools as organizations: Long-term permanence and short-term change. *Sociology of Education (extra issue),* 100–14.

Coburn, C., & Talbert, J. (2006). Conceptions of evidence use in school districts: Mapping the terrain. *American Journal of Education, 112*(4), 469–95.

Conley, S., & Enomoto, E. K. (2009). Organizational routines in flux: A case study of change in recording and monitoring student attendance. *Education & Urban Society, 41*(3), 364–86.

Cuban, L. (1993). *How teachers taught: Constancy and change in American classrooms, 1880–1990* (2nd ed.). New York: Teachers College Press.

DuFour, R. (2004). What is a "professional learning community"? *Educational Leadership, 61*(8), 6–11.

DuFour, R., DuFour, R., Eaker, R., & Many, T. (2010). *Learning by doing: A handbook for professional learning communities at work* (2nd ed.). Bloomington IN: Solution Tree.

DuFour, R., Eaker, R., & DuFour, R. (2005). *On common ground: The power of professional learning communities.* Bloomington, IN: Solution Tree.

Feldman, M. S., & Pentland, B.T. (2003). Reconceptualizing organizational routines as a source of flexibility and change. *Administrative Science Quarterly, 48*(1), 94–118.

Horn, I. (2010). Teaching replays, teaching rehearsals, and re-visions of Practice: Learning from colleagues in a mathematics teacher community. *Teachers College Record, 112*(1), 225–59.

Ikemoto, G., & Marsh, J. A. (2007). Cutting through the "data-driven" mantra: Different conceptions of data-driven decision making. *Yearbook (National Society for the Study of Education),* (1), 105–31.

Lave, J., & Wenger, E. (1991). *Situated learning: Legitimate peripheral participation: Learning in doing.* Cambridge: Cambridge University Press.

Levitt, B., & March, J. G. (1988). Organizational learning. *Annual Review of Sociology, 14*, 319–40.

Little, J. W. (2003). Locating learning in teachers' communities of practice: Opening up problems of analysis in records of everyday work. *Teaching and Teacher Education, 18*(8), 917–46.

Little, J. W. (2012). Understanding data use practice among teachers: The contribution of micro-process studies. *American Journal of Education, 118*(2), 143–66.

March, J. G. (1994). *A primer on decision making: How decisions happen.* New York: Free Press.

March, J. G., & Simon, H. A. (1993). *Organizations* (2nd ed.). Oxford, UK: Blackwell.

Maxwell, J. A. (2005). *Qualitative research design: An interactive approach* (2nd ed.). Thousand Oaks, CA: Sage Publications.

McLaughlin, M. W., & Talbert, J. E. (2001). *Professional communities and the work of high school teaching.* Chicago: University of Chicago Press.

Means, B., Chen, E., DeBarger, A., & Padilla, C. (2011). *Teachers' ability to use data to inform instruction: Challenges and supports.* Washington, DC: U.S. Department of Education Office of Planning, Evaluation and Policy Development.

Merriam, S. B. (1998). *Qualitative research and case study applications in education.* San Francisco: Jossey-Bass.

Mintrop, H. (2004). Fostering constructivist communities of learners in the amalgamated multi-discipline of social studies. *Journal of Curriculum Studies, 36,* 141–58.

Moss, P. A. (2012). Exploring the macro-micro dynamic in data use practices. *American Journal of Education, 118*(2), 223–32.

O'Day, J. (2009). Good instruction is good for everyone—Or is it? English language learners in a balanced literacy approach. *Journal of Education for Students Placed at Risk, 14,* 97–119.

Oláh, L., Lawrence, N. R., & Riggan, M. (2010). Learning to learn from benchmark assessment data: How teachers analyze results. *Peabody Journal of Education, 85*(2), 226–45.

Osterman, K., & Kottkamp, R. (2004). *Reflective practice for educators: Development to improve student learning* (2nd ed.). Thousand Oaks, CA: Corwin Press.

Schein, E. (2010). *Organizational culture and leadership.* San Francisco: Wiley

Servage, L. (2008). Critical and transformative practices in professional learning communities. *Teacher Education Quarterly, 35*(1), 63–77.

Spillane, J. P. (2012). Data in practice: Conceptualizing the data-based decision making phenomena. *American Journal of Education, 118,* 113–41.

Tyack, D., & Cuban, L. (1995). *Tinkering toward utopia: A century of public school reform.* Cambridge, MA: Harvard University Press.

Wenger, E. (1998). *Communities of practice: Learning, meaning, and identity.* New York: Cambridge University Press.

Chapter Nine

Teacher-Principal Collaboration

Partnerships or Power Plays?

Vivienne Collinson

Leader and follower are partners in the same dance.

(Bennis, 2009, p. 225)

Collaboration among teachers has been extolled for several decades. For example, following Lortie's (1975) observation of teacher isolation and Little's (1982) operational definition of teacher collaboration, teacher teaming in schools became more prevalent. In the 1990s, principals were encouraged to promote teacher-teacher collaboration, which was increasingly linked to improving teaching and student learning (e.g., Pounder, 1998). Literature on teacher-principal collaboration, however, was thin. Explanations suggested that collaboration could pose problems "for many school leaders who fear for their power as they worry about how far collaboration can go" (Hargreaves, 1994, pp. 9–10) or for principals who might not trust teachers enough to share authority and responsibility (Tschannen-Moran, 2001).

This chapter discusses teacher-principal collaboration from the perspectives of eighty-one secondary school teachers across the United States who participated in a study of exemplary teachers. Although the study focused on the concept of "exemplary teacher," 95 percent of the participants provided unsolicited information about their relationships and interactions with principals. The chapter summarizes what this group of teachers most appreciated and disliked about principals. Their comments indicated that as a group, the teachers preferred to collaborate with principals as partners for the ultimate purpose of helping students learn and experience success. However, they also described strategies they use when dealing with principals with whom they have difficulty collaborating in productive partnerships.

COLLABORATION AND GOVERNANCE

Much of education research in the twentieth century focused on individual learning for teachers (usually professional development) and individual leadership in schools (usually individuals with a formalized title and role). Research in the twenty-first century has increasingly directed attention to organizational learning and shared leadership. This shift in thinking emphasized continuous and shared learning for *all* professionals in school systems and embraced the perspective that all organizational members influence and share responsibility for learning—individually and collectively—as they work collaboratively to sustain purposeful improvement in response to a rapidly changing world (see Collinson & Cook, 2007).

Research also reflected the changing belief that leadership can "come from many places within an organization" (Senge, 1996, p. 45; Rost, 1991) and that people "follow to the fullest when leadership is based on expertness or an admirable goal, not because of a title or organizational status" (Kelley, 1992, p. 9; Gardner, 1990). At the same time, technology enhanced collaboration; learning could be shared quickly and groups such as professional learning communities (PLCs) were not limited by geographical boundaries of schools and school systems.

Shared learning and leadership are interconnected and both are closely related to collaboration (Collinson, 2008, 2012). Dixon (1999) observed that shared learning "creates equals, not subordinates" (p. 5); that is, "learning inexorably leads to shared governance and shared governance requires learning" (p. 221). Collaboration in this sense requires "true partnerships, [where] competent people join together to achieve what they could not achieve alone" (Kelley, 1992, p. 203).

Building a Foundation for Collaboration: Skill Sets and Trust

Collaboration does not simply happen. Few would dispute the importance of positive interpersonal skills and relationships for collaborative interactions, effective leadership, or learning for students, teachers, and organizations (Collinson & Cook, 2007; Conley, Fauske, & Pounder, 2004; Martin & Dowson, 2009; Stoll, Fink, & Earl, 2003). Some of the skill sets necessary for all professionals in schools include "communication skills, conflict management and resolution skills, consultation skills, [and] group process skills" (Donaldson, 2001, p. 116). Other skill sets that support collaborative learning include dialogue and questioning, collective inquiry (problem solving), argumentation (providing one's reasoning, evidence, explanation), and decision making (Collinson, 2008). Development of these skills requires years of practice and then further practice to refine them.

Although both principals and teachers influence the school environment, principals tend to carry responsibility for establishing and nurturing an environment hospitable to learning and innovation (Collinson & Cook, 2007; Rosenholtz, 1989; Stoll, Fink, & Earl, 2003). Moreover, because the development of collaboration requires "interpersonal relationships of mutuality, trust and respect" (McGregor, 2003, p. 123), principals also play a major role in teachers' levels of relational trust or distrust (Tschannen-Moran, 2001). "Collaboration and trust are reciprocal processes; they depend upon and foster one another . . . In schools where there was greater trust, there tended to be a greater level of collaboration" (Tschannen-Moran, 2001, pp. 315, 327).

Likewise, a recent survey suggested that both elementary and secondary schools "with higher degrees of collaboration are associated with shared leadership and higher levels of trust and job satisfaction" (MetLife Survey, 2010, p. 9). By contrast, Rosenholtz (1989) observed that in less collaborative or "isolated settings," principals exerted more control, learning and sharing decreased, and principals seemed to subvert teachers' opportunities for decision-making by what teachers perceived as "ego-defensive maneuvers" and "power plays" (p. 62). In another study, Robinson (1996) found that "trust comes, in part, from judgments about integrity" (p. 578); for example, trust can erode if someone displays a lack of respect and concern for the welfare of others or demonstrates inconsistency between words and actions. She also discovered that erosion of trust can be a potential catalyst for individuals' withdrawal of contributions to the organization or departure from the organization.

RESEARCH METHODS

This chapter presents findings of unsolicited data from a study whose purpose was to explore the concept of "exemplary teacher" at the secondary level (grades seven through twelve). Using the reputational method of purposive sampling to identify exemplary secondary school teachers across the United States, I asked a professional contact in each successive sampling round to form a local group of six to twelve peer nominators with extensive experience in their school district and regular opportunities to visit classrooms or work closely with teachers. Peer nominators comprised educators such as staff developers, subject specialists, school/university partnership liaisons, and regional laboratory personnel. Each local group compiled a pool of exemplary teachers in their region, allowing me to select a broad representation of subjects, grade levels, and schools (urban, suburban, rural) by the end of the sampling rounds (N=81; pseudonyms throughout).

Data were collected across three years and included a pre-interview survey (professional information) followed by an in-depth, semistructured, three-hour interview with each participant. Interviews were taped and transcribed. To supplement field notes, other data from the participants included artifacts such as student work; teacher-solicited feedback from students; notes and letters to the teachers; and books, articles, and materials they had published.

Analysis of surveys was captured in data displays and indicated that participants were avid learners and active leaders in their schools, local communities, and the profession (elaborated in Collinson, 2012). The method of constant comparative analysis was used to analyze interviews whose guiding questions built on the literature and were designed to extend understanding of exemplary teachers. Interviews were coded, searched for patterns, relationships, explanations and inconsistencies, and then integrated into categories and subcategories. During the coding process, a data display indicated that as the teachers responded to the interview questions, 95 percent talked about their principals—sometimes current principals, sometimes past principals, sometimes both.

This study did not set out to investigate teacher-principal collaboration, so the data may represent an incomplete portrait of the exemplary teachers' perspectives of secondary school principals and only a partial account of strategies they employed. Nevertheless, the extent and richness of the unanticipated data provide a glimpse into how this sample of exemplary secondary school teachers in the United States viewed and reacted to principals who influenced their professional life.

TEACHERS' PERSPECTIVES OF
SCHOOL ADMINISTRATORS

Extensive experience informed the exemplary teachers' perspectives of administrators. The majority had seen numerous principals and assistant principals come and go throughout their career, including the thirteen (16 percent) who had taught at only one school (generally the least experienced teachers or those in isolated areas). At the time of data collections, twenty-two teachers (27 percent) had taught at two schools, fifteen (19 percent) at three schools, eighteen (22 percent) at four schools, six (7 percent) at five schools, and seven (9 percent) at six to nine schools. Those schools were located in 164 school districts across the United States. Additionally, the teachers held voluntary roles that allowed them to observe, instruct, or converse with many colleagues inside and outside their school region (e.g., as department chair or team leader; higher education instructor; staff development trainer or presenter; member of district, state, or national committees; member or officer of state or national professional organizations).

The teachers appreciated that running a good school is very difficult and that "administrators are extremely important people. They can make or break your day" (Matthew). They can also make or break teachers: "I think if you really get right down to it, a fine principal makes many fine teachers" (Brendan). These teachers understood that in the absence of a "fine principal," they personally cannot do their best.

> To teach effectively, you really must have—well, it is very important to have a good administration to back you up. You'll teach, but the better the administration, the more effective you're going to be. . . . And we have an excellent administration.—Gabe

Excellence is not always the norm, however. Some environments create a difficult situation for these teachers who want to do their best with students and help their students experience success. The teachers especially disliked administrators' beliefs and behaviors that ran counter to what they were trying to model for students (also Huberman, 1995). Remarks included comments like "Thinking does not seem to be a real important goal at our school" (Toller) and "Sometimes you learn [from them] what *not* to do" (Natalie). Table 9.1 summarizes this sample's positive and negative perspectives of their principals.

Dealing with Principals

Researchers have long known that exemplary teachers are avid learners, take risks, enjoy novelty and variety, love both autonomy and collegial

Table 9.1   Exemplary Teachers' Perspectives of Their Principals

Positive Perspectives of Principals Who:

- prioritize learning and establish an environment hospitable to learning
- help teachers do their best (e.g., resources, relations with parents and the community, opportunities for teacher development)
- encourage risk taking, experimentation, and innovation
- foster collegial professionalism (i.e., competence and autonomy balanced with professional judgment and responsibility)
- have strong communication and interpersonal skills
- model respect for everyone
- know and care about students
- demonstrate fairness and consistency, especially with school budgets
- provide genuine, knowledgeable recognition and feedback

Negative Perspectives of Principals Who:

- engage in self-promotion or power plays (control over)
- demonstrate attitudes and actions that do not support learning or represent poor teaching practice
- issue rules as a substitute for problem finding and solving
- give the most difficult assignments and most undesirable schedules and classrooms to novices
- make unilateral hiring and instructional decisions (particularly if decisions show lack of understanding about learning and students)
- sabotage or cut successful programs
- issue arbitrary budget and structural decisions
- do not stay up to date
- mindlessly accept policies that ignore research
- are not visible ("phantom principal")
- conduct meaningless annual assessments/evaluations (minimal classroom monitoring and knowledge)

relationships, and seek self-imposed change or opportunities inside and outside their classrooms (e.g., Williams, 2003). The exemplary teachers in this sample are no different; they do everything they can to foster and improve learning for themselves and their students (e.g., they read and stay current, avidly pursue professional development opportunities, write grants for resources, establish business and university partnerships). That desire also appears to be a catalyst for their many collaborative efforts: developing collegial networks, participating as members or leaders of professional organizations, observing colleagues, team teaching, or sharing innovations with colleagues (Collinson, 2012).

They also enjoy collaborating in innovative endeavors. In addition to pedagogical innovations, many had piloted school-wide changes such as interdisciplinary curriculum, assessments, new schedules, mentoring programs and mentor training, school-community relations, and school-to-work programs. One teacher was thrilled to follow her principal and help open a new high school. She considered the challenge "exciting stuff because now we're really bridging between the community and business partnerships and higher education partnerships. And we're really understanding that schools cannot remain in isolation and go about their little academic roots anymore. It just doesn't work" (Gail).

Working as Partners

Teacher comments suggested that working with principals as partners is highly valued: "We have to work together. . . . In the site team, the principal's vote is no more important than the rest of the members" (Colleen) and "[My principal] really tried to do everything he could to make the teacher's life as happy a life as it could be. He was a fine man. And he treated me like a professional" (Matthew). Innovation to improve learning appeared particularly attractive to these teachers (also see Williams, 2003) and they enjoyed principals who served as catalysts to encourage experimentation and risk taking. For instance, one teacher praised

> a principal who knew how to plant seeds and let teachers run with them, which—many times, you don't find principals that will relinquish that iron rule over their teachers. . . . I think our administration gave us the license to take risks and to fail because they knew that we were going to bounce back

and find a way to succeed. It was not going to be a long-term failure, throw your hands up in the air, and say "Forget it." We were going to prove to ourselves that we could do it, and I think we have.—Janet

In another region, after a principal encouraged a teacher to "try something new" by giving a presentation to her peers, she then "did lots of new things with him. He'd say, 'Renee, you learn from failure too, so if this does not work, it's okay,' making it okay for me to fail so that I would take risks" (Renee).

Although collaboration with principals as partners was appreciated, not all participants had collaborative principals at the time of data collection or in prior schools. Apparently unwilling to accept that reality, 42 percent of the sample volunteered explanations of how they had dealt with a less-than-collaborative administrator. The nine ways they mentioned represent action: they model or pilot desired changes, reason with administrators, find alternative solutions or do it themselves, make unilateral administrative decisions work, work around administrators, alter administrators' rules, bargain with administrators, speak truth to power, or leave the school.

Model or Pilot Desired Changes

The exemplary teachers seem skillful in defining barriers to learning and finding helpful solutions. They routinely pilot or model innovations in their classroom and usually try to get administrators' support. For example, one teacher who started doing parent-teacher conferences for her own class said, "Our school doesn't do parent conferences. I'm working with the new principal to see if [he] can start" conferences as a school-wide practice (Juanita).

Some of the most irksome barriers seemed to involve principals' unilateral structural decisions such as budgeting or scheduling, especially if those structures demonstrated a lack of understanding of students, learning, or research. One principal chose "what was called a rotating schedule [of periods]. One week, it could be 1, 2, 3, 4, 5, 6. The next week it could be 1, 3, 6, 5, 4, 2 . . . Lunch wasn't even consistent. They [students] could have first lunch one week, second lunch [the next week]. These poor children!" (Fiona). Another said,

These scheduling people! Last year, I had a class that was forty-three minutes, one that was forty-eight minutes, one that was an hour and twelve minutes. . . . Well, [students] couldn't figure out where they're supposed to be or what time they were supposed to be there. And then [the administrators] wonder why they're tardy!—Claire

Another teacher who had been assigned forty-minute teaching periods for English classes said, "I just go insane because I teach [in] one of these districts that has to talk about everything for sixteen years" and in a school "with a lot of people that say, 'If it ain't broke, don't fix it.'"

If [teachers] are willing to stand up for what they believe in within their district and they're willing to model that belief, . . . the changes are going to come . . . I believe this in kids and I believe this in adults: they will learn by modeling. And teachers, even the ones that you're not very fond of, if they see something working and see something be successful, their chances of trying it are much higher . . . [I'm] big into piloting. I piloted eighty-minute blocks the year before anybody else would even look at it. . . . And all the teachers were saying, "Eighty minutes? Oh, my God! I can't teach for eighty minutes! What do you mean?!" So I did eighty minutes by myself for a year—just my class—the only one in the whole building. They watched me enjoy it and they listened to me brag about it all year. My whole building is that way now.—Glynis

Reason with Administrators

Because the exemplary teachers love to read, attend conferences, and experiment in their classroom, they have little difficulty marshaling research or evidence to persuade an administrator why an innovation would be good for the school. They also use knowledge of the administrator and careful language to influence a favorable outcome. For example, a math teacher wanted to increase networking capacity in the school and knew his administrator was interested in integrating math, science, and technology.

If you can convince a supervisor that they thought of your great idea, you stand a much better chance of its implementation. . . . When this whole technology idea came up, . . . I was looking at the [networking] idea being the context and his integration idea was in it. But instead, I turned [it] around and said, "Okay, your integration idea. Maybe we can use this kind of networking." And he's a technological klutz . . . [but] he's not a foolish man. He knows that when the tide is turning, people turn with the tide and don't try to fight it. So he thinks it's a good idea, and particularly when I said, "You know, with the math and science integration, there are resources that enter the building without [restrictions], to go anywhere. The kids can sit down and do what's called distance learning. They learn with other classrooms. We can connect with kids in Australia or France or Nova Scotia or British Columbia and talk about stuff. We can get projects going. There's all these funds available that we can write grant proposals for and bring the money in." . . . So he came around.—Andrew

Find Alternative Solutions or Do It Themselves

One teacher who was accustomed to providing leadership development at the state level looked for ways to improve difficult relationships between administrators and teachers in his own school.

> I started a conflict resolution program at the school. I provided an opportunity for teachers to be trained in conflict resolution. I think we've trained thirty-four staff members. And then I've written several grants so that we have a [student] peer mediation program. And then we also are working on a parent training program to offer. . . . I do some conflict resolution teaching as part of that teamwork building.—Toller

In other circumstances, teachers may simply act independently. One team leader who believes strongly in communicating explained:

> We have [a principal] now who's not the best communicator in the world, and that's a lot of what our [team] meeting was about that last day. You have to do it in spite of them. If they won't do it, you have to do it.—Sandy

The same teacher, whose students lived in poverty, also collaborated directly with teachers to write grants and with community businesses to secure resources to support learning. "The community [helps] if we just ask," she said. "I don't think we've [the team] ever asked them for anything they didn't try to do if they could."

Make Unilateral Administrative Decisions Work

Several teachers mentioned unilateral administrative decisions they profoundly disagreed with on the grounds that the decision negatively affected students' learning and prevented teachers from doing their best. When persuasion failed, they made the decision work for the sake of the students. Two cases involved class size. One was a first-year class of thirty-nine foreign language students. As department head, the teacher "took the class rather than assign it to one of my other teachers because I felt that I could deal with it better, and I didn't want to put that burden on someone else" (Esther). Another teacher was also given large classes, including one with thirty-eight honors students.

> The school did not get the funding for an English position, and . . . so the way the administration solved the problem [laughter] was to take the two honors classes and combine them into one. And . . . their thinking was, "Well, they're good students so it should be easy." Good students have a lot of questions. They need a lot of personal attention. But anyway, it did work. I mean, . . . I could tell sometimes the students would get frustrated if they didn't have as much of the one-on-one [interaction].—Helen

Work around Administrators

Instead of making a principal's decision work, teachers sometimes found ways to work around the decision.

> Part of it is when the principals, I find, have problems sharing power. . . . This power thing, there's no need for that. But by being there long enough and going through many things over the years, I've learned to adjust and adapt. If you cannot adjust—adapt or adjust—then you're going to have to move or die. So I can adjust. I work my way *around* the principal.—Emmett

Teachers seemed particularly inclined to work around principals' decisions if their experience and professional judgment suggested that student learning would be compromised.

> Teaching isn't static, and teachers kind of need to be flexible and open to new ideas. And yet, the way our school system is, you know, they [administrators]

come up with a new idea and they want you to abandon everything else. I think you kind of need to have some judgment there, and balance. But I think good teachers are willing to listen to new ideas and smart enough to keep what's good of the old [ideas].—Juanita

Several teachers of art, music, foreign languages, and vocational education noted dismissive administrator attitudes toward their subject. For instance, when a novice art teacher first arrived in a large rural area, she wanted to observe and talk with the only other art teachers in a distant northern part of the school district. She asked her principal for a day to observe them, but

> the principal looked at me and he said, "You're art. Nah, you don't have to do that. You're doing just fine the way you are." It was . . . hard. I did go up after school every now and then . . . [but] I would really like to have watched them teach.—Catherine

Alter Administrators' Rules

Professional judgment may also lead teachers to alter administrators' rules. Numerous teachers commented on the importance of the first day of classes for sending a message to students that their course involves interesting ideas and student engagement but is rigorous and demands work. However, many teachers were required to read the school rules on the first day, so students heard the same rules every period and from every teacher.

> I disagree with my principal on this. My principal does not believe in passing out books on the first day and does not believe in getting much work done on the first day. But in my classes, I assign homework on the first day. We [work] the first day. And you should see how fast I go though those class rules! . . . And at that point, [the students are] kind of like, "She's nuts. She has now gone through the four-hour school booklet in five minutes!"—Amy

If administrators' rules disrespect students, reflect unacceptable teaching practice, interfere with students' academic or attitudinal learning, or contradict professional judgment, teachers may give a nod to the rule only when absolutely necessary (also see Rosenholtz, 1989). For example, when one principal made a rule that teachers had to walk all students to the cafeteria because "some students were running, . . . we came up with the Protest Picnics . . . We'd eat in our room to keep from having to be walked to lunch" (Rachel). In one school system, administrators created a one-size-fits-all teaching requirement and then made it part of the teacher evaluation review to ensure compliance. A seasoned teacher gave me well-reasoned arguments why she disagreed "so strongly" with the rule and then said, "I don't run my classroom like you're supposed to for the evaluation instrument [laughter]" (Claire).

Bargain

Occasionally, teachers are so concerned with top-down decisions they perceive as egregious influences on learning that they bargain with administrators. One teacher who views bargaining as "politicking" was told through an intermediary that the school administrators were moving her class to a period that would cause her students to miss extracurricular activities. Knowing that the students' anger could affect their learning during that period, the teacher "immediately called the vice principal. . . . Even though I . . . said all the nice things, at the end, I knew that I had told them I was going to play hardball" (Wendy). Her leverage was that

> the principal owed me one. Well, why did she owe me? Because I did a favor for her [writing a grant the principal wanted, with no notice, the last week of school]. So part of politicking, my thinking is, is that *you* do what they want you to do at the right time too . . . I did [the grant] because it had to be done for my school. I mean, I would *never* let that fall through the cracks and . . . I knew she couldn't write it. So I said, "No problem. I will take care of it" because I didn't want to lose that for my school. It wasn't for me at all . . . But politics is definitely a part of the whole thing.—Wendy

Another teacher bargained with even higher stakes after administrators insisted she "teach to the test" when statewide annual testing was introduced.

> I did it one year. I did what they told me to do. And for six weeks, I bored my kids with handouts and exercises and drills for [the test]. And I lost my kids that year and I never got them back. They were bored. . . . When those kids understood that they couldn't trust me to provide them with interesting

learning material and that I'd sold out to the enemy by allowing my class time to be taken up with these stupid exercises, they didn't trust me ever again. And I learned a hard lesson that year and I'll never do it again. The next year I said [to the administrators], "See these [test exercises]? See this trash can? I'm not doing it, so fire me." And they said, "Oh! Well, what about your kids? They won't pass the [state test]." And I said, "Yeah they will. If they don't pass it, fire me," you know. And they did great on the [test].—Amber

Speak Truth to Power

Although speaking truth to power requires courage and may result in possible reprisals (Kelley, 1992), Bennis (2009) asserted that speaking truth to power is "the most important obligation as followers" (p. 225). Crowther (2009) also noted that "responsible professionals" are inclined to "challenge the status quo" and "do not to turn a blind eye when they perceive that barriers are diminishing the integrity of their school" (p. 17). In this sample, teachers tended to speak up when principals neglected learning or the well-being of students or faculty. One teacher said, "If I want something for a student [or] if I think they're [administrators] screwing around with my students' education, I'm right after them on where I stand" (Ted). Another teacher said, "I've got to have what I consider a knock-down, drag-out battle with the principal . . . over technology" (Mark). The teacher believed that his students who entered high school with high expectations could not advance appropriately because the high school's equipment was so inferior to the technology students had enjoyed in middle school.

Teachers may also resort to speaking truth to power when administrators override teachers' professional judgment—not to help students, but to serve their own interest; for instance, to appease parents or political groups.

This year, I had a *most* interesting, several most interesting cases . . . [It] was very interesting to be told by parents, "My child *will* be getting an A in [your] class" . . . And I had to tell my principal, "Here's my summer phone number." You know, "Call me. I'll be glad to come in to the meeting. I'm not changing the grade, no matter what, so if you want to divert it ahead of time, you go right ahead" kind of thing. So that was interesting.—Amy

Leave the School

Although the participants in general seemed to have a high incidence of changing schools, many of the changes were voluntary (e.g., to work with a good principal, challenge themselves with new grade levels, help open a new school). However, eight participants in this sample (10 percent) happened to mention situations in which they had voluntarily left their workplace as a last resort or final straw when leaders engaged in retaliation for speaking truth to power, allowed an environment that was antithetic to learning, prevented students or teachers from doing their best, asked them to do something unethical, or overlooked unethical behavior (also see Blase & Blase, 2004).

Four of the eight participants—two during a prior career and two others during their teaching career—left with no future job in hand. "You have to support the people that you work for. If you can't work for administrators, get out. Transfer. I did that once. I was recommended for [State] Teacher of the Year . . . and resigned two days later, with no job" (Arturo). Another teacher left a school where administrators allowed a culture that undercut excellence. Her beliefs shaken, she thought, "I've got to get out of here because this will destroy me as a teacher. . . . The things that I saw there—the attitudes that were held dear—were very, very frightening" (Tanith). One teacher spoke of seeing excellent colleagues change schools or leave the profession, explaining that "eventually, those impact teachers want to go someplace where—remember, they're humans too— where they're appreciated and where they *can* thrust their energies into something that's moving, where the train is moving" (Nate).

WHITHER TEACHER-PRINCIPAL COLLABORATION?

Recognizing that collaborative relationships and higher levels of trust tend to exist in schools where learning is emphasized and leadership is shared (e.g., Engels et al., 2008; MetLife Survey, 2010; Rosenholtz, 1989), the data in this study underscore the need to learn more about such relationships, especially about teacher-principal collaboration. Collaboration is a complicated construct that has become an umbrella term encompassing complex concepts like communication, relational trust, and a host of skills. Besides demanding intellectual and social skills, collaboration as a partnership seems to require attitudes that favor equality, respect for others, learning, sharing, risk taking, and a balance between autonomy and interdependence. Such skills and attitudes are forged and refined over time through life experiences and workplace practice. They cannot be left to chance. Rather, skills and attitudes that support collaboration are necessary for *all* members and could provide a blueprint for differentiated development for professionals during their career.

Tradition during the twentieth century typically separated principals and teachers for professional development and offered leadership preparation and development only to aspiring or practicing principals respectively. These structures seem to work against collaboration and shared understandings. Moreover, the teachers' choices to model and pilot innovations, reason with administrators, find alternative solutions, make decisions work, work around administrators, alter rules, bargain, speak truth to power, or leave the school reflect Gardner's (1990) assertion that titular "leaders are almost never as much in charge as they are pictured to be, followers almost never as submissive as one might imagine. That influence and pressure flow both ways is not a recent discovery" (p. 23).

About half of the teachers in this sample had worked with principals whom they admired. They spoke openly and positively about the character and actions of such principals who had clearly earned their trust and respect. However, negative perceptions of principals in this and other studies raise again the overt and covert aspects of principal selection and development that Rosenholtz (1989) uncovered. Most principals are selected from the teaching body, so we might legitimately insist on selecting only teachers who have a long track record of demonstrating high levels of desirable qualities and skills, including collaborative partnerships to improve learning.

We might also seek principal candidates who have a history of modeling and piloting innovations, for as Weick and Quinn (1999) noted, "to lead change is to show people how to be" (p. 3). In other words, leadership emerges from those who are willing to "first make deep changes in themselves" (p. 380). Then, as they change behaviors, they attract new behaviors from others. Under this "logic of attraction, . . . when leaders model personal change, organizational change is more likely to take place" (p. 380).

The connections among collaboration, trust, respect, and job satisfaction also raise questions about principals' influence on teacher retention, particularly retention of exemplary teachers who love to learn and innovate to help students experience success. It is doubtful whether the exemplary teachers in this study would challenge administrators so forcefully unless they felt confident about their deep understandings of learning and of their students. Exemplary teachers are recognized as being resourceful, but their energies should not be squandered on finding ways to deal with administrators who seem uninterested in promoting an environment that fosters learning and improvement.

When school administrators, unsupportive collegial relationships, or restricted opportunities for learning influence high-performing teachers to leave schools, these teachers take their talents to more vibrant schools. Put simply, "successful schools . . . attract more academically talented teachers than unsuccessful schools" (Rosenholtz, 1989, p. 140). There is already evidence in some American schools to suggest a pattern of "the rich get richer and the poor get poorer," a pattern that "has the potential to seriously diminish organizational learning and therefore student learning" (Collinson & Cook, 2007, p. 188).

The exemplary teachers in this study initiated and enjoyed many collaborative partnerships in the profession or beyond, including partnerships with admired principals. Their ability to work collaboratively (interdependently) in schools while simultaneously protecting autonomy (individual independence) in the classroom represents in microcosm the same challenges that today's global environment poses for countries at the macro level. The twenty-first century demands collaboration in schools, along with new skills, attitudes, ideas, discussions of what is desirable, and analysis of what school personnel can do about it. Some teachers and principals have already begun to demonstrate a different way of thinking and behaving. It clearly is not easy, but their insights are valuable and need further investigation.

REFERENCES

Bennis, W. (2009). *On becoming a leader*. New York: Basic Books.
Blase, J., & Blase, J. (2004). The dark side of school leadership: Implications for administrator preparation. *Leadership and Policy in Schools, 3*(4), 245–73.
Collinson, V. (2008). Leading by learning: New directions in the twenty-first century. *Journal of Educational Administration, 46*(4), 443–60.

Collinson, V. (2012). Leading by learning, learning by leading. *Professional Development in Education, 38*(2), 247–66.

Collinson, V., & Cook, T. F. (2007). *Organizational learning: Improving learning, teaching, and leading in school systems.* Thousand Oaks, CA: Sage.

Conley, S., Fauske, J. R., & Pounder, D. (2004). Organizational context, work design, and interpersonal processes: Testing predictors of work group effectiveness. *Educational Administration Quarterly, 41*(2), 144–69.

Crowther, F., with Ferguson, M., & Hann, L. (2009). *Developing teacher leaders* (2nd ed.). Thousand Oaks, CA: Corwin Press.

Dixon, N. M. (1999). *The organizational learning cycle: How we can learn collectively* (2nd ed.). Aldershot, UK: Gower.

Donaldson, G. A. (2001). *Cultivating leadership in schools: Connecting people, purpose, and practice.* New York: Teachers College Press.

Engels, N., Hotton, G., Devos, G., Bouckenooghe, D., & Aelterman, A. (2008). Principals in schools with a positive school culture. *Educational Studies, 34*(3), 159–74.

Gardner, J. W. (1990). *On leadership.* New York: The Free Press.

Hargreaves, A. (1994). *Changing teachers, changing times: Teachers' work and culture in the postmodern age.* London: Cassell.

Huberman, M. (1995). Professional careers and professional development. In T. R. Guskey & M. Huberman (Eds.), *Professional development in education: New paradigms and practices* (pp. 193–224). New York: Teachers College Press.

Kelley, R. E. (1992). *The power of followership: How to create leaders people want to follow and followers who lead themselves.* New York: Doubleday Currency.

Little, J. W. (1982). Norms of collegiality and experimentation: Workplace conditions of school success. *American Educational Research Journal, 19*(3), 325–40.

Lortie, D. (1975). *Schoolteacher: A sociological study.* Chicago: University of Chicago Press.

Martin, A. J., & Dowson, M. (2009). Interpersonal relationships, motivation, engagement, and achievement: Yields for theory, current issues, and educational practice. *Review of Educational Research, 79*(1), 327–65.

McGregor, J. (2003). Collaboration in communities of practice. In N. Bennett & L. Anderson (Eds.), *Rethinking educational leadership: Challenging the conventions* (pp. 113–30). London: Sage.

MetLife Survey. (2010). *The MetLife survey of the American teacher* (Collaborating for student success). New York: Author.

Pounder, D. G. (1998). Promises and pitfalls of collaboration: Synthesizing dilemmas. In D. G. Pounder (Ed.), *Restructuring schools for collaboration: Promises and pitfalls* (pp. 173–80). Albany: State University of New York.

Robinson, S. L. (1996). Trust and breach of the psychological contract. *Administrative Science Quarterly, 41*(4), 547–99.

Rosenholtz, S. J. (1989). *Teachers' workplace: The social organization of schools*. White Plains, NY: Longman.

Rost, J. C. (1991). *Leadership for the twenty-first century*. Westport, CT: Praeger.

Senge, P. M. (1996). Leading learning organizations: The bold, the powerful, and the invisible. In F. Hesselbein, M. Goldsmith, & R. Beckhard (Eds.), *The leader of the future: New visions, strategies, and practices for the next era* (pp. 41–57). San Francisco: Jossey-Bass.

Stoll, L., Fink, D., & Earl, L. (2003). *It's about learning (and it's about time): What's in it for schools?* London: RoutledgeFalmer.

Tschannen-Moran, M. (2001). Collaboration and the need for trust. *Journal of Educational Administration, 39*(4), 308–31.

Weick, K. E., & Quinn, R. E. (1999). Organizational change and development. *Annual Review of Psychology, 50*, 361–86.

Williams, J. S. (2003). Why great teachers stay. *Educational Leadership, 60*(8), 71–74.

Epilogue

Overcoming Teacher Isolation: Collaboration, Professionalism, and School Quality for the Future

Bruce S. Cooper

> Traditional school norms compose a culture antithetical to collegial interaction among teachers and between teachers and administrators.
>
> (Keedy & Robbins, 1993, p. 185)

In this epilogue, we discuss the barriers, the stimuli and paths to collaboration, and where we think teachers' professionalism is heading in the future. What will be the key steps in fostering teacher collaboration that will begin to break down the barricades and build on the professional culture that is so urgently needed in education? In addition, what might the future hold, as we strive to improve education by enhancing the preparation, work, and overall careers of those vital to education—the teachers? The two themes we identify in this book are (1) framing the problem and (2) understanding the need for teacher collaboration.

THEME 1: FRAMING THE PROBLEM

Today's reforms to increase testing of children for a more accountability-oriented education may also be another move away from teacher professionalism. More and more, teachers are expected to "perform" when teaching their students to matriculate, working virtually alone in their classrooms—with the doors closed. Arthur Wise (2012) recently called this "the tyranny of the classroom walls" (p. 32). For as we test and then evaluate *student* outcomes and improvements again and again, we may tend to ignore the classroom *teachers'* activities, methods, and pedagogical skills.

Cooper and Brown described how teachers should be functioning as professionals versus being treated merely as working cogs in a production-oriented education system. The importance of teachers and their pedagogy could not be clearer, as teachers are now the largest public sector employee group in the United States, if not the world, with about 4.1 million licensed K–12 teachers in our country.

The chapters in this book explored the benefits of enhancing teachers' collaboration such as (1) reducing teacher isolation (chapter 2); (2) improving the quality of instruction and outcomes for students (chapter 8); thus (3) lowering teacher turnover so that teachers do not "take their talents to more vibrant schools" (chapter 9); and (4) improving teachers' work lives (chapter 3) as adults who educate our nation's more than 53 million schoolchildren.

Starting with the vital sociological research of Dan Lortie (1969, 1975) and Amitai Etzioni (1969), we have shown the elements of teaching that have been traditionally characterized as semiprofessional: ease of entry, low status, isolation, unclear connections between teaching and students' learning, state-level control over teachers' work, and the traditional domination of the field by women, much like some other "semiprofessions," such as nursing and social work (chapter 1).

When education is compared, for example, to the professions of medicine, law, and engineering—fields traditionally dominated by men, with higher status and longer, more demanding training, assessments, career entry, and licensing—we see the "arcane knowledge" of these fields, to use Lortie's terminology (1969, 1975). It can be argued that unlike the medical and legal professions, the classroom rarely has a life or death consequence. However, this book suggests that the establishment of a collaborative atmosphere in the classroom, school, and district can affect the quality of millions of students' and teachers' lives.

The chapters in this book discussed efforts in the field of education to overcome the difficulties of teachers' work lives: their job isolation as well as for some, a sense of poor preparation (chapter 2); low professional esteem (chapter 1); and, less than optimal relationships with administrators (chapter 9). How can we strive to improve, increase, and facilitate the entry into the profession and to strengthen preparation, training, licensing, and, then over the years, the work environment itself? These reform efforts, if designed and implemented, would help to overcome the hit-or-miss socialization of becoming and "growing" as a teacher in the modern school.

In one sense, the collaboration discussed in this volume may provide a more accelerated and effective way to enhance the professionalism of teachers—through extensive, carefully crafted peer collaboration. As Seashore Louis, Kruse, and Bryk (1995) pointed out, "Society has traditionally seen teachers as individual workers rather than as a group . . . and this has helped to isolate teachers in classrooms" (p. 15). We have suggested different settings and conditions where teachers can work together to improve and support one another—again, breaking teachers out of the lonely "box" they call their classrooms.

This careful, collaborative approach stands in contrast to a more traditional process where teachers may slowly (and randomly) accumulate knowledge, skills, and abilities alone or in occasional staff development programs. This traditional approach—where the teacher operates mostly alone in the limited world of their own classrooms—results in often missing the potential benefits of knowing what of interest occurs two classrooms away, not to mention all across their profession, in their field.

For now we realize that teachers are working in modern hi-tech learning environments where they can hardly remain alone and be lonely for long, as the field of education is rapidly interconnecting and becoming instantaneous (chapter 5). These rapid hi-tech developments (iPad, Androids, Lenovo Ideapad, Kindle-for-Kids, etc.) are putting the technology and methods virtually at teachers' (and students') fingertips—online—as we move from the larger, heavier, more expensive computer to the more available, usable portable pad. With these innovations now readily available, teachers and students no longer work in isolation; they possess at the ready, literally, instant accessibility, interactions and involvement in the educative process anytime, anywhere!

This book points out ways we might bring professionalism (enhancing "collective participation in decision making, collegial assistance, and mutual responsibility for the quality of education," [Shedd, 1988, p. 417]) rapidly to greater numbers of teachers, new and experienced, as means for ending the loneliness and slowing the current teacher turnover factor. For teachers have been leaving the profession at increasing rates, often within the first five years of their service.

In fact, according to one estimate, 25 percent leave teaching before their third year (see Skaalvik & Skaalvik, 2011), creating a turnover rate unusual in the professions. (For example, an endocrinologist, as a medical specialist, will hardly work for ten to twelve years to become trained and licensed, and then quit three to four years later.) Simply put, it is harder to thrive when the job calls for work in an isolated environment and for further being ignored by one's field, colleagues, and community.

Also, ease of entry may restrict the ability of the field of education to insist upon, and oversee, the professionalism of their peers. For becoming a teacher is often accomplished too quickly and easily (e.g., a summer institute for preparation plus a student teaching semester, and the trainee is ready to teach). Meanwhile, becoming a quality, outstanding teacher is often left to teachers themselves within their individual circumstances and dependent on their own luck, tenacity, and talent. Thus, teacher collaboration is an important process in preparing new teachers, sustaining and improving the quality of colleagues' work and student outcomes— while supporting and recognizing professionalism across the field over a teacher's career.

THEME 2: UNDERSTANDING THE
NEED FOR TEACHER COLLABORATION

What is meant by teacher collaboration? Although much has been said about increasing teacher interactions and mutual support, observers often mean different things by the term. Hart (1998), for example, defines collaboration as "the cooperation of equals who voluntarily share decision making and work toward common goals" (p. 90).

In an earlier, significant volume on educator collaboration, Diana G. Pounder (1998a) provided a framework for examining organizational collaboration—its foundations, inter- and intra-organizational dimensions, and implications for practice. In one chapter, she conceptualized collaboration in terms of the design of teachers' work groups (Pounder, 1998b).

Pounder's (1998b) design is meant to "increase members' responsibility for the group's performance and outcomes, creating work interdependence and opportunities for self- management" (p. 65). She noted that the promise and quality of interdisciplinary instructional teams, in particular, rest with involving all school faculty, potentially changing the nature of teachers' work, affecting the instruction of students, and establishing a link between school restructuring and student outcomes.

In another chapter in the Pounder edited volume, Ann Weaver Hart (1998) examined collaboration across the full complement of different professional roles in schools. These efforts involve not only teachers and administrators but also counselors, school psychologists, and social workers. She observed that myriad school professionals often pursue their work in isolation with the resulting "compartmentalization of a student's problems and school experience" (p. 90).

Teachers are the primary educators in schools, but the values of other professionals involved in collaboration are also important. Within our volume, a range of collaborative models has been considered. These include collaborative teams (chapter 4), teacher grade level teams (chapter 6), professional learning communities (chapters 3 and 4), collaboration to learn computer technology (chapter 5), and subject-area departments (chapter 7).

Arthur Wise (2012) urges us to:

Contrast schools with other professional workplaces, where seasoned professionals and novices work together, incorporate technology into their work, see each other in action, and collaborate in ways that allow novices to contribute and to learn while senior professionals remain firmly in charge and accountable to clients for performance. (p. 32)

Wise recommended breaking the tyranny of the classroom and making the learning environment more involving, exciting, and engaging.

The chapters in this book examine collaboration from different perspectives: not only as drawing on different theoretical traditions, but also as general perspectives on how sharing can be accomplished in the classroom, school, and district. Indeed, collaboration may be viewed from different vantage points, including grade level teams, subjects-discipline groups and departments, collaborative teams based on interests, and principal-teacher collaboration.

The following steps appear important as the field works to be more effective—and professional by: (1) Striving for a skill set that defines high-quality teaching; (2) Building methods for observing and recording quality teaching; (3) Using accurate, practical measures for assessing—and providing resources to enhance—teaching quality, teacher performance, and school performance; and (4) Applying methods in real-life settings, districts, and states. These steps appear to relate key teaching activities to students' learning, performance, and overall satisfaction with their learning experiences.

How do districts and schools strive to recruit, train, support, and assess good teaching, around qualities of mutual support, collegiality, and collaboration? In what ways can schools be organized to allow teachers to work together for their mutual benefit and for the sake of their students? Also, what can schools and colleagues do to improve underperforming teachers and administrators—newcomers and old-timers who need help—or even perhaps to counsel (or push) them out of the profession?

We hope that teachers and school administrators will learn from this book because collaboration within and across schools appears attractive in meeting the needs of a changing education landscape and the growing demands for quality. High rates of teacher turnover are an indication that something is not going well as teachers feel lost or unsuccessful and leave their work.

Thus, this volume offers some directions and raises other lines of inquiry on this critical subject of how to make schools better with more professionalized teachers. We also hope that university faculty and staff will find our book of interest, both from a theoretical and practical standpoint, as they help to better train and maintain teachers' skills and work.

REFERENCES

Etzioni, A. (Ed.) (1969). *The semi-professions and their organization: Teachers, nurses, and social workers*. New York: The Free Press.

Hart, A. W. (1998). Marshaling forces: Collaboration across educator roles. In D. G. Pounder (Ed.), *Restructuring schools for collaboration: Promises and pitfalls* (pp. 89–120). Albany: State University of New York Press.

Keedy, J. L., & Robbins, A. D. (1993). Teacher collegial groups: A culture-building strategy for department chairs. *Clearinghouse, 66*(3), 185–88.

Lortie, D. C. (1969). The balance of control and autonomy in elementary school teaching. In A. Etzioni (Ed.), *The semi-professions and their organization: Teachers, nurses, and social workers.* (pp. 1–53). New York: The Free Press.

Lortie, D. C. (1975). *Schoolteacher: A sociological study.* Chicago: University of Chicago Press.

Louis, K. S., Kruse, S., & Bryk, A. S. (1995). Professionalism and community: What is it and why is it important in urban schools? In K. S. Louis, S. Kruse & Associates (1995) *Professionalism and community: Perspectives on reforming urban schools.* Long Oaks, CA: Corwin.

Pounder, D. G. (1998a). *Restructuring schools for collaboration: Promises and pitfalls.* Albany: State University of New York Press.

Pounder, D. G. (1998b). Teacher teams: Redesigning teachers' work for collaboration. In D. G. Pounder (Ed.), *Restructuring schools for collaboration: Promises and pitfalls* (pp. 65–88). Albany: State University of New York Press.

Seashore Louis, K., S. D., Kruse, & Bryk, A. S. (1995). Professionalism and community: What is it and why is it important in urban schools? In K. Seashore Louis & S. D. Kruse (Eds.), *Professionalism and community: Perspectives on reforming urban schools* (pp. 3–22). Thousand Oaks, CA: Corwin Press.

Shedd, J. B. (1988). Collective bargaining, school reform, and the management of school systems. *Educational Administration Quarterly, 24*(4), 405–15.

Skaalvik, E. M., & Skaalvik, S. (2011). Teacher job satisfaction and motivation to leave the teaching profession: Relations with school context, feeling of belonging, and emotional exhaustion. *Teaching and Teacher Education, 27*, 1029–38.

Wise, A. E. (2012). End the tyranny of the self-contained classroom. *Education Week, Commentary,* January 25, 2012, *31*(18), p. 24.

About the Contributors

Mary Antony Bair, PhD, is associate professor of education in the social foundations program at Grand Valley State University, Grand Rapids, Michigan.

Scott C. Bauer, PhD, is associate professor in the Education Leadership Program at George Mason University in Fairfax, Virginia.

S. David Brazer, PhD, is associate professor and director of Leadership Degree Programs at the Stanford Graduate School of Education.

Carolyn A. Brown, PhD, is associate professor of educational leadership and policy and recently elected division chair at Fordham University Graduate School of Education in New York City.

Vivienne Collinson, PhD, previously served as a primary and secondary school teacher and as a professor in the Graduate School of the University of Maryland, College Park, and Michigan State University.

Sharon Conley, PhD, is professor of education in the Gevirtz Graduate School of Education at University of California, Santa Barbara.

Tanya F. Cook, MA, is a former strategy consultant to various corporations and has worked to develop school and nonprofit partnerships. She is a graduate of Harvard University and the University of Maryland, College Park.

Bruce S. Cooper, PhD, is professor of educational leadership and policy at Fordham University Graduate School of Education in New York City.

Terrence E. Deal, PhD, previously held professorships at Stanford, Harvard, Vanderbilt, and University of Southern California and resides in San Luis Obispo, California.

J. John Dewey, PhD, is principal at Garden Street Academy in Santa Barbara, California.

Frank C. Guerrero, EdD, is an assistant principal in the Oxnard School District in Oxnard, California, and a graduate of University of California, Santa Barbara.

Donna Redman, EdD, is assistant professor of education in the College of Education and Organizational Leadership at the University of La Verne in La Verne, California.

Robert G. Smith, PhD, is associate professor in the Education Leadership Program at George Mason University in Fairfax, Virginia, and served previously as the Superintendent of Schools in Arlington County, Virginia.

Michelle D. Van Lare, PhD, is assistant professor in the Education Leadership Program at George Mason University in Fairfax, Virginia.